T0326926

# THE
# LEGENDS
## OF THE
# PYRAMIDS

# THE
# LEGENDS
## OF THE
# PYRAMIDS

—◦◦◦—

## MYTHS AND MISCONCEPTIONS
## ABOUT ANCIENT EGYPT

## JASON COLAVITO

**RED ⚡ LIGHTNING BOOKS**

*This book is a publication of*

RED LIGHTNING BOOKS
1320 East 10th Street
Bloomington, Indiana 47405 USA

redlightningbooks.com

*Manufactured in the
United States of America*

First printing 2021

*Library of Congress
Cataloging-in-Publication Data*

Names: Colavito, Jason, author.
Title: The legends of the pyramids :
    myths and misconceptions about
    ancient Egypt / Jason Colavito.
Other titles: Myths and misconceptions
    about ancient Egypt
Description: Bloomington,
    Indiana : Red Lightning Books,
    [2021] | Includes index.
Identifiers: LCCN 2021002617 (print) |
    LCCN 2021002618 (ebook) |
    ISBN 9781684351480 (hardback) |
    ISBN 9781684351497 (ebook)
Subjects: LCSH: Pyramids—Egypt. |
    Egypt—History—To 332 B.C.—
    Historiography. | Egypt—In popular
    culture. | Egypt—History—
    Errors, inventions, etc.
Classification: LCC DT63 .C568
    2021 (print) | LCC DT63
    (ebook) | DDC 932/.01—dc23
LC record available at https://
    lccn.loc.gov/2021002617
LC ebook record available at https://
    lccn.loc.gov/2021002618

# CONTENTS

# NOTE ON THE TEXT

In 2012, one of the stars of the History Channel series *Ancient Aliens* took to Twitter and made a bizarre claim about a medieval book by an Arab-Egyptian author that provided evidence space aliens had inspired the building of the Great Pyramid. My efforts to explore why he was wrong led me to devote seven years to investigating the astonishing untold story of how medieval myths and legends built on ancient history and presaged modern pseudohistorical fantasies. I chronicled my discoveries on my blog, and the book you are about to read contains revised, rewritten, and updated versions of some of the reporting first published online.

Many of the people discussed in this book lived in cultures that did not use the Roman alphabet. Generally speaking, for familiarity, I have elected to use the most common modern forms of their names. So, for example, I have called the Byzantine monk Γεώργιος Σύγκελλος by the common English version of his name, George Syncellus, rather than the less familiar Georgios Synkellos. Similarly, Arabic names are given as they are usually used in modern English texts, which hew closer to the Arabic, rather than old-fashioned Latinate versions no longer used: so, Jalāl al-Dīn al-Suyūṭi rather than the medieval Gelaldinus. Exceptions occur when the Latin name is better known or standard. However, due to the lack of a standard English transliteration of Arabic, inconsistencies are inevitable. My goal is to focus attention on the individuals' contributions by favoring familiarity rather than creating unnecessary distance or confusion with too rigorous an application of orthography.

Unless otherwise noted in the text, all translations are my own.

# THE
# LEGENDS
## OF THE
# PYRAMIDS

# INTRODUCTION

IN FEBRUARY 1924, THE EDITOR OF THE PULP FICTION MAGA-
zine *Weird Tales*, J. C. Henneberger, wrote from Chicago to one of his
regular authors, H. P. Lovecraft of Providence, Rhode Island. Henneberger proposed that the up-and-coming horror writer ghostwrite a
tale for the world's most famous magician, Harry Houdini, to run in
Henneberger's magazine. Houdini had begun a regular "Ask Houdini"
feature in *Weird Tales*, and Henneberger hoped to build an audience
with more content from the celebrity escape artist. The great excitement
spawned by Howard Carter's opening of King Tutankhamun's tomb in
1922 had refused to die down now that the newspapers were filled with
stories about the "curse of the Pharaohs" that had struck dead several of
the men who worked on Tut's tomb; something on an Egyptian theme
seemed quite appropriate for a magazine specializing in the weird and
the macabre.

Lovecraft accepted the commission, and Henneberger sent him the
details of an adventure that Houdini claimed to have had in Egypt. It
concerned a "hideous experience" that Houdini coyly hesitated even to
discuss involving some unexplained unpleasantness that occurred when
in 1910 some "Arabs" kidnapped him and dumped him into a tomb in

the shadow of the Great Pyramid of Giza. Houdini told the story orally to Henneberger, who wrote up a summary for Lovecraft. But it took the horror writer virtually no time to discover that Houdini's story was a fake. Lovecraft asked Henneberger for permission just to make up his own story since Houdini's was already a fictitious tale. Henneberger agreed.

Lovecraft quickly churned out a lurid tale about a paranormal experience Houdini might have had when he pretended to have been captured by pirates and held in a chamber near the Sphinx. In the story, the fictional version of Houdini is kidnapped by a tour guide who looks like an antique pharaoh. He is thrust into a massive underground cavern in the desert, where he meets an army of reanimated half-human mummies and the horrific, tentacled animal-human hybrid that is but the paw of a more massive monster that inspired the ancients to carve the great leonine statue in its image and honor. In the story, Houdini waves away the events as a hallucination, but Lovecraft hints at the end that the tour guide is the undead leader of the mummy army.

Lovecraft had an aversion to typing; he considered it a chore to turn his well-nigh unreadable longhand into crisp typed pages. This story in particular was a nightmare. Lovecraft lost the typescript for "Under the Pyramids." With the publication deadline looming, he and his new wife, Sonia Greene, spent their honeymoon following their March 3 wedding retyping the manuscript to ensure it would be in the hands of the publisher in time for a May 1924 publication.

Retitled "Imprisoned with the Pharaohs," the story hinted darkly that something was amiss with the chronology of Egypt as we received it from Egyptologists and experts. Building off the (incorrect) assertion of the famed Egyptologist Auguste Mariette that the Sphinx was originally a statue of the sun-god Armachis carved long before Egypt had dynasties and kings, Lovecraft five times made Houdini say that the impassive visage of the famous statue was not originally that of the pharaoh Khafre (Khephren) as Egyptologists believed: "There are unpleasant tales of the Sphinx before Khephren—but whatever its elder features were, the monarch replaced them with his own that men might look at the colossus without fear." He spoke, too, of "legends of subterranean passages beneath the monstrous creature" that were older than Egypt itself, and at the story's climax, Houdini finds himself face-to-face with powerful demon gods in just such an underground chamber.

Houdini loved the story, and after reading it invited Lovecraft to his apartment for dinner. With more than a little irony, the two men discussed their shared disbelief in the supernatural.

"Imprisoned with the Pharaohs," alongside Universal's 1932 horror movie *The Mummy*, starring Boris Karloff, embodies the way a particular set of ideas about ancient Egypt live on in modern pop culture. When you imagine ancient Egypt, what do you see? According to pop culture, ancient Egypt was a world of pyramids and tombs, of mummies and magic. It is a place where booby traps and mystical guardians kept the dead safe in their sarcophagi, and every pyramid and crypt contained astonishing treasures. Fantastical stories of Egyptian magic, secret wisdom, and high technology are almost as old as Egypt itself. The sense that the impossible antiquity of Egypt possessed incredible wonders, wisdom, and wizardry became ingrained in popular consciousness over the centuries before Howard Carter opened the boy-king Tutankhamun's tomb in 1922. It was hardly a surprise that the massive wave of Egyptian-themed pop culture inspired by Carter's astonishing discovery would draw equally on the imaginary history of Egypt as it did the country's true history and heritage.

## ABOUT THIS BOOK

This book intends to look at the forgotten part of the story of ancient Egypt—the way people imagined (and outright fabricated) Egyptian history from Alexander's conquest in 332 BCE down to the present. In doing so, we will explore several important and recurring themes. We will look at the role of religious belief in bending history to its demands. We will look, too, at the many ways that race, ethnicity, nationalism, and culture have contributed to efforts to revise Egyptian history to favor certain groups over others. Above everything, we will trace the influence of a powerful and compelling—but fictitious—idea that the pyramids had a deep and abiding connection to the forbidden knowledge of supernatural creatures across centuries, witnessing the myriad ways that this idea gave rise to nearly all of the stories told about the pyramids today. Finally, we will explore the tension between the ideas of the political, social, and religious elites on one hand and the popular notions of everyday people on the other. We will examine how those tensions created divisions between "official" ideas about Egypt and those that large numbers of people widely believed.

Each chapter will proceed chronologically from antiquity to today. We will explore how the Greeks and Romans got some details wrong but basically understood Egyptian history, and we will look at how Jewish, Christian, and Islamic scholars systematically undermined the real history of Egypt in the hope of bringing it in line with the stories and beliefs that had grown up around the Abrahamic faiths. We will examine in particular the unusual story told in the Islamic world that placed the construction of the Great Pyramid before Noah's flood and associated it with the lost science and technology of a vanished prehistoric world of magicians and giants. We will trace this occult history of Egypt through time, watching as scholars, entertainers, mystics, and frauds transformed the story into a bewildering array of fantasies about ancient Egypt, and we will explore the ways this story continues to influence pop culture's vision of ancient Egypt. Our exploration will take us from the deserts of Egypt to the farthest reaches of outer space and introduce us to colorful characters, frightening monsters, ancient spirits, and even space aliens. And at every turn, we will ask why so many chose the fantasy over the real history of Egypt.

To do so, however, we need to understand a little bit about the real history of Egypt.

## ANCIENT EGYPT AND ANCIENT TEXTS

For most of recorded history, the true history of Egypt was lost under layers of myth and legend, the ancient land's written records all but unreadable and its heritage scattered before rulers from beyond its borders and new faiths that held the old gods in contempt. The Egyptians themselves had kept records of their history—albeit from the biased perspective of the kings—in texts inscribed on the walls of temples and tombs and written on papyrus. The last priests capable of reading Egyptian hieroglyphs died around 500 CE, and after that, the records of Egypt were closed for more than a thousand years. As late as the early 1800s, much of what Western scholars knew about Egyptian history was little more than scraps of lore from classical authors and whatever could be gleaned from references to Egypt in the Hebrew Bible. To fill in the gaps, even the greatest scholars of the 1600s and 1700s turned to folktales, myths, and legends.

This book will explore those legends as they existed in parallel with a scientific and scholarly effort to revive the history of Egypt and to understand the ancient land and its many wonders. The most important source for understanding Egypt before French scholar Jean-François Champollion deciphered hieroglyphics using the famed Rosetta Stone in the 1820s was the work of the ancient Egyptian priest Manetho, who wrote a book in Greek around 280 BCE called the *Aegyptiaca* that explained Egyptian history to the Greeks. His work survives only in fragments, mostly copied by Christian writers, most of whom rewrote his history of Egypt to suit their own needs, shortening his thousands of years of history into a few centuries to match what they saw as the short period between the biblical flood and their own time. The result was that any chronology of ancient Egypt that followed Manetho was, at best, an approximation, though it was the best approximation to be had until the deciphering of the hieroglyphs.

When Champollion unlocked the secrets of Egyptian writing, suddenly thousands of inscriptions were no longer silent and could tell their stories. Archaeologists rushed to translate as much material as possible. In so doing, they discovered striking confirmation that much of what came down to us from Manetho was an accurate reflection of Egyptian records. Evidence from inscriptions contemporary with various rulers as well as papyri surviving from ancient times has allowed modern historians to develop an intricate chronology of ancient Egypt. Taken together, they help historians fix particular kings in time. Ancient and medieval people had few of the tools modern Egyptologists possess, and this is one reason that their attempts to imagine Egyptian history slid further and further away from the truth the farther that ancient Egypt slipped into the mists of time.

## ANCIENT EGYPT AND ARCHAEOLOGY

Fortunately, written sources are not our only window into ancient Egypt. We also have the discoveries of archaeology, and these help us put the events of ancient Egyptian history into order. In addition to the remains of temples, tombs, and villages, which tell us how the Egyptians lived and imagined their lives beyond death, we also know about their daily lives through the remains of the tools they used and even the foods they ate.

The result of two centuries of investigation and analysis of Egyptian history is a fairly comprehensive understanding of why the Egyptians built the pyramids and how the pyramids developed over time. According to Egyptology, the pharaohs were originally buried in single-story mudbrick tombs called *mastabas*, which were rectangular in shape and had walls that sloped slightly inward as they rose, culminating in a flat roof, giving them a bench-like shape. (*Mastaba* is Arabic for "bench.") The mastaba sat atop the grave, which was placed in an underground chamber. In time, the Egyptians began using stone rather than mudbrick to make the structures more durable. The pharaohs of the Early Dynastic Period and the beginning of the Old Kingdom—Manetho's First and Second Dynasties—made use of these tombs, and they remained popular with the nobility for a thousand years after kings began to build pyramids.

A major innovation, however, came when Imhotep, the architect to Third Dynasty king Djoser (ca. 2650 BCE), devised a plan to make the king's tomb much grander than those of his predecessors and the other nobles. His innovation was to place a series of five progressively smaller mastabas atop the large mastaba originally built for Djoser (see fig. I.1). In so doing, he created a step pyramid, the very first in Egypt, and the final 62.5-meter (205-foot) structure sat atop a veritable 6-kilometer (3.7-mile) labyrinth of hidden halls and chambers. The pyramid sat within a massive complex of temples and halls.

Djoser's step pyramid was so impressive that later pharaohs were inspired to try to outdo him. The founder of the Fourth Dynasty, Sneferu (or perhaps his predecessor Huni), attempted to build a larger pyramid. Djoser's had six steps, so Sneferu's pyramid at Meidum would have seven. In the process of building the pyramid, the plans were changed to make

**Figure I.1.** The step pyramid of Djoser, the first pyramid constructed in Egypt.
*Library of Congress Prints and Photographs Division, LC-M305- SL17-879.*

the building more impressive. The finished step pyramid was encased inside a layer of limestone that filled in the steps and transformed the structure into the first smooth-sided true pyramid. Not every effort worked. Two of Sneferu's three pyramids were failures, for example. But the third, or Red Pyramid, was a success.

This gradual process of innovation led to the creation of the greatest of all the pyramids, the Great Pyramid of Giza, constructed by Sneferu's son, Khufu, around 2580 BCE. A true pyramid like the Red Pyramid, it featured complex interior chambers quite similar to those in Sneferu's pyramids and was in many ways a larger version of them. Its slope split the difference between Sneferu's Bent and Red Pyramids and came in

**Figure I.2.** The Great Pyramid of Giza, the largest of the ancient Egyptian pyramids, seen here with the nearby Nile River. *Library of Congress Prints and Photographs Division, LC-M32-8932.*

at 51.5 degrees, and its height reached 139 meters (455 feet), making it the tallest building on earth until it was finally surpassed in 1311.

In many ways, the Great Pyramid represented the height of Egyptian architecture (see fig. I.2). Its sides aligned almost perfectly to the cardinal directions, and its stonework was so fine that it was said that the thinnest blade could not fit between the massive blocks of its polished limestone casing. The pyramid was likely robbed in the Middle Kingdom, a century or so after Khufu, and any remaining artifacts removed under the Arabs in the 800s CE. Its casing stones came loose in the great earthquake of 1303, and the Arab rulers of Egypt removed them from the

1300s to the 1800s to build the fortresses, palaces, and mosques of nearby Cairo. Nevertheless, the massive pile that remains more than testifies to the power and the grandeur of Egypt's Old Kingdom and more than earns the legendary inscription that medieval people imagined had been carved on it by its builder, whom they called Sūrīd: "I, Sūrīd, the king, built these pyramids at such and such a time. I completed the building in six years. Let anyone who would come after me and believe himself a king as great as I destroy them in six years, for all know that it is easier to destroy than to build."

The pyramid builders lived 4,500 years ago, and yet science has only understood their history and culture in something approaching our modern view of Egypt for about two hundred years. This is an extraordinarily short time when you compare it to the millennia that the outlines of Roman history have been known and understood, for example.

## THE SECRET OF THE PYRAMIDS

This book will provide you with the 100 percent genuine true secret of the pyramids—or, rather, the mystical and occult lore that esoteric groups have passed off as the true secret of the pyramids for the past two or three centuries. It reveals the hidden history of Egypt—or, rather, the fictitious history of Egypt that occultists, mystics, and gurus have relied on for the revelations they claim to offer about Egyptian history. For, as it happens, almost everything you've seen about ancient Egypt in pop culture is the result of thousands of years of failed attempts to make the real history of Egypt match up with science-fiction fantasies and what was basically Bible fan fiction.

This book is the story of why pop culture sees Egypt as a land of walking mummies, booby-trapped tombs, ancient wisdom, and powerful magic. It is the story of how history is invented and rewritten to serve contemporary ends, and more than anything, it is the story about the power of storytelling to transform reality in its image.

# 1

## ANCIENT TESTIMONIA

WHEN THE GREEK HISTORIAN HERODOTUS ARRIVED IN EGYPT sometime around 454 BCE, the Great Pyramid of Giza was already two thousand years old and the preeminent wonder of the world. The Halicarnassus-born writer had come to Egypt among the train of Athenians who had arrived to help repel Persian forces, which were then in control of the country. Although some modern historians believe that Herodotus may have faked his entire trip to Egypt, the stories he told about the country's history remain an important, if challenging, source of Egyptian history: They are among the first narrative accounts written by a non-Egyptian. Naturally, when Herodotus wanted to talk about the history of Egypt, he wrote extensively about the Giza pyramids. However, the information he claimed to have learned from Egyptian priests was not exactly accurate, and it would cast a shadow across Egyptian history for thousands of years.

His account, along with those of other writers from the Greek and Roman periods, would set the foundation for modern pyramid myths. Like so many stories about the pyramids, these first tales tended to be an odd mixture of fact and fantasy, laying the groundwork for what was to come.

## Herodotus and the Antiquity of Egypt

Herodotus said that Egyptian priests showed him more than three hundred wooden statues, each representing one of the 341 generations that had lived since the first king reigned in Egypt. The priests reckoned that the first three hundred generations lived ten thousand years and the next forty generations lived 1,340 years, for a total of 11,340 years of Egyptian history. But although the priests traced their history back to inconceivable depths of time, the details of that history didn't quite filter down to Herodotus accurately. They said, for example, that the builders of the Giza pyramids, whom Herodotus named Cheops (Khufu), Khefren (Khafre), and Mykerinos (Menkaure), lived after Rhampsinitos. This last pharaoh was Ramesses III, of the Twentieth Dynasty, who lived seven centuries after his Fourth-Dynasty predecessors.

### HERODOTUS AND THE PYRAMIDS

In the second book of his *Histories*, Herodotus says he spoke with the priests of Egypt, who kept records dating back to a fabulous antiquity of more than ten thousand years. His account, however, contains many errors. He places Cheops, his name for Khufu, around seven hundred years too late. Although Herodotus's chronology is a bit out of whack, his description of the pyramids and their construction almost certainly reflects genuine traditions that circulated among the Egyptians in the Late Period. The Middle Kingdom Westcar Papyrus, discovered only in 1823 or 1824, depicts Khufu as a cruel tyrant in its fictitious tales of magic, and this same characterization appears in Herodotus, indicating that it was a real Egyptian tradition. According to the story they told, Cheops broke the eternal peace, prosperity, and order of Egypt by closing the temples, forbidding worship of the gods, and conscripting all the people in the tireless work of building the Great Pyramid. One hundred thousand men at a time he impressed into service, forcing them to travel afar to quarry stone, ship it back to Giza by boat, and lift the stones into position with "machines," which Herodotus fails to describe fully. Ten years were spent building the long causeway leading from the Nile to the pyramid, and twenty in building the pyramid itself. But this was nothing compared with the stories he heard about what lay within.

According to the rumor Herodotus picked up, the inside of the pyramid contained an underground burial chamber with an artificial lake fed by a secret channel from the Nile. In the center of the lake was an island on which stood the king's sarcophagus. It was among the first fanciful lies about hidden pyramid chambers to gain wide currency in the Western imagination.

Herodotus wrote that the pyramid was erected by stacking stones atop one another in layers until it reached its full height and that casing stones were then added from the top down to smooth the sides into a perfect

### The Island Tomb

No funeral island exists under the Great Pyramid like the one Herodotus described. However, unbeknownst to scholars until the twentieth century, there was in fact such a tomb at Giza, the so-called Osiris Shaft underground near the Sphinx, which archaeologist Zahi Hawass has interpreted as an underground cenotaph, or symbolic tomb, of Osiris. It featured a sarcophagus he believes was surrounded by a water-filled trench, similar to the cenotaph of the god Osiris at Abydos, which also surrounded the grave with water. Herodotus's informants might have spoken of this Giza grave or some similar much later grave as though it were the ancient burial chamber of the Great Pyramid.

pyramid. He claimed that the pyramid was covered in inscriptions documenting the construction and that he had an Egyptian interpreter translate the writing for him. It seems the interpreter was pulling his leg when telling Herodotus that the inscriptions covering the Great Pyramid recorded Cheops's grocery bill: 1,600 talents of silver spent on radishes, leeks, and other vegetables for the workmen. Cheops allegedly spent so much money on vegetables, supplies, and other pyramid-building necessities that he prostituted his own daughter to raise money for the massive edifice. The Egyptians didn't tell Herodotus how much a roll in the hay with a princess cost, but he said that she secretly charged extra—the cost of one more stone—to raise money for a pyramid of her own.

The Greek historian had many more stories to tell of Egypt—of the wickedness of Khefren and the piety of Mykerinos, and of the fantastical Labyrinth, actually a massive mortuary complex at Hawara of such complexity as to awe the Greek traveler. He wrote, too, of the pharaoh Sesostris (likely based on Senusret III), who supposedly conquered an empire that stretched deep into Europe.

He also recorded some unusual myths that spoke to the fact that at this date, so early in Greek history and so late in Egyptian, history had already started giving way to myth. He wrote that the Greeks believed, wrongly, that Menkaure's pyramid was actually the tomb of Rhodopis. Although he does not tell her story himself, we know from other authors that it was the earliest Cinderella story: the pharaoh finding a slave girl's sandal, falling in love with the shapeliness of her foot, and searching the kingdom to find her and make her his wife. The story probably attached itself to the pyramids, as H. R. Hall argued, because *Rhodopis* means "rosy-cheeked" and the Greeks mistakenly thought the red-painted face of the Great Sphinx of Giza was a portrait of her. Herodotus spoke, too, of Nitocris, an infamous but possibly fictitious female pharaoh at the end of the Old Kingdom; she killed her brother's murderers in a dramatic act of revenge by inviting them to a feast and flooding the underground banquet hall with Nile water. And he preserves an unexplained anecdote that the Giza pyramids were called by the name Philitis, a shepherd who pastured his flocks beside them, because Khufu and Khafre were so wicked as to be anathema to the Egyptian tongue.

## LATER GREEK AND ROMAN PYRAMID STORIES

Herodotus's mixture of fact and fiction set the template for the telling of Egyptian history and influenced other ancient authors, who spoke of the pyramids and their history with the same confluence of reality and fantasy. Strangely, though, the pyramids were of much less interest to Greek and Roman authors of antiquity than you might think. According to the Roman writer Pliny the Elder, besides Herodotus, the Greek writers Euhemerus, Duris of Samos, Aristagoras, Dionysius, Artemidorus, Alexander Polyhistor, Butoridas, Antisthenes, Demetrius, Demoteles, and Apion all wrote something about the pyramids; however, he added that most of what they wrote was about their size and how many vegetables the pharaoh had to buy to feed his workers. They were really fascinated by produce. Of these authors, few agreed as to who built the pyramids, but very little of their work survives to know whom they credited.

The later authors typically provided similar information to that given by Herodotus. In the first century BCE, the historian Diodorus Siculus wrote of the pyramids in the first book of his *Library of History*, devoted to all things Egyptian. His account is nearly the same as Herodotus's but with a few unexpected differences. He calls Khufu by the name of Chemmis instead of Cheops, using the Greek word for chemistry. This perhaps reflects the growing Greco-Egyptian tradition, which we'll explore later, that Khufu was a Hermetic alchemist. He claimed that the Great Pyramid was either 1,000 or 3,400 years old, that 360,000 men worked on it, and that it was constructed in just twenty years. And like Herodotus, he alleged that the pyramid was covered in details of Khufu's 1,600-talent grocery bill.

More important, though, is his claim that the perfection of the pyramid's construction made it seem to be a work created by supernatural forces rather than human hands—an early anticipation of later allegations that the pyramid was the work of God or space aliens. He also shared some of the bizarre stories that were current among the Egyptians of his era, three centuries after Herodotus. The story given to him—which he considered strange—was that the pyramids were built by heaping up giant mounds of salt and saltpeter that the workers then used for dragging the stones. Then they channeled the Nile to the pyramid and

**Figure 1.1.** The three major Giza pyramids with their satellite pyramids. From left, the pyramids of Menkaure, Khafre, and Khufu. *Library of Congress Prints and Photographs Division, LC-M305- SL17-868.*

simply washed away the mounds, which were as big as the pyramids themselves!

Diodorus also repeats the legend that Khufu and Khafre were hated tyrants; he also places them much later in time than they should be—alongside a pharaoh of the Twenty-Fourth Dynasty. But he adds a new wrinkle. While Herodotus writes that Khufu's body lay on an island in a chamber beneath the Great Pyramid, Diodorus says that he and Khafre were so hated that the people threatened to mutilate their corpses, so they were secreted away to some hidden spot and not buried in their pyramids at all. But Diodorus also speaks of the confusion that had begun to creep into the popular understanding of Egyptian history. Like other authors, he noted that there was no real agreement on who built the pyramids. A competing theory held that three men, Armaeus, Amosis, and Inaros, built them and that the third pyramid was—just as Herodotus had reported—Rhodopis's tomb (see fig. 1.1). Similarly, Diodorus's near contemporary, the geographer Strabo, gave much the same description of the pyramids and also repeated the Rhodopis story.

Pliny the Elder spoke of the pyramids as universally famous and repeated the story about Rhodopis, but he was more interested in the neighboring Great Sphinx, about which he recorded an unusual account. Pliny said that the people of the area around what is now Cairo claimed that the Sphinx was itself a divinity and a tomb, for buried within was the king Armais (i.e., the Armaeus of Diodorus), the last king of the Eighteenth Dynasty, around 1300 BCE. They also claimed that Armais brought the Sphinx to Giza from a distant land. Pliny scoffed at the stories, for he knew that the Sphinx had been carved in place from solid bedrock.

Other notices of the pyramids tended to be brief accounts of their size or summaries of what these authors had said, but the bottom line had become clear: while some genuine traditions were preserved in written records, fictitious legends had grown around the pyramids, and fact and fiction were no longer easy to disentangle.

### GREEK IDEAS ABOUT EGYPT

For the most part, the Greeks, for several centuries after Herodotus, did not devote too much effort to understanding Egyptian history. Greek mythology imagined Egypt as the land originally ruled by fictitious figures from the family of Perseus, such as Belus, the son of Poseidon, and his grandson Aegyptus, for whom the country received its Greek (and eventually English) name. In reality, the Greek word derived from *aigyptos*, meaning "burned faces," in reference to the Egyptians' darker complexions. The Egyptians themselves called their country alternately the "Two Lands" or *Kemet*, meaning "the black land" for its fertile Nile valley soil. After Alexander the Great conquered Egypt and the country became a Greek kingdom under the Ptolemies, Greek writers became much more interested in Egyptian history and struggled to reconcile their mythic stories about fictitious Egyptian kings with what they learned about Egyptian history from the Egyptians themselves. This resulted in complex stories about Greek and Egyptian gods and their many, varied actions at the dawn of Egyptian history. This was also the period when Manetho wrote his history, composed for a Greek audience to teach them about Egyptian history from an Egyptian perspective.

Beside Manetho, one of the most important of these accounts was that of Leon of Pella, as he is conventionally known. Sadly, Leon's book of Egyptian history is lost, and so little is known of him that is it debatable whether he was a Macedonian from Pella or an Egyptian priest. We don't even know when he lived, except that it was around 200 BCE. Only a few fragments remain, quoted in works by later writers. They tell us that Leon published a fictitious letter from Alexander to his mother, Olympias, in which Alexander revealed the real secret of Egypt: the gods of the Egyptian pantheon weren't deities at all, but rather the kings of old, whom the people came to worship as gods. Civilization, according to Leon (or, rather, as the Roman schoolboy known as Hyginus wrote of Leon in his homework assignment on astronomy that has come down to us) was the gift of Osiris, whom the Romans identified with Liber, also known as Bacchus, the Greek Dionysus.

As we have seen from Pliny's list, many other books about Egypt did not survive. Among these was a curious volume called the *Egyptian Theology* by a certain Palaephatus the Egyptian, who may have lived around the time of Aristotle. This book took the opposite tack and claimed that the gods of Egypt were symbols of earthly emotions, including sexual attraction. Another, more rigorous book was the *Aegyptiaca* by an unknown author called Mosmes from the time of Aristotle. This work claimed the Egyptians were the first people to live on the face of the earth, if we can judge by the summary given by a commentator on the *Argonautica* by Apollonius of Rhodes. Too little, however, of such books remains for us to draw firm conclusions about all their views of ancient Egyptian history.

On the other hand, some survived in full. Plutarch told the history of Isis and Osiris in his *Moralia*, describing Osiris as a culture hero who civilized Egypt during his reign as an earthly king. When Diodorus Siculus told the rest of Egyptian history beyond the tale of the pyramids, he, too, had the good fortune of having his discussion survive. That's why we know some pretty wild stories were already in circulation in the centuries after Alexander that combined Greek mythology, Egyptian history and legends, and the rationalizing tendency to rewrite the stories of the gods as though they happened to human kings.

Plutarch presented the Egyptian myth of Osiris as the Greco-Egyptians had told it to him, but Diodorus presented an unusual version of Egyptian mythology, assigning gods to the lights in the sky. Osiris and Isis, he claimed, were the sun and moon. He wrote that Hephaestus was the first king of Egypt and that the common people mistook the first generation to live in Egypt for a race of gods, whom they later worshiped. He assigned to the god-kings the traditional roles given them in Egyptian mythology: Dionysus (Osiris), for example, gave the arts of civilization. Hephaestus (Ptah) invented fire, while Hermes (Thoth) created language and writing.

### THE GOD PAN AND THE ALCHEMISTS OF AKHMIM

Diodorus also reported that the Egyptians held the nature god Pan in high esteem and had a major temple to him at Chemmis, also called Panopolis (i.e., "the city of Pan"), known across the Greek world as the city of alchemy. It would retain its reputation as a center of alchemy into the Middle Ages and eventually play an essential role in the development of pyramid myths and legends, as we will see in chapter 3.

Pan was the local Greek interpretation of Khem or Min, the god of orgiastic sex and powerful erections. The upper Egyptian city of Akhmim was known to the ancient Egyptians as Apu or Khent-min, the latter name corrupting into the Greek Chemmis (Χέμμις). The city was the capital of the ninth nome (province) of the country, and it was home to a cult of Khem. He was a fertility god whose cult was celebrated with sexual rites and whose followers depicted him as a man with an engorged phallus. His sacred vegetable was the Egyptian lettuce, whose tall, straight heads emitted a milky substance when stimulated, like Khem's penis.

This story would merely be an unusual sidelight in a Greek literature full of colorful but unimportant anecdotes, except that Chemmis would soon become an important center of Hermetic alchemy. It would one day be considered the repository of ancient wisdom from before the time of Noah's flood. We can conclude from Herodotus's naming the place as Chemmis that this was Akhmim, known to later centuries as a "veritable mountain" and the hall of records of the antediluvian world. But Herodotus knew nothing of these later stories, for good reason. Hermeticism hadn't been invented yet. Instead, he only knew ancient Chemmis as the home of the Gorgon-slaying hero Perseus (i.e., Min), and Neapolis, the new city, as the Greek quarter founded near the old city. Thus, these accounts prove that Hermes wasn't a part of the legends of Akhmim in the 400s BCE, but that a Greek presence was long associated with the site.

## Perseus in Egypt

The Greeks had long associated Perseus with Egypt—his mother was a descendant of Aegyptus, the legendary founder of Egypt— and the association can likely be traced back to the Greek Dark Ages and perhaps as far back as the Mycenaean period. Many scholars have concluded that Perseus was identified with Min at Akhmim, though A. B. Lloyd argued more persuasively in 1969 that Akhmim's Perseos Ouranion (Perseus of the sky) was the Greek interpretation of Horus at Akhmim. A legend from the next major city over, Antaeopolis, even identified sandals as the spoils of Horus's fight with Seth, accounting for Herodotus's reference. Lloyd also concluded, probably correctly, that by this early date, the people of Chemmis were heavily Hellenized, in all probability due to intermarriage with the Greek colonists of Neapolis. This identification of Horus with Perseus is unorthodox, as the standard *interpretatio graeca* identifies Apollo with Horus, but that didn't occur until around the fifth century, and the Greek community in Akhmim was decades or even a century older than that.

(An alternative explanation identifies Neapolis with Cenae and holds that Herodotus confused Chemmis with Coptos.)

By the time of the Ptolemies, the association with Hermes had begun. The Greek quarter, Neapolis, gave way to a new Ptolemaic settlement, Ptolemais Hermiou, around 312 BCE, founded five miles from Akhmim as the new capital of the nome and as large as Memphis (Strabo 17.1.42). By this point, the Greek rulers of Egypt had identified the wisdom god Thoth with the messenger god Hermes, and a bewildering variety of legends emerged to account for the contradictions and confusions that resulted from tying the two together. Some proposed that *several* men and gods were named Hermes, of whom there were at least five in Greco-Roman mythology (Cicero, *De natura deorum* 3.22). But according to Cicero, the various divine Hermes characters shared elements in common with Min: one had a perpetual erection like Min; another was chthonic like Min; and another had a sacred unspeakable name among the Egyptians. Diodorus (*Library* 1.27) similarly identifies Hermes as a human mistaken for a god, the author of primordial stelae, and a master of science. We'll deal with him in detail in chapter 3, but for now it's important to recognize that the Greek writers captured a period of transition where native Egyptian history, religion, and mythology had begun to merge with Greek influences, resulting in something new, something Greco-Egyptian.

## GRECO-EGYPTIAN TALES OF MAGIC

The Greeks, too, read Egyptian literature and adapted popular stories of commanding pharaohs on sacred quests for power and occult books into their own magical systems. Old Egyptian myths and legends became fodder for new Greco-Egyptian stories of magic and mystery. "The Story of Setna," written around the fourth century BCE, is one of the most famous. It is a Hellenistic tale incorporating elements of history and mythology dating back to the New Kingdom. It is not an accurate guide to New Kingdom beliefs; nevertheless, it preserves a rare account of how the late Egyptians viewed magic, which was inherited by the late antique Greco-Roman Egyptians and the believers in Hermeticism.

## "The Story of Setna"

"The Story of Setna" speaks of a mysterious *Book of Thoth* that contains forbidden occult secrets known only to the gods themselves and is said to have been written by the hand of Thoth (Greek: Hermes), the god of writing and wisdom. In the story, this book grants the power to listen to animals' speech and the power to see the gods themselves. Ramesses the Great's son Setna seeks out the book in a prince's tomb, only to learn from the dead royal's ghost that it is locked in boxes nested within boxes nested within a box of iron at the bottom of the Nile. Setna obtains the forbidden book and studies its secrets, but the dead prince's ghost haunts him and kills his wife and son before the book is returned.

As we shall see, "The Story of Setna" created a template that the Greek-influenced occult history of Egypt would follow for 2,300 years. Its themes of revivified mummies, ancient vengeance, and buried books of occult secrets became highly influential in the late antique and medieval periods and found a second life among novelists like Marie Corelli, through whom it went on to influence *The Mummy* (1932) and its various sequels and knock-offs. The theme of the book of forbidden knowledge is especially important in later myths and legends, particularly those of the Arabs, and seems to find an origin point in this popular story.

Nowhere was this transition to a mysterious and occult understanding of history more evident than at Alexandria, the Greek capital of Egypt founded by Alexander, expanded by the Ptolemies, and distinctly Greco-Egyptian in character. Its most famous god, and the patron of its world-famous library, was Serapis, whose very name was a Greek corruption of the Egyptian Usherapi, or Osiris-Apis, a combined form of Osiris and the sacred Apis bull. This deity was artificial, created by Ptolemaic decree in an effort to unite the Egyptian and Greek peoples. Despite his name, he

**Figure 1.2.** The large size of carvings like these at Dendera led some to conclude Egyptian temples were covered with magical formulae and references to mythical giants. *Library of Congress Prints and Photographs Division, Lot 13552, no. 80.*

was more Greek than Egyptian, and in time, much of Egyptian culture would follow suit.

Within a few centuries, knowledge of the sacred of writing of Egypt, the hieroglyphs, had all but vanished from the country, leaving the ancient inscriptions as little more than awe-inspiring carvings that visitors and locals alike imagined as secret repositories of ancient wisdom—and possibly occult magic spells. By the late 800s CE, Ibn Khordadbeh even wrote that the pyramids of Giza themselves were covered in the secrets of magic, reflecting the common belief going back to late antiquity that hieroglyphics were magical formulae. According to Diodorus Siculus (1.26.6), by the Hellenistic period, the Greeks believed the carvings on the temple walls represented the giants of Greek mythology, who were identified with the biblical giants of the book of Genesis known as the

Nephilim by the Hellenized Jews of Alexandria and later the Christians (see fig. 1.2).

The most famous example of Egypt's vaunted place in the Greek imagination occurs in two of the great philosopher Plato's dialogues on the fictitious lost continent of Atlantis, written around 360 BCE. Today, almost everyone knows the story of Atlantis, the island home of a lost civilization that had a high level of culture, stretched its reach across the known world, and vanished in a day and a night beneath the Atlantic Ocean, never to be seen again. To give the tale of his fabulous, ancient island kingdom a kind of spurious plausibility, in the *Timaeus*, Plato attributed the whole story to the Egyptians, claiming it had been written on pillars in an old temple and known only to the wise priests. These priests revealed the story to Plato's ancestor Solon around 600 BCE, using it as an object lesson in the inferiority of Greek history to the incredible records of Egyptian civilization. *Compared to us*, they said, *you Greeks are merely children*. The story of Atlantis, they said, was nine thousand years old.

According to Plato's story, Solon heard from the priests that Egypt had recorded several disasters that had destroyed the whole of the earth, most caused by fire or water. They said that their millenniums spent observing the heavens and history showed them that fire and flood occurred at regular intervals, according to the movements of the stars. Egypt, they said, was largely immune from the calamities that wiped out life elsewhere on Earth, positioned as it was in the ideal location, safe from fire thanks to the Nile and safe from flood thanks to good drainage. As a result, Egypt does the world a service, recording on the walls of the great temples the history of the world, even those histories that are no longer remembered elsewhere thanks to the destruction by fire and flood. Atlantis, they said, was one such forgotten kingdom, located in the Atlantic Ocean, beyond the Pillars of Hercules (traditionally, the Strait of Gibraltar), opposite Africa, for its history occurred before the greatest flood of all, the one that destroyed the world.

The priests related to Solon the story of Atlantis: of the way it had grown and prospered under the rule of Poseidon's sons; how it had spread its power across the known world; how it had come into conflict with Athens; and how it was destroyed in a single day and night when

### Atlantis and the Theme of Divine Wrath

In the *Critias*, Plato goes into more detail about the culture and history of Atlantis, describing its wonders and building toward a discussion of why Atlantis sank. According to Plato, the Atlanteans had grown corrupt and no longer honored the gods or followed divine commands. Overtaken by decadence and vice, they lost the divine spark and were all too human. Zeus, the chief god, announced his intention to punish the Atlanteans and called the gods together to enact his plan. Sadly, the dialogue breaks off at this point, but the extremely close parallels between these events and the role of Zeus in bringing about the great flood that destroyed the world show that Plato almost certainly intended Zeus to announce that he would flood Atlantis. Parts of the story can be found in Apollodorus's *Library*, Ovid's *Metamorphoses*, and Lucian of Samosata's *Syrian Goddess*. The last of these is the most interesting because Lucian explicitly notes that the story he tells is a composite of Greek material and the same flood story known to the peoples of Mesopotamia and the Jews. As chapter 2 will show, the peoples of Mesopotamia had a story of a great flood featuring a hero called Xisuthros that predates the Jewish flood myth featuring Noah.

In all of these stories, key elements repeat: a formerly satisfactory people anger a divine being through disobedience, causing the divine being to vow to flood the world and punish humanity. A small number of people are saved in some sort of box or ark and repopulate Earth, promising to live by divine commandment.

it sank beneath the ocean, leaving behind only a muddy waste. In his unfinished dialogue *Critias*, Plato seems to be using elements of Greek and Mesopotamian myths of the great flood and heavily implies that the destruction of Atlantis occurred because the Atlanteans had angered the god Zeus.

The final lines of Plato's *Critias*, when read with the sinking of Atlantis in the *Timaeus*, suggest that Plato was planning to use the story of the great flood as the model for Atlantis's destruction. It was a pregnant choice and one that did not escape the notice of later Jewish, Christian, and Islamic commentators, all of whom saw in this choice a reason to associate Atlantis with the antediluvian world that existed before Noah's flood—and to attribute some of the surviving ancient wonders, such as Egypt's Great Pyramid, to this lost world.

Nothing in the Greek flood myth is Egyptian in origin, but Plato's mixing of Greek mythology with Mesopotamian elements under the fiction of an Egyptian origin was a fateful step in the creation of modern pyramid legends: it unintentionally provided the blueprint for associating Egypt's greatest wonders—the pyramids—with Noah's flood. It is therefore somewhat unsurprising to see that the same mixture of Near Eastern myths and Egyptian history didn't just occur in Greece but also had taken root among the Jews of Judea.

# 2

# WHY ARE THE PYRAMIDS NOT IN THE BIBLE?

*circa 500 BCE–200 CE*

THE ANCIENT GREEKS AND ROMANS WROTE QUITE A BIT about the pyramids, but the story was quite different for the other major set of ancient documents that influenced Western civilization: Jewish and Christian religious writings. Egypt looms large in the biblical imagination, but surprisingly, neither the Hebrew Bible nor the New Testament makes any mention of Egypt's pyramids, despite the large shadow that Egypt casts over the Bible. This oversight would encourage religious thinkers to find some odd ways to try to shoehorn the largest buildings in the world into what they considered the most important book ever written. The thinking seemed to be that such massive monuments had to have a connection to God—or at least to hell—to explain why such buildings could exist. But the result was to forever connect the pyramids to Noah's flood, giants, and apocalyptic prophecies.

## EGYPT IN THE BIBLE

Both the Hebrew Bible and the New Testament mention Egypt. It was the land where Joseph ruled as Pharaoh's vizier, where Moses lived as a prince of Egypt, and where Jesus, Mary, and Joseph fled from Herod at the direction of an angel. The books of Genesis and Exodus describe the servitude of the Hebrews in the land of Egypt, when the New Kingdom pharaohs made the Jewish people slaves and forced them to build the great works of the kings and to toil for the Egyptians. The stories told in the Bible describe Egypt as a powerful land filled with wise men and magicians who are possessed of some of the secrets of creation (albeit in a corrupt form marred by polytheism). In Genesis 41, the priests of

### Egypt and the Exodus

The most famous of the biblical tales of Egypt is, of course, the Exodus. Although there is no archaeological evidence that the Hebrews were ever enslaved in Egypt or that Moses ever led the Jewish people out of Egypt to the Promised Land, the narrative has served as a touchstone for thousands of years. In the narrative, Joseph's brother Jacob (also called Israel) came to Egypt to live beside his brother, and his family and household—the Israelites—grew to such numbers that Pharaoh ordered all newborn boys killed. Only Moses survived when his mother placed him in a basket and floated him down the Nile, where a princess of Egypt discovered him and raised him as a prince. As an adult, Moses received a revelation from God that the Israelites were to be free. He demanded Pharaoh let his people go. When Pharaoh refused, God sent ten plagues, including an invasion of frogs, the Nile turning to blood, and the death of firstborn Egyptians, to punish Pharaoh, whose heart God had hardened and made heavy. The Israelites left Egypt, crossing the Red Sea, which Moses had magically parted. God killed Pharaoh by closing the sea over him when he attempted to follow.

Egypt perform dream interpretations. In Exodus 7, Egyptian priests turn a staff into a living serpent, and in Exodus 8–9, they perform magical feats such as using their magic to duplicate God's plagues on Egypt to prove their power.

The biblical tales established a baseline for how Jews, Christians, and Muslims would come to view Egypt. All three faiths considered the story of Joseph important. The book of Genesis tells how Joseph's brothers sold him into slavery and how he ended up in Egypt. Imprisoned there, he developed a reputation for interpreting dreams, and Pharaoh's cupbearer brought him to Pharaoh to interpret the king's dream of seven lean cows consuming seven fat cows. Joseph told Pharaoh that seven years of famine would follow seven years of abundance, and he counseled Pharaoh to prepare for the worst. Pharaoh made Joseph vizier, and in that role Joseph built storehouses (traditionally called granaries), which he filled with surplus grain, thus providing enough food to feed all of Egypt and the surrounding lands during the seven years of famine. When he died, he was buried in Egypt, but Moses later took his bones to Canaan.

### THE JEWISH AND PAGAN FLOODS

The biblical stories show great familiarity with Egypt. Pharaoh's heavy heart in the Exodus story, for example, references the Egyptian belief that a man's heart must be lighter than a feather to gain a place in the afterlife. But while these stories were foundational for establishing how the Abrahamic faiths would imagine and interpret Egyptian history, they were not enough to fully integrate Egypt into the developing Judeo-Christian worldview.

These were stories of the Egypt of the New Kingdom to be sure, but as the Jewish world came into contact with the Hellenistic world of the Greeks, Jewish writers became aware that Egypt was vastly older than the stories told of it in the Bible. But if Manetho was right that there had been dynasties before Joseph was a gleam in his father's eye and the Greeks were correct in asserting that Egypt's history went back thousands of years, how could this square with the biblical fact that Egyptian history should not go back any further than Noah's flood? The Masoretic text of the Bible places the Great Flood 1,656 years after creation, and the

## The Many Flood Stories

The story of the Great Flood is today the best-known flood myth, but it is not the oldest. That honor goes to the Mesopotamian flood myth, which had Sumerian, Assyrian, and Babylonian versions. The story, so similar to Noah's, involved one man and his family being saved from a flood the gods sent to destroy the world when one god directs him to build an ark. So similar were the stories—even in minor details like the use of birds to gauge the end of the flood—that most scholars believe the Abrahamic version (shared by Jews, Christians, and Muslims) either derives from a Mesopotamian original or shares a common origin with them.

All of the ancient peoples, however, believed the flood had really happened. The priest Berosus, writing in the 300s BCE, reported that the Babylonians believed Xisuthros's ark to have landed on Mount Judi, and locals mined wood from the supposed wreck to make healing amulets. The Greek historian Nicolaus of Damascus, writing in the last years BCE, equated the Babylonian and Jewish flood stories and said that the ark on Mount Judi was probably the one of which Moses wrote in Genesis. This belief slid easily into Christianity, and in the 300s CE, Faustus of Byzantium reported that Saint Jacob of Nisibis had recovered wood from the same ark on the same mountain. Only later did Mount Masis, today called Ararat, replace Mount Judi in the popular imagination as the landing place of the Ark.

Greek Septuagint text of the Bible places it in *anno mundi* 2262, somewhere between 2200 and 3500 BCE, depending on which authority did the calculating. There wasn't really a lot of agreement.

There was, however, broad consensus that the Great Flood was a real event. The many peoples surrounding the eastern Mediterranean shared a common belief that a world-destroying flood had occurred. The

Babylonian version of the flood story recorded in Greek by the Babylonian priest Berosus, though, adds an important detail not found in the biblical story of Noah: the flood-hero, Xisuthros (a Greek transliteration of the Sumerian name Ziusudra), inscribed tablets with all the wisdom of the preflood world and buried them at Sippar to recover after the flood, preserving knowledge for posterity. This Mesopotamian story would filter down into pyramid mythology in a roundabout way when these tablets of wisdom influenced stories about ancient Egyptian wisdom. No matter which version of the story one knew, the common belief across the Near East was that the Great Flood really happened.

## COMPARING JEWISH AND PAGAN HISTORIES OF EGYPT

But there was a problem. For as long as anyone could remember, the Jewish people claimed that the first king of Egypt after the Great Flood was Mizraim, the namesake of the Hebrew name for the land of Egypt. This name was so old that it could also be found in the texts of Assyria and Ugarit, suggesting it was the common name used by all the Semitic peoples. This name was the dual form of the word *Misr*, meaning "land," and thus a literal translation of Egypt's native name, the "Two Lands." According to Genesis 10, Mizraim ("Egypt") was one of the sons of Noah's son Ham, born after the Great Flood, and therefore the founder of Egypt. A writer passing falsely under the name of the Jewish historian Eupolemus claimed that the Babylonians considered Mizraim the progenitor of Egypt and a descendant of Babylon's founder, Belus. Jewish scholars often equated Mizraim with the first human king of Egypt on Manetho's list, Menes.

Although the oldest direct reference to the Jewish story occurs only in a Hellenistic text quoted later by George Syncellus around 800 CE, the same information can also be found in the Phoenician priest Sanchuniathon's account of Phoenician mythology, the only such account to survive from antiquity. In the surviving account, as quoted by later writers, a certain Misor's son Taautus was known in Egypt and became Thoth (Hermes), while Manetho claimed Menes's kingdom went to his son Athothis. Misor may be a reflection of Misr or Mizraim. The repetition

## Is Sanchuniathon's Mythology Real?

Down to the middle nineteenth century, Sanchuniathon was considered a reliable source. Afterward his veracity was doubted, with many scholars arguing that his Phoenician cosmology was a fabrication from Greek sources. The translation of Bronze Age texts from Ugarit, to the north of Phoenicia, in the 1920s and after demonstrated that Sanchuniathon's work contains genuine Semitic elements that had been revised and rewritten by Philo of Byblos, a Hellenistic writer of Phoenician extraction. Philo translated and probably rewrote the original to make the gods into mortal kings, in keeping with the scholarly understanding of mythology in his day.

of names and relationships suggests that the Semitic peoples claimed Mizraim as the first ruler of Egypt at an early date.

However, the Greeks told of Egyptian history dating back nearly fifty thousand years, according to Diogenes Laërtius, and Manetho spoke of periods when gods ruled for untold thousands of years. The Bible could not be wrong, but Manetho could not be entirely dismissed without eliminating the best source for the more recent history of Egypt. Even conceding that the Greeks and Egyptians were liars or fools about the time before the Great Flood, it was obvious that Egypt was so old that its history could not be contained entirely in the centuries allotted between Noah and Moses. Why, for example, were the pyramids not in the Bible?

### EGYPT'S PILLARS OF WISDOM

To fix the problem, Jewish scholars adapted a myth that had grown up around the biblical patriarchs Seth and Enoch, who lived before the Great Flood. The Jewish historian Flavius Josephus, who lived in the first century CE, recorded a popular but apocryphal story in his *Antiquities of the Jews*, albeit one that did not make a whole lot of sense by itself and confused many readers for centuries. He also recorded another story, largely ignored until the Renaissance, that the Jews had built the pyramids while slaves in Egypt. But that is a story for later.

Josephus wrote that in the time before the flood, the world was divided into two groups born from two of Adam and Eve's children: good people descended from the saintly son, Seth, and sinful people born of the murderous son, Cain. Josephus reported that at the end of Adam's life, he prophesied that either fire or flood would destroy the world and that the sons of Seth feared what this would mean. In Josephus's words, as William Whiston translated them, the sons of Seth took steps to protect the wisdom of the antediluvian world from the coming disaster, so "they made two pillars, the one of brick, the other of stone: they inscribed their discoveries on them both, that in case the pillar of brick should be destroyed by the flood, the pillar of stone might remain, and exhibit those discoveries to mankind; and also inform them that there was another pillar of brick erected by them. Now this remains in the land of Siriad to this day." The Greek word Josephus used for *pillar—stela—*was also used by the Christian bishop Eusebius to describe the pyramid-shaped monuments of Helena of Adiabene, suggesting that pillars and pyramids were not necessarily seen as distinct. Importantly, *Siriad* referred to the "land of Sirius," the Dog Star, sacred to the Egyptians who used it to govern their year. Josephus had said that a large stone structure covered in ancient wisdom existed somewhere in Egypt.

But to understand what exactly Josephus's story is all about requires a detour into the complicated and sometimes completely bonkers efforts to interpret a single sentence of the book of Genesis—one that forever and totally by accident changed the way the West thought about the Egyptian pyramids.

### FALLEN ANGELS AND GIANTS

The opening chapters of Genesis give the Jewish account of the primeval history of the world. It starts with the Creation and proceeds through the expulsion of Adam and Eve from Eden and the lineages that sprang from their sons Seth and Cain. Seth's line became righteous patriarchs, but Cain's line founded cities and invented the mechanical and industrial arts, which the pastorally focused Genesis associates with decadence and corruption. In the sixth chapter of Genesis, we read about an unusual event made more mysterious by its brevity. Into this world before the flood came an unexplained group called the *banê hā'ĕlōhîm*, translated as the sons of God, who chose wives from the "daughters of men." Verse 4 gives the results of that marriage, the single-most influential sentence in the entire primeval history given in the Bible: "There were giants in the earth in those days; and also after that, when the sons of God came in unto the daughters of men, and they bore *children* to them, the same *became* mighty men which *were* of old, men of renown." What exactly this sentence meant—and who exactly the giants, known in Hebrew as the Nephilim, were—became the subject of intense controversy from the time of its composition around 500 BCE to today. One of the first controversies surrounded exactly *who* the "sons of God" were supposed to be.

The oldest interpretation of the text identified the sons of God as angels and concluded that the passage referred to angels who had left heaven and broke God's divine law by mating with human women, giving rise to horrible giants (see fig. 2.1). Other cultures around the Levant had similar stories. Ugarit spoke of a godly council, the *bn 'il*, who were the sons of El, the chief god. Similarly, Sanchuniathon reported that the Phoenicians told a similar story, albeit in different arrangement, that the gods invented the arts of civilization and had gigantic sons. They discovered that human women had become sexually libertine, and they had intercourse with the giants, giving rise to the authors of civilization. Interestingly, these giants were associated with the Anti-Lebanon mountains, where the Jewish people believed that fallen angels lived and the Babylonians—hated enemies of the Jews—claimed that their gods, the Anunnaki, walked. The scholar Amar Annus noted that this was unlikely to be a coincidence and the Jewish story probably was intended as a diabolizing of the pagan myths of their neighbors.

This version of the story, with fallen angels, appeared in several influential texts written during what is known as the "intertestamental period," or the time after the composition of the Torah but before the time when the Christian New Testament emerged. For our purposes,

**Figure 2.1.** In Judeo-Christian lore, angels were often envisioned as descending from heaven to alight on mountains, as in this scene from Milton's *Paradise Lost*.

the most important of these texts were the Book of Enoch, the Book of Jubilees, and the Book of Giants. Of them, the Book of Giants survives only in fragments, and Enoch and Jubilees are known primarily through copies preserved in the Ethiopian liturgical language of Geʻez. We know, however, that Enochian literature (as such books are known) was extremely important because the Epistle of Jude in the New Testament quotes from the Book of Enoch, and 2 Peter discusses the fallen angels in terms likely borrowed directly from Enoch. Many of the church fathers wrote about the book approvingly, and several believed that it was the work of Enoch himself, preserved by Noah from the time before the Great Flood. (Even though the book carries the name of the prophet Enoch and is written in his voice, it is pseudepigraphal, meaning that the author's name is a fake.)

The form of the Book of Enoch that we have today was probably assembled sometime between the first century BCE and the first century CE, but the sections of interest to us—about the fallen angels—come from an older text, often called the Book of the Watchers, that was copied into Enoch. This material might date back as far as 300 BCE, around the same time that Manetho was writing his Egyptian history.

The early chapters of the Book of Enoch attempt to explain what Genesis 6 *really* meant by giving a fuller account of the story. Some scholars, like Józef Milik and Matthew Black, hold that the tale at 6:1–4 was inserted into Genesis in response to the Book of Enoch. But I would agree with scholars such as Pierluigi Piovanelli, who wrote in 2007 that the Enoch narrative presupposes and requires familiarity with Genesis and the two need to be seen as in intertextual conversation. Either way, the Enochian version of the tale is much longer and a great deal stranger than the Genesis version. It's important to discuss it in detail because later pyramid legends will utilize parts of the story to explain the Great Pyramid.

## FALLEN ANGELS IN THE BOOK OF ENOCH

Starting with its sixth chapter, the Book of Enoch relates what begins as the Genesis narrative, but the sons of God have been substituted for angels who are also called the Watchers (or *Egregori* in Greek), in reference to a type of angel discussed in the biblical book of Daniel. The protagonists are fallen angels who teach the arts of civilization to humanity before the Great Flood and are punished with the flood for their lack of chastity. Under the leadership of the angel Semjaza (also called Semyaza, Semiazas, and a number of other variations), a group of two hundred

**Figure 2.2.** The summit of Mount Hermon, where the angels were believed to have fallen from heaven and later the sons of Seth were thought to have lived. *Library of Congress Prints and Photographs Division, LC-M32- 50943-x.*

horny angels descended to Mount Hermon in the Anti-Lebanon range and bound themselves together by an unbreakable oath to abandon heaven and marry human women (see fig. 2.2). Upon each angel taking a wife, Semjaza taught their wives plant-based charms, enchantments, and medicines. An angel named Azazel—a name from Leviticus associated with scapegoats and sacrifice—taught men to forge weapons and how to make jewelry and taught women the use of makeup and how to dye clothes. Other angels taught other evil arts, including astrology and various forms of soothsaying and prophecy. In the biblical perspective, violence, vanity, and magic are all impure arts.

Their wives bore children to them, and these were giants, but not just the "men of renown" from Genesis. In the Enochian version, these giants were pure evil. They were 3,000 ells (4,500 feet) high (according to the Ethiopian text—the surviving Greek fragments omit this detail) and ate everything on the earth, eventually turning on humanity and eating them in a ravenous blood feast. When there were too few humans, they cannibalized each other.

According to the Book of Enoch, God could not abide the evil of the giants, and God placed the blame on the Watchers for having sex with humans. Enoch seems to have a composite of two stories, one where Semjaza is the leader and the other where Azazel is, so in various parts one or the other is considered the more diabolical. In Genesis, God considered all of creation to be sinful and sent the flood to kill it all, but in this version the flood was designed specifically to kill the giants and eliminate any knowledge of what the archangels called "the eternal secrets" of heaven that the Watchers had given to humanity (astrology, presumably, rather than makeup!). Humans were collateral damage of this effort to cleanse the earth. God ordered the Watchers bound and hidden away under the earth or in the stars, but of their sons, these dread giants' ghosts would be allowed to haunt the earth as evil spirits and torture future humans. This would last for seventy generations, until the Watchers and all who sin would be consumed in an abyss of fire to last until the end of all creation.

### THE PROPHECY OF ADAM

All of this was intimately tied with a related myth, the so-called prophecy of Adam, in which Adam predicted that the world would be destroyed by either fire or flood. The prophecy was an adaptation of a Babylonian astrological belief, recorded by Berosus in the 300s CE (and preserved by the Roman writer Seneca), that a world-destroying conflagration occurs whenever the "planets" (meaning the sun, moon, and five visible planets) align in Cancer and a flood when they align in Capricorn. Plato wrote about a similar belief in world-ending fires and floods among the Egyptians in his *Timaeus*. This common motif among ancient peoples found expression in Judaism as Adam's prophecy, though it came in many versions across extra-biblical Jewish literature. Sometimes the prophecy was delivered by Adam's son Seth, or by Enoch, or even the archangel Michael. Although the details change from writer to writer, the two destructions remain constant, as does the injunction to create two stelae or tablets, one of stone and one of brick, so something of ancient wisdom would survive the coming disasters.

The prophecy of Adam and the fall of the angels merged when the identity of the sons of God started to shift away from wicked angels and toward holy men who were accidentally corrupted because . . . well, because sexist ancient people thought women were inherently corrupting and wicked.

## THE LATER MYTH OF THE PILLARS OF WISDOM

At first, later literature followed the example set by Enoch. The Book of Jubilees, written around 200 BCE, retold the story in very similar language, but it added some new wrinkles. For one thing, it limited the number of evil spirits of the giants to just 10 percent of their number, the others being confined to the underworld. More importantly, in Jubilees, Enoch visits the Watchers in the years before the flood and attempts to convince them to give up their wicked ways. He fails, but in chapter 8, after the flood, Cainan, son of Arphaxad, otherwise mentioned only once in the Bible as an ancestor of Mary's husband, Joseph, in the book of Luke, discovers inscriptions made by antediluvians covered with the secret science of predicting the future using the sun, the moon, the planets, and the stars. This is the wicked wisdom of the Watchers, carved according to their teachings. By reading the forbidden wisdom, he "sins." He transcribes the text into a book, which (it is implied) becomes the evil magic of the pagans. Similarly, the Book of Giants tells of Enoch's visit to the giants to discourage their sin and describes tablets written by Enoch foretelling the future.

The story of the Watchers was extremely popular among the Jewish people in its time, and the Book of Enoch enjoyed broad popularity both in Judea and abroad. Not only do fragments of the book appear in the Dead Sea Scrolls, the only ancient fragments of the Greek text to survive from antiquity were discovered in Egypt, at Panopolis (Akhmim), where the myth of antediluvian pyramid wisdom would take shape. We also know from Saint John Cassian, writing in the 400s CE, that the Jews living in Egypt originally believed the Enochian story that the sons of God were fallen angels who taught humanity the civilizing arts and that after the country became Christian in the early centuries CE, the belief remained "common," even though educated Christians and Jews had come to reject it. That Enoch's version of the Watchers remained the common belief in Egypt down to the Middle Ages would play an important role in the development of pyramid myths and legends.

Another key factor that would contribute to later pyramid legends was also a direct outgrowth of the Enochian story. A different legend had emerged that the giants had survived the flood and built Babylon, the great city of sin, home to the Tower of Babel—the gigantic construction that reached to the heavens, not unlike the Great Pyramid. A writer pretending to be the Hellenistic Jewish historian Eupolemus around 158 BCE was the first to record this story. He added that Abraham had been born in Babylon, where he developed astrology, claiming it to be the invention of Enoch, and took that science to Egypt, where he taught it to the priests at Heliopolis. Pseudo-Eupolemus went on to say that the Babylonians claimed that the Egyptians' ancestor Mizraim was the descendant of their own first man, Belus, and the Greeks identified Enoch with the titan Atlas, who held up the heavens, for both invented astrology.

Regardless of the details, the general thrust of the Enochian story was gradually coming to imagine Egypt as the repository of secret wisdom. It would, however, require another change to the story to start putting the parts together.

## TAKING THE ANGELS OUT OF THE STORY

Flavius Josephus bears witness to the transition that began occurring in the last century BCE. His account of the story contains two different versions. One (*Antiquities* 1.73–74) is the familiar story of how the angels fell, mated with human women, and gave rise to giants. But the other (*Antiquities* 1.68–72) retells the same story differently. He very briefly relates that the progeny of Seth were holy men of excellent virtue until they became "perverted" and wicked, leading the whole world into sin. The two sections don't mesh perfectly; clearly Josephus was trying to merge two very different traditions. But we don't get the whole story of the progeny of Seth until later writers, mostly medieval, began to

## Misogyny and the Giants

The new sons of God story was baroque and complex, and it drew on the same elements as the Enochian version but removed the supernatural aspects; religious scholars of the time had come to believe that angels could not actually engage in sexual intercourse. This was perhaps best expressed by Eutychius, a medieval writer who summarized the argument in his *Annals*: "For if the angels could have sex with women, there would not be one virgin left uncorrupted among the daughters of men." While this reads like a laugh line, it hides a darker truth: a vicious streak of misogyny had infected theology, and the story of the giants had come to be seen as proof that women were, as Eutychius said, wanton whores who couldn't stop fornicating unless they were controlled by godly men. As early as the Book of Jubilees, the shift had begun. In that book, the angels selflessly descend to help humanity, but sexually irresistible women corrupt them with all their brazen carnality. The Book of Enoch had located the corruption in the angels' lust, but it was Jubilees' version of female temptation that carried over to the new theology.

record tales that had circulated orally for centuries before being elevated to formal theology. That said, since the early Christian chronographer Julius Africanus chides those who believed the sons of God to be angels rather than Seth's family when he wrote in 221 CE, we know that the new interpretation spread quickly, but it competed with the angelic version into the Middle Ages.

According to the story, as related by sources as diverse as Eutychius, Agapius, *The Book of the Cave of Treasures*, Saint John Cassian, Julius Africanus, and many more, humanity had been divided into two families: the saintly and holy sons of Seth, known as sons of God for their righteousness, who lived chastely in all-male monastic splendor atop Mount

Hermon, and the lustful, orgiastic progeny of Cain, who lived in the valley below Mount Hermon. The men of the family of Cain "resembled stallions neighing in lust," and the women were worse. Some authors suggested that demons inhabited the women and made them wanton. Incest and orgies were common. So wild and indiscriminate was their sex that no woman knew the father of her children. Worst of all (according to a Syriac tradition), they played music at all hours of the day and night, and the sounds of their rocking out to the lute and lyre reached the sons of Seth atop Mount Hermon. The sons of Seth were so turned on by the sexy music that they abandoned their mountain stronghold over the patriarch Jared's objection. When they saw that the daughters of Cain were beautiful and running around naked, they experienced lust for the first time in their holy lives. The daughters of Cain loved how tall and handsome the sons of Seth were and immediately seduced them. The women became pregnant and gave birth to giants, taller than their fathers. The sons of Seth tried to return home to Mount Hermon but found the path barred and the mountain turned to flame in punishment for their sins. From here, the story progresses as in the Enochian version, with the Watcher Semiazos (Semjaza) given as the name of the first king of the sons of Seth now living with the daughters of Cain.

The new version did more than just blame women for seducing men into sin, and it did more than blame sex for literally bringing about the end of all flesh. It also attempted to merge the story of the Watchers with that of the Pillars of Wisdom in a way that absolved the pillars of the charge of harboring evil forbidden knowledge. Since the Watchers were now the godly sons of Seth, corrupted through the wicked works of women, their wisdom was that of the righteous and could safely be considered holy truths from God.

## THE WATCHERS IN EGYPT

This version of the Watchers story, which we might call the "Sethite" version, made its way to Egypt, where it found a foothold among the Jewish population as well as the Christian one. According to Saint John Cassian, the abbot Serenus of Alexandria railed against Egyptians who believed in fallen angels and told all the Hellenized Egyptians who would listen that the holy wisdom of Seth had been corrupted in the years before the Great Flood and the books of ancient wisdom were full of sinful secrets. Noah's wicked son Ham wrote it all down on metal plates and stone tablets to preserve evil knowledge from the flood; afterward, he and his offspring hunted down all these tablets to restore evil magic and sin to the world.

Agapius of Hierapolis informs us that later writers had retroactively made the Egyptian priest Manetho endorse elements of the story. A version of one of his books—probably a forgery—supposedly claimed that Enoch had been the true originator of Egypt's astronomical and astrological wisdom and magic. Another forgery, the so-called *Book of Sothis*, written by Christians under Manetho's name, similarly adapted the Watchers story for an Egyptian context. The forged text, preserved only by George Syncellus, claimed that in the "Seriadic land"—the Siriadic land of Josephus, that is, Egypt—stood pillars with inscriptions carved by the god Thoth, or Hermes, in the time before the flood. These were translated into Greek and kept in the temples of Egypt, where Manetho found them. So similar to the story of Cainan in Jubilees, the tale would serve as a bridge between the Enochian legend and Egyptian history.

The upshot of all of this was to tie the pyramids ever more closely to the Judeo-Christian tradition of preflood wisdom and all of the magic and evil associated with it because the pyramids, in their sheer size, were the most obvious candidates for the Pillars of Wisdom. Making that final connection, though, only became possible when the knowledge of the classical world slipped from memory to be replaced with fantasies and myths.

# 3

## LATE ANTIQUITY

IN OUR PREVIOUS TWO CHAPTERS, WE EXAMINED ANCIENT attitudes about Egypt from two perspectives. First, we looked at how the Greeks and Romans viewed the pyramids. Then we examined the Judeo-Christian myths about Enoch and fallen angels that indirectly placed the pyramids in the midst of an epoch story centered on Noah's flood. These two perspectives eventually merged during the waning days of the Roman Empire. Ancient knowledge and Judeo-Christian legends coalesced around the figure of Hermes Trismegistus because some Jews and Christians had come to believe that this mystical figure was none other than Enoch. This merger of pagan and Abrahamic perspectives would help the pyramids become the focal point for magic and the mystical in ways the ancient Egyptians would scarcely have recognized once writers of late antiquity began to speculate that Hermes had built the monuments of Egypt and medieval thinkers concluded the pyramids were his work.

### HERMES IN CHRISTIAN EGYPT

The Hermes we encountered carving inscriptions on pillars before the flood in chapter 2 was not the Greek messenger of the gods known to earlier generations. Instead, he was a new figure, Hermes Trismegistus, the "thrice great," a composite of Egyptian and Greek influences who would come to be seen as the guardian of all wisdom and eventually as the patriarch Enoch himself. This melding of Egyptian, Greek, and Judeo-Christian cultures seen in the Trismegistus figure's many variations symbolized the cultural crisis that affected Egypt in the long twilight known as late antiquity, the period from the decline of the classical world to the rise of the medieval one. In this heady period, when cultures merged and meshed seemingly at will, the legends of the pyramids escaped history and joined religion, creating a distinctly faith-based ancient history of Egypt in the process.

But this development was a long time in coming, as the story of Hermes demonstrates. It takes place against a changing land of Egypt, where the classical world gave way to a Christian one. Egypt had always been home to a sizable community of Jews. The Hellenized Jews of Alexandria created the greatest of the Greek translations of the Bible, the Septuagint, under the Ptolemies in the third century to the second century BCE. This helped lay the foundation for the Christianization of the country. As early as 200 CE, Alexandria had become a major center of Christianity. It was also a hotbed of religious diversity, with Christians vying against Gnostics, Manicheans, and many others, all of whom had opinions on giants and angels. Christian writers like Origin and Clement wrote of the Watchers in their treatises on faith. Many spoke of the Egyptian and Greek gods as demons sent to deceive humanity, implicitly equating the fallen angels with the pagan deities in whose honor Egypt's monuments had been raised. By the time the Eastern Roman emperors ended the persecution of Christianity and established it as the state's faith, it had become the majority religion of Egypt; this required a suitable new history to place Egypt firmly in a Christian context.

Over the next few chapters, we'll watch Hermes Trismegistus absorb that new history and grow from a Greco-Egyptian philosopher into a Christian and Islamic prophet who saved civilization from Noah's flood by building the pyramids of Giza. But this development took nearly a thousand years, so we need to start at the beginning.

## THE DEVELOPMENT OF HERMES TRISMEGSISTUS

Hermes Trismegistus has an obscure origin. He is a combination of Thoth the wisdom god and Imhotep, the deified polymath and architect of Djoser's step pyramid, both assimilated to the Greek Hermes, in his role as psychopomp leading souls to the underworld. The Roman orator Cicero testifies that a figure very much like him had formed by the last century BCE, known as the fifth Hermes, who taught Egyptians their laws and writing and who was named Thoth. The records of the Ibis Cult from 172 BCE speak of him by name. The *Kore Kosmou* ("The Virgin of the World"), an early Hermetic text of the first century CE, testifies to the existence of Hermes Trismegistus as a syncretic philosopher who allegedly possessed the wisdom of the ancients and had inscribed it on pillars of stone. In both cases, the character is more Thoth than the alchemical philosopher of later centuries, but the core is recognizable. His

### From Min to Hermes

The actual identification of Min with Hermes is obscure, but it may be related to a late collapse of distinctions between characters in the Egyptian and Greek versions of the myth of Osiris, Isis, and Horus. In the Egyptian sources, Min plays almost no role. Plutarch (*Isis and Osiris* 14) assigns Pan, that is, Min, the role of having first learned of Osiris's death at the hands of Set and reporting the news to Isis. Hyginus (Fabula 196) gives Pan the role of providing the gods with a clever ruse to hide themselves from Set. In some places, Min and Thoth shared some titles. A third-century votive inscription at Akhmim from a soldier "to the great god Hermes Trismegistus" is one of the earliest records of the god's name.

name comes from Ptolemaic usage, where Thoth was dubbed "*megistos kai megistos theos megas*," or "the greatest and greatest great god," and as "thrice-greatest Hermes" took on the added descriptor to distinguish the Egyptian version from the Greek messenger god. The church fathers refer to Hermes Trismegistus in the early centuries CE, and by the third century CE, a papyrus identifies "*trismegistos Hermes*" as the god of Hermopolis, Egypt's largest cult center of Thoth, succeeding the original Hermes as the Greek version of Thoth (see fig. 3.1). At first, however, Hermes Trismegistus was simply a Hellenized Thoth.

For our purposes, the most important developments occurred at Akhmim (Panopolis), where the traditional worship of the old gods Min and Thoth had started to change into the veneration of Hermes Trismegistus as Egyptian culture became increasingly Hellenized. If we are to accept the rather unusual and highly syncretic word of John Malalas (*Chronicle* 1.13), a sixth-century Greek chronicler living in Syria who drew on earlier material, the reason for the identification is rather obscure and complex: The (fictitious) Assyrian king Ninus had a brother named Picus Zeus—an attempt to combine and revise the old Latin god Picus, the son of Saturn, and Zeus (Jupiter), the son of Kronos (Saturn), into a single human king—who reigned in Italy. He was, basically, one of the Enochian Watchers, an astrologer and magician who seduced women into believing he was a god by using machinery to simulate magic. He had a son named Faunus whom he nicknamed Hermes after the planet Mercury (Hermes in Greek). Hermes's brothers conspired to kill him, so he decamped to Egypt, having raided the Italian treasury. He set himself up in Egypt, where he acted arrogantly, practiced philosophy and reason, foretold the future, and was worshiped as a god. He was companion of the Jewish Mizraim, the first king of Egypt after the flood, and ruled Egypt after Mizraim's death.

This story, heavily influenced by Christianity, contains some Greek elements and many Judeo-Christian ones. It does, however, suggest the kind of inventive stories that circulated in Egypt as antiquity gave way to the Middle Ages. It also points to another important aspect of this merging of cultures: Hermes Trismegistus did not long stay a Hellenized form of Thoth. The Greeks turned him into a guru possessed of tremendous wisdom, a philosopher above all others. But the people of

**Figure 3.1.** Hermes, *top center*, in a 1702 engraving of alchemical processes, became the god of alchemy in late antiquity, probably in Egypt. *Library of Congress Prints and Photographs Division,* LC-USZ62-75101.

Egypt also began to see him as part of the Enochian story that was so popular in and around Akhmim, as the fragments of the Book of Enoch found there attest.

## THE MERGER OF ENOCH AND HERMES

The question then revolves around how exactly the biblical patriarch Enoch came to be identified with the pagan culture hero Hermes

Trismegistus, himself an amalgamation of Hermes and Thoth. The technical reasons for the identification are easy enough to ascertain. Thoth, Hermes, and Enoch were all revered figures associated with the invention of writing and the promulgation of sacred books and inscriptions. Both Hermes and Enoch had astronomical connections—Hermes supposedly recorded 36,525 books or lived that many years, while Enoch lived 365 years, numbers recalling the number of days in the solar year or in the Sothic cycle—the annual path of the star Sirius, which the Egyptians held sacred because they used it to predict the annual Nile flood. In later Judeo-Christian lore, Enoch and the other descendants of Seth were said to have built two pillars inscribed with prophetic wisdom in the land of Sirius, which was, of course, Egypt.

It's also fairly clear that the connection between Enoch and Hermes emerged among Christians in Egypt in the first centuries CE, presumably after Flavius Josephus recorded the legend of Enoch's pillars in 96 CE and before two very important Christian monks—Annianus and his contemporary Panodorus—wrote around 400 CE. We can see the connections starting to form in the 300s CE. Lactantius in the *Divine Institutes* 2.15 (ca. 311 CE) asserts that Hermes knew that demons were ἀγγέλους πονηροὺς, or evil angels. Around 300 CE, the influential pagan alchemist Zosimus of Panopolis wrote in a passage of his book *Imouth*, which survives only in a medieval quotation, that Hermes described in one of his books the story of a group of supernatural beings who descended and had sexual relations with women, which he compares to the biblical story of the sons of God. This suggests that the conflation was underway by then. But he doesn't make the identification of Hermes and Enoch explicit. It may also be that alchemists, perhaps at Panopolis, purposely "Christianized" Hermes as Enoch to give a Christian gloss to their "pagan" practices and avoid persecution by government authorities.

The geographic distribution of Hermeticism seems to coincide quite closely with that of the Jewish myth of the Pillars of Wisdom the progeny of Seth and/or Enoch allegedly built. Weirdly, this isn't simply due to Greco-Roman culture making room for both, for it extends far beyond the borders of Greco-Roman civilization. According to Kevin van Bladel, a historian of the medieval Near East, a document identifying Hermes as a prophet coequal with Enoch and Seth was found as far afield as

Chinese Turkestan, and a hotbed of Hermeticism was ancient Iran. Van Bladel argued in his book *The Arabic Hermes*—convincingly, I think—that Greco-Roman Hermetic texts were translated into Middle Persian perhaps as early as the time of Shapur I (reigned ca. 240–270 CE).

According to the handful of modern scholars who have written at any length on the issue, the most likely candidate for the source of the conflation is the *Book of Sothis*. One reason is that the very few fragments of the *Book of Sothis* that survive—all in excerpts made by George Syncellus, probably copied from Annianus or Panodorus—conflate Egyptian figures with biblical counterparts. So, for example, Menes, the first king of the first human dynasty according to the genuine Manetho, becomes Mestraim, an alternate transliteration of Mizraim, the son of Ham in Genesis 10 and also the Semitic name for Egypt. Eusebius, in his *Chronicle*, similarly identifies Menes with Mizraim and declares Ham's son to be the founder of Egypt. If one biblical figure could be substituted for a pagan one, the argument goes, it is likely the full *Book of Sothis* gave Semitic counterparts to other legendary Egyptians.

## Alexander and the Secret Persian Wisdom

Persian translations of Greco-Roman Hermetic material occurred because the Persians had come to believe that Alexander the Great had stolen ancient Persian wisdom and stored it in Egypt. Therefore, Hermetic texts were "really" Persian ones. The Persian sage Ostanes started the process of "recovering" their patrimony through translation. Part of the reason for this belief was that Greek literature falsely attributed the invention of magic to the Persian mage Zoroaster—and thus the reason that medieval Europeans equated him with the wicked Ham and the Pillars of Wisdom. The bottom line is that early on, Hermeticism came to be seen as intimately tied to Enoch and the Watchers.

## THE DECLINE OF HIEROGLYPHICS

The development of the Egyptian god Thoth into the composite figure of Hermes Trismegistus could not have become possible without another major development of late antiquity: the loss of hieroglyphic literacy. As hard as it is to believe, the entire educated class of Egyptians gradually forgot how to read the language of the pharaohs. Hieroglyphics fell out of regular use by the Roman period, with the last traces dying out in the fourth century during the Christianization of Egypt. This created an air of mystery around the old inscriptions, which few could read, and almost none fluently. The consequences were dramatic for the development of myths and legends around Egypt, for the effort to explain the hieroglyphs created whole new stories about the ancients and their wonders.

Sometime around the end of late antiquity, a man named Horapollo wrote a book explaining hieroglyphics for posterity. Nearly everything in the book was wrong.

### Who Was Horapollo?

According to the Byzantine encyclopedia called the Suda (s.v. Ὡραπόλλων), a certain Horapollo was one of the last of the pagan priests of Egypt, living in the reign of the Emperor Zeno (r. 474–475, 476–491). He allegedly converted to Christianity. In the Renaissance, however, our author was identified with the Suda's other Horapollo, a grammarian from Phaenebythis, famed for his expertise gained from Alexandria in Egypt in the time of Theodosius II (r. 408–450). Chances are that neither was the actual author. Rumor had it, though, that Horus was the true author, or perhaps the biblical Pharaoh, or maybe that it was the sacred book of Suphis (as we recall, the name Manetho gave for Khufu), at least according to the occultists of the era.

The extant text, in two books of bad Greek, claims to be a translation from the Coptic made by an unknown Philippos. Scholars are divided on its ultimate origins. The consensus seems to be that Book II is a Greek or Byzantine concoction, made up of traditional Greco-Roman authors' works on animals. However, Book I is believed to be based on real knowledge of Egyptian hieroglyphs, though reported through a fog of corruption and confusion. Some have argued that it represents a genuine living tradition from the last Egyptian priests to understand hieroglyphs. One argument is that the Greek translator misunderstood an original work and adapted it badly into his language. Another argument has it that the Greek "translator" is actually the author, reporting in his own words material learned in Egypt but only partially understood.

Whatever the real source, Horapollo's work preserves legends of Egypt that fed directly into the stories familiar to us from their Arabic-language form several centuries later, when they became the core of medieval pyramid myths. For example, he declares that a sphinx is the Egyptian symbol for "the terrible," because (in A. T. Cory's translation) "this animal, being the most powerful, terrifies all who behold it" (1.20). Amazingly, the Arabs called the Great Sphinx the "Father of Terror" in the Middle Ages. In the very next section after the discussion of sphinxes, Horapollo wrote about the Nile flood and why it was associated with a hieroglyphic of a lion. In his view, the flood was connected with the constellation of Leo—an impossibility because Leo was a Greek constellation unknown to ancient Egypt, but a claim that would have important consequences later, when medieval and early modern writers mixed and matched Horapollo's words to create an astrological legend for the Great Sphinx. (See chap. 7.)

## FINDING BIBLE GIANTS IN EGYPT

But still more potent legends came from those who claimed no knowledge of the hieroglyphs and instead viewed them as mysterious invocations of magic (see fig. 3.2). Some early Christians noticed that the Egyptians drew some figures much larger than others, especially the strange ones with animal heads. They were unfamiliar with the practice called hieratic scale, by which a picture's size correlated to its importance

**Figure 3.2.** After knowledge of hieroglyphs was lost, impressive temples like this one came to be seen as mysterious repositories of magic wisdom. *Library of Congress Prints and Photographs Division, Lot 13550, no. 49.*

rather than its real height. Instead they wrote that the temples of Egypt recorded images of the giants of Genesis, the men of renown, and their strange wisdom. The pagans were no less moved to tie hieroglyphic inscriptions to occult secrets. A soldier-writer, Ammianus Marcellinus, who served under the last pagan emperor, Julian the Apostate, wrote a history of the Roman Empire in the 380s CE. He reported a new tradition that had grown up in late Roman Egypt. The hieroglyphs, he said, were meant to preserve religious knowledge from a predicted flood. As C. D. Yonge translates: "There are also [in Egypt] subterranean passages, and winding retreats, which, it is said, men skilful, in the ancient mysteries, by means of which they divined the coming of a flood, constructed in different places lest the memory of all their sacred ceremonies should be lost."

Ammianus was a pagan, so it is not clear what flood he had in mind, but the reappearance of this same story in connection with Noah's flood in the Middle Ages suggests that at this early date, Egyptian history and Christian historiography were already starting to merge.

## MERGING BIBLICAL AND EGYPTIAN HISTORY

This merger of the Christian and the pagan showed up most clearly in the work of the Christian chronographers—a group of early churchmen who attempted to create universal histories of the world demonstrating that the Bible wasn't just true but that all of the histories of the pagans supported the biblical narrative. One of the first to do so was Sextus Julius Africanus, who wrote a history of everything from Creation to 221 CE that survives only in fragments quoted by later chronographers. In his discussion of Egypt, he drew heavily on Manetho, and it is to him we owe the preservation of Manetho's king lists. But he was not happy with Manetho's massive numbers for the reigns of kings or those of Egyptian history that Plato attributed to Egyptian priests, so he decided that the Egyptians confused lunar months for years and all the numbers should be divided by twelve. He included a discussion of the Watchers as a key event in the history of creation, though he thought them the sons of Seth, one of the first Christians to do so in writing. He also wrote that while touring Egypt, he had heard that Suphis (Khufu) was the author of a sacred book: "Suphis (reigned) for 63 years. He built the Great Pyramid, which Herodotus says was constructed by Cheops. He became contemptuous toward the gods and also wrote the Sacred Book, which I acquired on my trip to Egypt because of its great renown." Many books of magic passed under Khufu's name in those years, and they became a precedent for the Great Pyramid's creator having sacred and secret knowledge. It wouldn't be long before someone would get the bright idea of looking for the so-called real sacred book in the texts inscribed on pyramids and temples.

Two Alexandrian monks of the fourth century, Panodorus and Annianus, were heavily influenced by the popularity of Enochian material in Egypt and considered it wrong that earlier chronologists had minimized the role of the Watchers. In their own works, they created a monumental and epic new history of Egypt and the world in which the fallen angels would take precedence as one of the turning points around which all

## Eusebius and Manetho

Africanus was a major influence on the bishop Eusebius of Cae-
saria a century later. Eusebius's *Chronicle* was, for its time, the most
ambitious effort to marry pagan and Christian histories ever attempted. He raided virtually every known book of pagan history
and lore for facts and evidence to support his case. Eusebius also
claimed that Manetho mistakenly spoke of lunar months as solar
years, which meant that the 24,900 years attributed to the gods
and spirits who reigned before Menes were suddenly made into
2,206 solar years, nearly the same, he said, as the 2,242 years between Adam and the Great Flood. (This is the calculation of the
Septuagint, which Eusebius used.) The Bible and Manetho had
been brought into harmony. He was, however, silent on the pyramids and the Watchers, and he dismissed texts claiming to relate
antediluvian history as unknowable speculation.

history revolved. It would be wonderful if we possessed their work to
know exactly how they did it, but, sadly, neither chronicle survives except in excerpts made by later writers and in later chronicles that were
explicitly based on their work. Of the two, Annianus is the better attested
because his work was shorter and traveled farther, but a lot of reconstruc-
tion is necessary to understand what they said and believed.

As we have seen, the Jews of Egypt had been interested in Enochian literature. But their community had been largely suppressed by the middle
of the second century CE (177 CE, to be specific), not to reappear again
until the 300s CE, at which point any interest in Enoch and Hermes goes
unrecorded. One would think they would have produced their own texts
reacting to Enochian and Hermetic texts; their Christian neighbors were
obsessed with apocryphal texts. However, the period from 70 to 600 CE
saw the suppression of the Enochian tradition among Jewish communities across the ancient world almost completely, reemerging only after

around 700 CE, for reasons that are not entirely clear. But the Christians, too, were starting to have second thoughts about fallen angels. In 367 CE, the Christian bishop of Alexandria, Athanasius (served 328 to 373 CE), bore witness to the fact in an angry missive known as Festal Letter 39. In it, he railed against Hermetic, astrological, and apocryphal literature, particularly that passing under Enoch's name, claiming that such texts were a threat to orthodoxy. Unfortunately, Festal Letter 39 is a textual mess, with one big chunk preserved in Greek and several more in Coptic. In the Coptic fragments, Athanasius complained about the books passing under Enoch's name, arguing that they had fooled the "common" people into believing the impossible—that there were scriptures older than the Bible, written before the Great Flood. Here Athanasius provides testimony that the people of Alexandria had been exposed to Enochian material and through it had been seduced into heresy, echoing the testimony of the abbot Serenus and the alchemist Zosimus that such beliefs were widespread.

## THE RETURN OF THE WATCHERS

The picture painted by the Egyptian writers of the fourth century is one of a Christian community divided between an orthodox elite and common folk who were much more heterodox and open to apocryphal texts that pretended to be coequal to the emerging body of canonical scripture—Athanasius is the first, for example, to enumerate the canonical books of the New Testament.

All of this makes it less surprising that the monk Panodorus of Alexandria, who wrote his world chronicle around 412 CE, attempted to create a grand synthesis of human history by appealing to the Book of Enoch. It was a choice that in another context might have seemed heretical or bizarre, but in Alexandria of his day would have been in keeping with the popular understanding of human history. In this, Panodorus created a true innovation in Christian historiography (or, rather, mythology). Earlier chroniclers had mentioned the fallen angels, but Panodorus was the first to introduce the Watchers as the explanation for the problem of chronology. He wrote that the Egregori, or Watchers, fell from heaven in the year 1000 after creation and taught astrology and astronomy. He

## Reconstructing Annianus

Unfortunately, despite its popularity around the medieval world, Annianus's chronicle is lost to history. Reconstructing what we can about Annianus's ideas about preflood history requires us to collate a large number of quotations and summaries from authors writing in Greek, Syriac, Arabic, and other languages, including the historians George Syncellus, Agapius, Michael the Syrian, Bar Hebraeus, and Al-Juzjani. Fortunately—because in the Middle Ages, Annianus was considered the ultimate authority on the world before the flood across the Near East—they tended to quote overlapping passages of the same material about the Watchers, which makes it relatively easy to see what Annianus had to say by putting all the pieces together in order.

placed the blame on early humans for therefore becoming obsessed with lunar months, mistaking them for years. The fault was not in the stars but in the sinful humans who loved the moon.

Panodorus added one more innovation, as best we can tell from the admittedly uncertain fragments of his lost world chronicle: he identified the gods who reigned among the pagans as the Watchers. We don't know for certain that he invented this concept, but his contemporary Annianus, who wrote a chronicle that was half summary and half critique of Panodorus and that survives in greater fragments, took over this idea and passed it on to the Middle Ages.

When comparing the two chronologists, a few points stand out. First, Panodorus seems to have believed the sons of God, or Watchers, to be fallen angels, and he wrote of them as a focal point of history. But all of the sources that cite Annianus testify that he believed the sons of God to be the children of Seth. More interesting, but less relevant to us, is that Annianus named the kings of the sons of Seth, and he gave them the same names as the kings of Babylon before the flood in the works of the Babylonian priest Berosus. Annianus had solved a major problem in Christian prehistory by accepting Babylon's mythic kings but making them into the sons of Seth, harmonizing Chaldean and Christian accounts of antediluvian times. To this, he made the kings of the fallen ones the evil angels from the Book of Enoch, starting with Semiazos. Much more important is a sentence in Bar Hebraeus almost certainly paraphrasing Annianus, which tells us that the Greeks believed Enoch to be Hermes Trismegistus, most likely because Annianus and Panodorus both mistakenly believed the *Book of Sothis* to be a genuine work of Manetho and accepted its equation of biblical and pagan figures.

But Annianus wasn't done. He was an Egyptian, not a Levantine, so he wanted epochal, world-shaking events to rival those of Israel taking place in his homeland. The Book of Jubilees had established a tradition that Enoch was taken to Eden rather than to heaven when God snatched him up in Genesis 5. Prior to this, as 1 Enoch 65:2 and 106:8 state, he lived at the ends of the earth, which Annianus seems to have taken as a reference to Upper Egypt, perhaps on the strength of the apocryphal tradition that Enoch made his home beyond the civilized world and beyond a great desert (as the mutilated Book of Giants put it in 4Q530 7 ii 5). Annianus may have tried to harmonize this with 1 Enoch 12:2, where the patriarch is said to have dwelt with the Watchers, following the longstanding tradition (still current in medieval times) that Egypt had been populated before the Great Flood by the giant Nephilim.

The medieval historian Agapius likely quotes from Annianus when he says that "Manetho" (i.e., the *Book of Sothis*) said that Enoch had traveled to the heavens and taught astrology and the science of foretelling the future through the stars, writing a book on the occult nature of the heavens. Bar Hebraeus agrees, but several Arabic-language writers give the same material attributed to Hermes Trismegistus, suggesting that Annianus had already equated the two. Whatever it was, as Kevin van Bladel argued in *The Arabic Hermes*, a Persian astrologer named Abū Ma'shar, whom we shall meet soon, appears to give one more key claim from Annianus's lost work, drawing on Ammianus's legend of the preservation of knowledge, Hermeticism, and the Enochian tradition of the predicted end of the world. So important is this passage, preserved by Ibn Juljul and Ṣāʿid al-Andalusī, that it is worth quoting in full, minus the material Abū Maʿshar probably added to the original:

> It is also said [among the Egyptians] that Hermes was the first to predict the Flood and anticipate that a celestial cataclysm would befall the earth in the form of fire or water. He made his residence in Upper Egypt, and chose it to build pyramids and cities of clay. Fearing the destruction of knowledge and the disappearance of the arts in the Flood, he built the great temples; one is a veritable mountain called the Temple in Akhmim, in which he carved representations of the arts and [scientific] instruments, including engraved explanations of science, in order to pass them on to those who would come after him, lest he see them disappear from the world.

These lines, which can be traced in some form back to Annianus through a highly complex collation of Arabic, Persian, and Syriac texts, would serve as the template for most later myths of Egypt's occult wisdom. But it is interesting to see how they were first centered on Akhmim (Panopolis), a center of alchemy and Hermetic philosophy.

When Annianus closed the book on his chronicle, he would have no idea that his Christian contemporaries would basically throw it in the garbage or that his ideas would find their florescence only with the rise of Islam centuries after. Before we get *there*, we need to see why Christians were so eager to dump Hermes as a pyramid builder in favor of a, well, *ridiculous* new legend.

# 4

# THE EARLY MIDDLE AGES

AS WE LEAVE THE LATE ANTIQUE WORLD BEHIND AND MOVE ahead to the Middle Ages, you're probably wondering why the ancients didn't tell too many stories about the pyramids. The answer is fairly straightforward: everybody knew the real story of the pyramids, and most people in the Greco-Roman world would have at least secondhand knowledge of what Herodotus or Diodorus or Pliny had to say about them. Even the competing stories about other kings besides Khufu having built them weren't *that* far from the real history of Egypt. That's why so many myths about Egyptian magic and ancient wisdom tended to cluster around the less massively obvious parts of Egypt—the temple walls, obelisks, tomb paintings, and so forth.

That started to change, however, as the early Middle Ages set in and Christianity became more militant about ensuring that the pagan past gave way to a more religiously correct one. In this chapter, we start to get into the meat of the story. As the real history of Egypt faded from memory, new legends took its place, especially the odd belief that the pyramids had been giant grain silos and the more exotic claim that they were repositories of preflood wisdom.

## CHRISTIANITY AND THE PYRAMIDS

Early medieval Christians had a hard time figuring out what to do with the pyramids. The Greeks and Romans considered them a wonder of the world, but Christian writers dropped them from their lists because of their being pagan works. Christian thinkers especially disliked that the pyramids were the tombs of dead pagan kings, whom they felt deserved no special honor. Worse, as we have seen, the Bible made no mention of the pyramids. To fix that oversight, a new Bible-based speculation arose in the late 300s CE—right around the time Panodorus and Annianus were furiously turning Egypt into a land of fallen angels and astrological secrets. In the 380s CE, a pilgrim named Egeria wrote a long account in Latin to her friends back in the West (exactly where isn't known) of her pilgrimage to the Holy Land. In describing her visit to the pyramids en

### The Pyramid and the Ark

Interestingly, at the same time the church fathers also identified Noah's Ark as being pyramid shaped, suggesting a reason that late antiquity came to view the pyramids as arks in stone that preserved knowledge, just as the wooden Ark preserved life. Origen in Genesis Homily 2, Philo in Questions and Answers on Genesis 2.5, and Clement in Stromata 6.11 all claimed that the Ark was pyramidal in shape. They derived this from the account in Genesis, which claims that the Ark was three hundred by fifty cubits at the base but rose to a window embedded in a peak just one cubit square. They concluded, therefore, that the ship must be pyramidal to fit those measurements. The same claim appeared in the Dead Sea Scrolls, and the belief lasted well into the Renaissance. A pyramid-shaped Ark appears on the Florentine Baptistery's Gates of Paradise by Lorenzo Ghiberti (completed in 1452), confusing tourists to this day.

route, she offered a shocking account. They weren't tombs of dead kings. Instead, "Joseph built them for storing grain," referring to the biblical story of the storehouses Joseph supposedly built in Egypt to store grain for seven years of famine.

Imagine what it must have taken to believe this: one had to imagine the pyramids were hollow and to actively reject every bit of evidence for their real purpose. It required a leap of faith, and faith is what led so many Christians to set the unfortunate precedent of believing fantasies about the pyramids that simply could not be true.

But the idea spread fast. In the Cotton Genesis, a Greek illuminated manuscript of the book of Genesis from the fourth or fifth century, Joseph's granaries were drawn as the Giza pyramids. The image doesn't survive, but it is believed to have inspired the similar mural at Saint Mark's Cathedral in Venice, where it can still be seen today. (Many murals in the cathedral match images from the Cotton Genesis, so the rest are assumed to be copies of its missing pages.)

JOSEPH'S GRANARIES

But this sidelight paled before the spotlight created by the glamour of Joseph's granaries. Sometime before the year 500 CE, a student of Julius Honorius, a Roman teacher, took notes about his master's geography lecture and recorded that Honorius had told his students that the pyramids were the "storehouses of Joseph." The claim appears again in the commentaries of Pseudo-Nonnus in the first half of the 500s. Gregory of Tours wrote in 594 CE in the *History of the Franks* 1.10 that Joseph's granaries were made of stone, wide at the base, and narrow at the top. Although he had never seen the pyramids, they are clearly his inspiration. In 825 CE, the monk Dicuil, writing in the *Liber de Mensura Orbis Terrae* 6.13, described the monk Fidelis's visit to the pyramids and identified them as Joseph's granaries. The claim appears as well in the commentaries of Nicetas of Heraclea in the eleventh century and the Byzantine *Etymologicum magnum* of the twelfth century (among other sources); in both, the word *pyramid* is falsely said to derive from the Greek word for grain because of Joseph.

The reason for this belief is a little unclear. Some of it is likely due to sheer ignorance at the end of antiquity, when Egypt was slowly falling out of the increasingly isolated West's orbit. Although the Byzantines had the legend, it was never as popular in the East, where classical views of the pyramids in Greek competed with Christian views. The succeeding Islamic authors dismissed the granaries claim as unfounded—but because they believed the pyramids too old. Another reason is probably cultural appropriation. Reassigning the pyramids from pagan Egyptian tombs to holy granaries of a biblical patriarch Christianized them and made them an acceptable monument to the Judeo-Christian heritage in the years when Christianity finally overcame paganism in Byzantine Egypt.

But the clearest and best explanation is an inference that can be found in Rufinus, who reported in his translation of Eusebius's *Ecclesiastical History* 11.23 that Christians and Jews in Egypt both identified Joseph with the Greco-Egyptian god Serapis, whom we remember was a form of Osiris, and the Jews said that a statue of Serapis the grain-giver actually depicted Joseph. This claim can be found as far back as Tertullian in *Ad nationes* 2.8 (197 CE). Thus, some scholars have argued that the sarcophagus of the Apis bull (in this period, an aspect of Serapis) became identified with the sarcophagus of Joseph, and both Joseph and Osiris-Serapis were said to have had their coffins drowned in the Nile (the former in a Jewish tradition repeated by Christians and Muslims). But most importantly, we can conclude from this that because the pyramids were known to be tombs and the late antique Egyptians associated death with Serapis, the inference is that pyramids were seen as the realm of Serapis. Thus, some scholars have concluded that for Christians and Jews, these became the structures of Joseph, and since Osiris-Serapis was identified with grain in Egypt (as Plutarch reported in *Isis and Osiris*), it's a small inference to call the pyramids the place where the grain-giving Joseph operated.

Whatever the cause, the belief was by no means universal even in the West (Isidore of Seville correctly knew the pyramids to be tombs in the early 600s CE, for example), but it *was* frequently repeated by medieval chroniclers. Famously, Sir John Mandeville—the fictitious author of a plagiarized travelogue—described two options for what the pyramids *really* were. Some thought they were the tombs of kings, he said, but that couldn't be true because all the natives of Egypt—meaning the Coptic Christians—said that they were the granaries of Joseph and recorded the same in their holy books and their history books. Mandeville was perhaps the first doubter of the tomb theory to ask why, if these pyramids were tombs, they were all empty. (The empty pyramid myth persists to this day despite the discovery of broken pieces of mummified remains in multiple pyramids left behind by looters.) His answer, though, reflected a widespread Christian claim, more popular in the West than, as he claimed, in Egypt itself.

### EMPTYING THE GRANARIES

But that was the high point of the granaries theory. It went out of fashion quickly once the struggle against Islam settled into a stalemate after the fall of Constantinople in 1453 and travel to Egypt became, if not easy, somewhat easier for Westerners. In 1484, no less pious a fellow than a Catholic canon from Mainz, Bernhard von Breydenbach, visited the pyramids on his way back from a tour of the Holy Land—he was as religious as they come. He took one look at the pyramids and wrote the following, published in 1486 in a medieval bestseller called *Peregrinatio in terram sanctam*: "Beyond the Nile we beheld many pyramids, which in ages past the kings of Egypt caused to be built over their tombs, of which the vulgar say that these are the granaries or storehouses which were built there by Joseph in order to store grain. However, this is clearly false, for these pyramids are not hollow inside."

That final sentence effectively ended the granaries claim for several centuries, as every scholar thereafter—whatever his or her beliefs—recognized that solid blocks of stone with, at best, one or two tiny rooms would make ridiculous storehouses. Well, almost. One late edition of Cesare Ripa's *Iconologia* published in the mid-1700s illustrated the story of Joseph's granaries with a picture of a pyramid. Nevertheless, as the number of European travelers to Egypt increased in the 1500s and 1600s, the idea of granaries became increasingly insupportable in light of observation. If there were any remaining doubt, the famed professor John Greaves quashed it in his monumental *Pyramidographia* (1646), the most important work on the pyramids between ancient and modern times. He called the claim "most improper" because pyramids are the wrong shape to maximize storage. He said that facts like the small number of rooms in an otherwise solid building "utterly overthrow this conjecture."

Such was the fate of the first major pyramid myth.

## EGYPT IN THE EYES OF THE BYZANTINE EAST

The granaries of Joseph saw their greatest popularity in the West, but in the East, much more interesting developments combined pagan and Christian ideas in unique ways. In the third or fourth century, a now-forgotten Christian historian named Bouttios or Bottios composed a

### Annianus and the "Italian" History of Egypt

The story of Picus Zeus and Hermes is bizarre, but it is the culmination of a long tradition that probably passed to us through Annianus. The hypothesis that Annianus stands behind the early chapters of Malalas's *Chronicle* was put forward by Heinrich Gelzer in his classic study of Sextus Julius Africanus in the nineteenth century, but has, so far as I know, never been superseded by a better one and is still accepted in modern literature. My own reading of Malalas suggests a clear similarity. This is confirmed by a somewhat more logical version of the story appearing in George Syncellus (*Chronicle* 200), where the identification with Hermes is confirmed and attributed to an anonymous "some," who are probably Annianus and Panodorus, Syncellus's main sources. An earlier version of the story, recorded by Eusebius (*Chronicle* 1.106) makes no mention of Hermes, but Diodorus's brief account in the fragments of his lost Book 6 (chapter 5) do identify Faunus with "Hermes" (the planet Mercury, not the god), but without discussing a trip to Egypt.

history that fused rationalized Greco-Roman mythology with biblical material. (Some think he may be the same as the Bruttius cited in Eusebius's *Chronicle*.) His work does not survive, but it was copied by two Byzantine world chronicles of the early Middle Ages, the so-called *Excerpta Barbari Latina* and the *Chronicle* of John Malalas. The former, whose name means "Excerpts in Bad Latin," is a poor Latin translation of a Greek world chronicle that the Byzantines gave to the Franks as a gift; the latter is the oldest Byzantine chronicle to survive in full in the original Greek. Both are very, very weird when writing about Egypt.

Despite a few differences, they tell basically the same bonkers story about Egypt, which we reviewed in chapter 3, concerning the Italian king Picus Zeus, whose son Faunus, also called Hermes, fled to Egypt and set himself up as a sage and a god. He was a companion of Misraim, the first king of Egypt after the Great Flood, and ruled Egypt after Misraim's death. The *Excerpta* specifically identifies this Hermes as Hermes Trismegistus.

John Malalas also told stories from the forged *Book of Sothis* about what "Manetho" said of the first kings of Egypt before the Great Flood. These stories are not terribly interesting, except for their Christian influences. But one peculiar thing stands out: Malalas was obsessed with chastity and wrote that Hephaestus and his son Helios both imposed laws of absolute chastity on the Egyptians, who cheered at the restrictions on their sexual freedom.

## THE VIEW FROM MEDIEVAL JUDAISM

Nor were the Greeks alone in inventing stories about antediluvian Egypt. An Egyptian Jew, Rabbi Barachias Nephi, or Abenephius, may have written a treatise on Egyptian magic, rituals, and legends from a Jewish perspective around this time. I say *may have* because no one knows for sure whether he existed. His book is lost, and it is known only from a few quotations made by the Renaissance scholar Athanasius Kircher, who may have made him up. Kircher showed a friend a page of Abenephius's book, but he refused to let anyone see the whole thing. From the fragments, my instinct is that it might well be an Arabic translation of a late antique or an early medieval Hellenized Jewish text on Egyptian mysteries.

**Figure 4.1.** Abenephius associated Enoch's Pillars of Wisdom with the obelisks of Egypt, like this one at the temple of Luxor. *Library of Congress Prints and Photographs Division, Lot 13552, no. 81.*

Whether or not Abenephius existed, the legends attributed to him fit the context of Jewish culture in medieval Egypt after the coming of Islam. He offers some fanciful explanations of the hieroglyphs and speaks of antediluvian times, albeit with a focus on obelisks rather than pyramids (see fig. 4.1). "Hermes was the first who erected these columns, which they call the needles of Pharaoh, and on these he inscribed the sciences which he had discovered," Abenephius writes, echoing the myth of Enoch and the Watchers. He speaks, too, of a king named Sothis (i.e., the star Sirius), who created books of wisdom and pillars of the same. This seems to reflect the Suphis of Manetho, but Abenephius has given his name and the names of other pharaohs as those of stars and planets. Archaeologists and historians report that the Jews of medieval Cairo produced vast numbers of magical amulets and grimoires, part of the Islamic elite's patronage of Jewish magical practitioners for the "forbidden" arts. In that context, and given that amulets are explicitly discussed in the opening of Abenephius's book, his treatise looks less like a history of Egypt and more like a guide for how to carve (fake) hieroglyphs on amulets for fun and profit.

## EGYPT IN THE EYES OF EARLY ISLAM

Roman Egypt passed to the East Roman (Byzantine) Empire and remained a Christian province, except for the brief Persian interlude under Khosrau II, down to the Islamic conquest, which began in 639 CE under the caliph 'Umar. As Muslim soldiers, administrators, and scholars poured into the country, they struggled to integrate the newly conquered territory into a distinctly Islamic cultural context. At first, this meant that they expressed little interest in the pyramids beyond what the locals told them. When the first Muslims came to Egypt, they found little memory of the history of the pyramids. Ibn 'Abd al-Ḥakam, the first Muslim historian of Egypt, reported that no one knew anything about them. They were simply too old. An unknown Muslim writer famously said of the Great Pyramid, "For every building, I fear the ravages of time, but as for this monument, I fear for time." Another writer said that the pyramids must predate Noah's flood or else someone would know something about them. A few visitors claimed to see a line on the Great Pyramid about midway up marking where the flood's waters reached.

In the early 800s CE, when the Caliph Al-Ma'mūn arrived in Egypt, he ordered the Great Pyramid of Giza opened. Unable to find the entrance in the perfect casing stones, he blasted a hole in the side, at about the level of the imagined floodwaters, using heat and vinegar to crack the stones and burrow into the pyramid. According to later Arabic writers (whose mixture of fact and fiction is hard to separate), he discovered inside either empty rooms or a rich array of treasures (allegedly the exact amount,

**Figure 4. 2.** Looking out of the Great Pyramid from the entrance. *Library of Congress Prints and Photographs Division, LC-M305- SL17-860.*

in gold coins, no less, spent to break into the pyramid!) and a mummy clutching an occult text. Lacking the ability to read the text, there was little that could be said about the pyramids, which remained a mystery for the curious caliph. Al-Ma'mūn allegedly regretted the effort to investigate the pyramids, having spent beyond his resources to do it, and he declared an end to all pyramid exploration to save money.

That did not mean that the Arabs lacked for material to build a history —it just wouldn't be based on real facts. Abū Sahl al-Faḍl ibn Nawbakhtī, writing in the late 700s CE, reported that Hermes Trismegistus lived in Babylon under a Persian king and was sent from a college of sages to rule over Egypt because of his wisdom. The Persian king's college of wisdom persisted until the time of Alexander, who conquered Babylon. According to Ibn Nawbakhtī, Babylon's walls had been built by the antediluvian giants, and Alexander the Great had Persia's books of wisdom copied into Egyptian and Greek and then destroyed. Only centuries later was the ancient wisdom restored under the caliphs. Ibn Nawbakhtī had taken a traditional, pre-Islamic Persian legend and rewrote it to make the ancient

### The Rivals of Hermes

There were also a number of other stories about antediluvian wisdom circulating in the Islamic world. A traditional Persian story held that a king named Tahmurath, like Enoch, had received a warning of the coming flood and ordered all of the books of science buried in a secret place to keep them safe. Another story, current in Islamic Baghdad, claimed that the antediluvian kings of nearby Babylon learned of the coming flood from their astrologers and built fortresses on high hills to preserve themselves and their knowledge. Such stories, of uncertain vintage, were derivatives of the story of Enoch and the Pillars of Wisdom. But the majority of such stories attached themselves to the legendary figure of Hermes Trismegistus.

wisdom acceptable to Islam, changing it from Zoroastrian scripture to
Hermetic books of science. The discussion of Hermes had a polemical
purpose, too, to make the sage into a Babylonian and thus a subject of
the Persian Empire, therefore making Persia the origin and elder font
of Egyptian wisdom. And yet it bears an almost uncanny resemblance
to the story told more than a century earlier in Byzantium, recorded by
John Malalas and the *Excerpta Latina Barbari*. Both the Byzantines and
Ibn Nawbakhtī had access to Greek and Syriac Christian chronographic
works, particularly the fourth-century world history of Annianus, so
there is likely a common source.

According to later legend, when Al-Ma'mūn encountered the ancient
pagan star worshipers of the Mesopotamian city of Harran, now in Tur-
key, around 830 CE, he told them that since they were not Jewish, Christian, or Muslim, they would need to convert or be killed. The Harranians
hired a lawyer, who advised them to tell Al-Ma'mūn that they were Sabians, a religious group granted protection by the Qur'an but not defined or explained in the text. By claiming to be Sabians, the Harranians
outwitted the caliph, and they based their claim on their veneration of
Hermes Trismegistus, whom they held for a prophet, because Muslims
recognized Hermes as being the same as the patriarch Enoch, who was
also the Islamic prophet Idris.

The Harranians helped create a new legend for the pyramids of Egypt.
As Ibn al-Nadīm reported in his *Fihrist* in 998 CE, the story popular
among the common people near Giza was that the pyramids of Khufu
and Khafre were really the tombs of Hermes and his wife or his son. Abd
Al-Latif al-Baghdadi, writing much later, gave the more common form of
the story, that the ancient books of the Sabians identified the two pyramids as the tombs of Hermes and Agathodaemon, these being the Greek
names for Enoch and Seth. The Sabians, all agreed, made pilgrimages
to Giza to pay respect to Hermes. There they burned a rooster alive and
used its death throes to predict the future under Hermes's guidance. But
as the tombs of Seth and Hermes, these pillars of stone could not help but
recall the Jewish legend of the Pillars of Wisdom that Enoch and Seth
were thought to have erected in Egypt. Menkaure's pyramid, according
to al-Dimashqi, belonged to Sāb, the (imaginary) son of Hermes and
founder of the Sabians.

## LEGENDS OF THE HIDDEN TEMPLE

By the end of the ninth century, this new legend had merged all but seamlessly with the stories circulating about temples and tombs as archives of Egyptian wisdom against the flood. When the great historian al-Mas'udi traveled to Egypt in the early 900s CE and inquired how the pyramids were built for his book *Meadows of Gold,* he was quite sensibly told that the Egyptians stacked stones upon stones. But when he asked about the great temple at Akhmim, now a center for alchemy and veneration of Hermes Trismegistus, he received a story that quite obviously combined the Pillars of Wisdom with alchemy and ancient Egyptian magic. He heard that a man named Abū'l-Faïd Dū'l-Nūn al-Misri al-Ikhmimi claimed to be able to read the hieroglyphs on the temple walls—though his so-called translations were only bland aphorisms—and he was told that the builders of the temples in Akhmim—buildings known as *berabi* (singular: *berba*) in Arabic—were astrologers and that their study of the stars predicted that the world would end by fire or by flood: "In fear lest the sciences should be annihilated with the people, they constructed these berabi and disgorged their knowledge into the figures, the images, and the inscriptions which adorned them. They built them either of stone or of earth, separating these two kinds of constructions. If the foretold catastrophe, they said, is of fire, the edifices built of earth and clay will

### Temples and Pyramids

The scholar Okasha El Daly has suggested, not wholly implausibly, that medieval people conflated the *berba* (temple) name with the Coptic word *brbr,* which refers to the capstone of a pyramid, called a pyramidion, which was derived from the Egyptian name for a pyramidion, *ben ben,* thus making it easy to transfer legends of the temples to the pyramids through a confusion of terms.

harden like stone, and our sciences will be preserved. If, on the contrary, it is a deluge, the water will carry away that which is built out of earth, but the stone will subsist."

It was exactly—almost word for word!—the story of the Pillars of Wisdom, but with the pillars turned into a temple, perhaps due to the association of the temples with the Greek and biblical giants, as Diodorus had reported.

This story, which had probably been current in Egypt since late Christian times, cross-pollinated with the stories being told of Hermes Trismegistus and his stelae. These stories harmonized with another story circulating around Hermes's alchemical discipline. Jābir ibn Hayyān, the great eighth-century alchemist, said that all of the great elixirs of alchemy were hidden in the pyramids. When Ibn Wahshiyya wrote a treatise on alphabets and magic before 900 CE, he wrote that Hermes built "treasure chambers"—meaning the temples, in their new capacity as repositories of wealth and wisdom—in upper Egypt and erected stones inscribed with magical formulae. This story reflected a new tradition by which Hermes would become the builder of temples and pyramids alike.

## THE BIRTH OF THE MEDIEVAL PYRAMID MYTH

That version of the story belonged to the greatest astrologer of the Middle Ages, Abū Maʿshar al-Balkhi, who wrote a lost book called *The Thousands* in which he attempted an astonishing feat: to demonstrate that the whole history of the world—past, present, and future—followed the conjunctions of the planets, which governed every event. Abū Maʿshar inherited Greco-Roman and Jewish stories about the destruction of the world by fire and flood. In *The Thousands*, he developed a complex astrological system whereby he imagined that the entire universe ran on a clock of interlocking cycles, which could then be used to predict events until the End Times. *The Thousands* attempted to prove the accuracy of this system by presenting a chronology of world history drawn from Christian and Persian historiography and showing that each event coincided with an astrological conjunction. The Great Flood was the most important, occurring, he said, in 3101 BCE during a specific conjunction in Aries.

## Calculating the Flood

Later sources, including the anonymous *Akhbār al-zamān* and *The Remaining Signs of Past Centuries* of al-Bīrūnī, preserved Abū Ma'shar's astrological dating of the Great Flood. According to Abū Ma'shar, the flood occurred "when the heart of the Lion would be in the first minute of the head of Cancer, with the planets occupying the following positions: the moon in conjunction with the sun would be in the first minute of Aries; Zaus [Zeus], that is to say, Jupiter, would be at 29° of Pisces; Mars 28° 5' of the same constellation; Aphrodite or Venus at 29° 3'; Hermes or Mercury at 27°; Saturn in Libra; and the apogee of the moon at 5° and a few minutes of Leo." These calculations, he said, had been made before the flood by Hermes Trismegistus and the priests of Egypt.

His astrological system drew not just on Greek sources but others, too, including Babylonian, Persian, and—crucially—Indian materials. The mathematical details are kind of painful to get into and complicated enough to need whole articles and books to explain, so forgive me for oversimplifying a bit. Basically, Abū Ma'shar wanted to take the Babylonian/Greek zodiac of 360 degrees and make it work with the 4.32 billion years of a Hindu *kalpa* and the 360,000 years of a medieval Persian "world-year." These numbers occur in the surviving fragment of *The Thousands* given by al-Sijzī, where al-Sijzī tells us that Abū Ma'shar used the Persian world-year of 360,000 years and reckoned the kalpa as twelve thousand Persian cycles. He adopted, though, the Hindu belief—not found in Persian sources—that at the beginning of the kalpa, all planets were conjoined at the 0 degrees mark, which, when he translated it into the Babylonian or Greek zodiac, placed them at 0 degrees of Aries.

These cycles could work together because they all, basically, boiled down to multiples of twelve. The twelve months gave rise to the idea of twelve as a sort of perfect factor for units of time, and Abū Maʿshar developed the most elaborate system of interlocking Greek, Persian, and Hindu cycles. The math was a little wonky—he didn't know that he based his world system on a bad estimate of how fast the heavens churn—but his system, and the texts that supported it, spread like wildfire. Not to belabor the point, but Abū Maʿshar's system was extremely influential and could be found from Spain to the Hindu Kush—wherever Islam spread.

This is important because Abū Maʿshar defended his astrology with historical details about antediluvian times taken from Annianus and framed it, according to al-Masʿudi, around a study of the most important buildings of each thousand-year period. His work spread the story of Hermes predicting the Great Flood and building the temples and pyramids of upper Egypt, particularly the *berba*, or temple, of Akhmim, all across the Islamic world and, eventually, the West as Abū Maʿshar's book found new readers. So influential was his astrological analysis of the history of the flood that the writer who created the most famous of all medieval pyramid stories copied Abū Maʿshar's material wholesale and placed it into his own book.

### INTRODUCING KING SŪRĪD

He did so because Abū Maʿshar said that a man named Sūrīd had a dream three hundred years before the flood that the moon had descended to the earth in the form of a woman, that the earth had been overturned, and that the sun had gone into eclipse. This caused the priests to calculate the coming of the Great Flood and the Egyptians to build the pyramids of Giza to guard against the disaster. Ibn Wahshiyya, writing at the same time, tells us that this Sūrīd was a philosopher who inscribed divine wisdom on the walls of the Egyptian temples in a secret alphabet and that another man, Philaos—possibly the Philemon of later legends—built treasure chambers in the pyramids and filled them with scientific instruments, magical devices, and astrological texts and set traps to guard them. Ibn Wahshiyya transferred the story from Hermes to Sūrīd and Philaos because he had come to believe, as John Malalas had (and probably from Greek sources), that Hermes had actually lived *after* the Great

Flood. Ibn Wahshiyya believed Hermes served as king of Egypt, eventually inspiring Khufu, whom he calls King Kimas (i.e., the Chemmis of Diodorus), to write two hundred books of Hermetic alchemy.

Abū Ma'shar disagreed on Hermes, believing that one Hermes lived before the flood and one after, but if we can take the testimony of the writer of the *Akhbār al-zamān* and also that of the thirteenth-century historian Murtaḍā ibn al-'Afīf at face value, Abū Ma'shar had also known of the philosopher Sūrīd and his prophecy of the coming flood and attributed to him the building of the Giza pyramids. However, he considered the pyramids to be much less important than the Akhmim temple, which he called the most important building of its millennium.

However, later generations reversed this. They would promote Sūrīd to king of Egypt and make the Great Pyramid the focal point of all history.

# 5

# PYRAMID LEGENDS IN MEDIEVAL ISLAM

NOW THAT ANTIQUITY HAD GIVEN WAY TO THE MIDDLE AGES, the real history of Egypt had been forgotten. Myths and legends took the place of the facts, and the stories told about the pyramids only grew more elaborate over time. Abū Maʻshar had provided the template by linking pyramids to Hermes's preservation of preflood knowledge. But what remained was to rewrite the story to move the action from Egyptian temples, now disappearing beneath the sand or being dismantled for construction materials, to the pyramids, whose size and bulk seemed a more impressive place to store the secrets of creation. Medieval Islamic scholars had a much less negative view of the antediluvian world, and they did not share the Christians' worries about assigning too much glory and prestige to the ancient giants.

## AN EXPLOSION OF LEGENDS

Around the same time that Abū Maʻshar wrote his *Thousands,* the Christian chronographers of Byzantium, such as George Syncellus and George Cedrenus, wrote entire histories of the world detailing the history of Egypt without mentioning the pyramids, except in brief quotations from

Manetho. But on the other side of the shifting border that separated Christendom from the Islamic *umma*, or community, the pyramids held a deep fascination that reached from Iberia to Persia, and increasingly they had come to be seen as the last surviving remnants of the world before Noah's flood, the very embodiment of ancient wisdom. The trouble was that nobody could quite agree on who had built the pyramids.

The Sabians' suggestion that the Great Pyramid was the tomb of Hermes Trismegistus eventually developed into the belief that Hermes had built the Great Pyramid itself. But it was hardly the only claim of its kind. The popular Christian belief that Joseph had constructed them remained current in Islamic Egypt into at least the thirteenth century, as Sibt ibn al-Jawzī reported before 1256 CE. According to the sheiks living around Giza, the pyramids themselves had an inscription on them carved four thousand years before Cairo was founded stating that the pyramids had been built when the "Swooping Vulture" (Vega) was in Cancer, a time Sibt ibn al-Jawzī dated to either thirty-six thousand or seventy-six thousand years before Muhammad's birth in 571 CE. He added that other stories in circulation suggested that the pyramids were built after the Great Flood, either by Nimrod—the biblical hunter believed in popular tradition to have built the Tower of Babel under demonic influence—or by Daluka, the fictitious queen who reigned after God drowned Pharaoh in the Red Sea during the Exodus. Some later Islamic writers asserted that a book by the Italian Jew Joseph ben Gorion attributed the pyramids to Aristotle, who built them as tombs for himself and Alexander the Great—though no surviving Arabic copy of his *Josippon* says this.

These stories, however, were fairly uncommon. Much more widespread was the belief that Shaddād bin 'Ād (and/or his brothers and sons) had built the pyramids during the time of the Hyksos pharaohs, around 1600 BCE. Shaddād was the legendary king of Iram of the Pillars, an Arabian city that the Qur'an states God destroyed for its arrogance and corruption. Some legends had Shaddād lead an invasion of Canaan that forced the Hyksos into Egypt. It was therefore easy to expand the story and imagine that Shaddād pursued them into Egypt and built pyramids as tall as the pillars of Iram. But although every Arab historian reported that Arab-Egyptians embraced a story that attributed Egypt's greatest wonder to Arabs, they also noted that the Copts—the descendants of the native Egyptians—disputed the story and denied that Shaddād had ever entered Egypt. They proudly told the Arabs that Egypt's magical talismans kept out every ancient invader except Nebuchadnezzar, and they suggested that the Arabs confused Shaddād with the (fictitious) pharaoh Shaddāt ibn 'Adīm, whom they claimed had built Sneferu's pyramids at Dahshur. The similarity of names was, of course, not accidental.

This clash of cultures between Arab-Egyptians and native Coptic Egyptians created competing narratives about the history of Egypt before the Muslim conquest. But over time, they tended to settle into a rough consensus, at least among the medieval Muslim community. It was generally accepted among Arab-Egyptians that Hermes was involved with the temples of Upper Egypt, particularly Akhmim, and Shaddād with the pyramids of Dahshur, which left an opening for a new story to help explain the Giza pyramids. This one tended to combine Coptic and Islamic views and drew on Abrahamic lore, late antique legends, and Hermetic mysticism.

### EARLY ISLAMIC ACCOUNTS

The first Muslim historians of Egypt, such as Ibn Abd al-Hakam, denied any history of Egypt before the Great Flood, but knew that Egypt was special, since it is the most-mentioned country in the whole of the Qur'an. As the scholar Ulrich Haarmann noted, the medieval historian al-Idrisi quotes al-Hakam's brother Muhammad (d. 875) as saying that Muhammad, the Prophet, himself had rejected the idea of an antediluvian history of Egypt, making a break with Christians and Jews who speculated at length about the preflood world. Down to around 900 CE, Muslim writers generally followed the convention that Egyptian history began with Mizraim after the flood. After this time, as Islam absorbed Greek and Syriac literature, bits and pieces of antediluvian lore found their way into Islamic historiography. We have already seen how Abū Ma'shar made use of Annianus's antediluvian lore, and after him the floodgates opened.

As historian Michael Cook documented, Muslim efforts to write the history of Egypt took three different forms. The three types of history

## Medieval Islamic History Books

Many medieval Islamic history books were not histories in the sense we know them today. Instead, they were more like anthologies of interesting stories. Their books collected anecdotes about strange, marvelous, or wonderful things, known as 'ajā'ib, and linked these anecdotes about wonders into loose narratives. Abū Ma'shar, for example, used stories about wondrous buildings as his framework in *The Thousands*. Most of the Egyptian wonders discussed by later writers were exaggerations of real objects, such as the magic mirrors and lighthouses modeled on the Pharos at Alexandria; standardized stories of protective charms and talismans; and tales of magical lost cities, mostly fantasy.

used many of the same stories and fictitious figures but interpreted them in different ways. The first, and least important to us, involved commentary on a corrupt and distorted account of Manetho's king list inherited from late antique sources. It appears primarily in the works of al-Birūnī and al-Maqrīzī but has nothing to say about the pyramids. The second type was what Cook called the "Traditionalist" history, being a set of stories and anecdotes building on the Qur'anic history of Egypt. It starts with Mizraim after the flood. The final and most important approach was what Cook called the "Hermetic" history of Egypt, focusing on life before the flood and centering on the occult and magical wonders created by Hermes and the Nephilim giants. The scholar Mark Pettigrew suggests that this division is too neat, but for our purposes it is a useful way to distinguish between histories that included antediluvian material and those that did not.

The history of Egypt these sources provide is almost impossible to summarize, both because of its enormous complexity and because there is little coherent narrative. Instead, all the versions offer impressionistic accounts based on magic, wonders, and entertaining anecdotes. We

## Medieval Arabic King Lists

Arabic writers had their own list of kings of ancient Egypt that was very different from those known to ancient Greeks and Romans. The antediluvian kings seem to bear little resemblance to Manetho's list. The legendary pharaohs who reigned before Menes were not preserved in most late antique and medieval copies of Manetho, so this is in some measure to be expected. The weird list of postdiluvian pharaohs preserved in the various Arabic authors under a bewildering variety of names, descend, in roundabout fashion, from Manetho's list of pharaohs, albeit with many corruptions and much confusion. Many of the Arabic king names seem to have Greek endings, and in some cases, later writers mistook Greek words for royal names. Because of this, it seems likely that the Arabic king lists had, at least in part, an underlying Greek source.

find stories of statues that could heal, murder, or detect lies. We read of fabulous temples and tombs laced with impossible treasures, guarded by automatons and ghosts. And most of all, we read that some kings were pious and believed in the one true God, while the evil and corrupt kings were seduced by *djinn*—the Islamic version of demons—into idolatry. The Hermetic writers counted about twenty kings before the flood, starting with Naqrāūs (or Baqrāwīs), a giant who led seventy Nephilim into Egypt, where they built "the tallest buildings" and many monuments. The list ended with Far'ān (i.e., "Pharaoh"), a corrupt and venal man who died at the Great Pyramid trying escape the flood. After the flood, the story resumes with Mizraim. His sons Qobṭīm, Ashmūn, Atrīb, and Ṣā were personifications of the regions of Egypt, whose names they shared. Each was thought to have fathered a dynasty, whose descendants they traced down to the pharaohs of Joseph and Moses and afterward through some of the kings listed by Manetho. Many of the kings were credited with pyramids, temples, and tombs, and all were said to have possessed occult knowledge from the angels and the djinn.

In general, in all three types of history, the further back in time an author looked, the more fanciful and fictitious his material became. In these histories, the role of Hermes Trismegistus has been minimized and his attributes reassigned to men like Naqrāūs. He is still present, but only around the edges of the narrative. In the Hermetic history, *Hermes* becomes a title rather than a person. It was the title of the (fictitious) Egyptian priest Shāon of Ashmūn, who traced the source of the Nile and erected eighty-five water-pumping statues there to regulate its annual flood. Hermes is sometimes called a king, even though he doesn't appear in the king list—a remnant of the old Byzantine traditions the Arabic-language sources drew upon. Hermes's lesser role reflected changing views in the Islamic world about magic and alchemy. Hermeticism was widespread in the early centuries, but both it and alchemy gradually fell into disrepute, particularly after the fatwa issued against the Hermetic Sabians in 933 CE. It never entirely vanished, though. Each successive writer after 933, however, was a little less Hermetic and moved away from mysticism toward, if not history, then a religious approximation of what history would have looked like if Abrahamic legends had really happened.

## SŪRĪD AND THE ANTEDILUVIAN PYRAMIDS

All of this set the stage for the development of the last and greatest Islamic legend of the pyramids. This story made use of the philosopher Sūrīd, traditionally seen as a priest of Egypt before the Great Flood. The new story promoted him to the greatest king of Egypt before the flood and a special recipient of a divine message about the coming catastrophe. In his efforts, he was joined by the priest Filīmūn or Aqlīmūn—apparently an Arabic transliteration of the Greek name Philemon—who used astrology to discern the future of Egypt.

Dozens of medieval Muslim writers told Sūrīd's story, but most were copyists, rarely changing more than a few words. The three most important sources for the Sūrīd story are (1) the *Akhbār al-zamān*, an

## Who Was Ibrāhīm ibn Waṣīf Shāh?

Little is known of the life of the writer known variously as Al-Waṣīfi and Ibrāhīm ibn Waṣīf Shāh, traditionally ascribed to the early 1200s CE. Neither the date of his birth nor his death is recorded, and even his name is the subject of dispute. Al-Waṣīf is the first version cited, given by al-Qifṭī around 1250 CE, but he is better known by the more elaborate name under which the most extensive extant fragments of his work are quoted by al-Maqrīzī, who calls him "the Master" (al-Ustād). Many scholars traditionally declared Ibn Waṣīf Shāh's text to be one and the same with the *Akhbār al-zamān*, but although the excerpts quoted by al-Maqrīzī, totaling about two-thirds of the *Akhbār al-zamān*'s second part, on Egypt, are nearly identical to the parallel passages in this book, they are not entirely the same. Where they differ, ibn Waṣīf Shāh has the inferior reading, sometimes quite garbled, and his version has apparently been redacted, with references to giants and Hermetic material minimized or eliminated. The *General Estoria* of Spain's King Alfonso X preserves under the name of Alguazif lengthy accounts of what was apparently the next volume of ibn Waṣīf Shāh's *History of Egypt*, covering the period from Moses to Alexander the Great.

anonymous history of Egypt written around 950–1000 CE; (2) the *Egyptian History* of the scholar Murtaḍā ibn al-'Afīf, a close parallel to the *Akhbār* made around 1200 CE by copying a rotted and incomplete manuscript but preserving a few correct readings absent from the *Akhbār*; and (3) the excerpts of Ibrāhīm ibn Waṣīf Shāh's *Great Book of Marvels*, possibly from around 1200 CE, preserved in al-Maqrīzī's *Al-Khitat*, all nearly verbatim identical to the *Akhbār*. It appears that all three texts are copies of a lost original, one probably composed around 900 CE.

Because of the great importance of this story for pyramid legendry, we need to look at the Sūrīd story as it is given in these sources. Below is my translation of the longest and most elaborate of the Arabic pyramid legends, as it is given in the *Akhbār al-zamān*, with a few corrections from Murtaḍā ibn al-'Afīf and Ibrāhīm ibn Waṣīf Shāh.

### THE STORY OF SŪRĪD FROM THE *AKHBĀR AL-ZAMĀN*

The first to build pyramids was Sūrīd, son of Sahlūq, who ruled Egypt three hundred years before the Flood. This king had a dream in which he felt as if the earth was overturned with all its inhabitants, the men fled in all directions, and the stars fell and clashed against each other with a terrible noise. He was moved by this dream and conceived a great fear; he nevertheless imparted his foreknowledge to no person, but he knew that some terrible event would happen in the world. Then he dreamed that the fixed stars descended on the earth in the form of white birds; these birds caught men in flight, and threw them between two high mountains which then closed over them; then the stars darkened and were eclipsed. This dream renewed his terrors. He entered the Temple of the Sun and began to pray and worship God in the dust, and wept.

When morning came, he ordered the chief priests to come together from all parts of Egypt. One hundred and thirty of them met, and he secretly consulted with them on the visions he had seen. The priests praised him and glorified him, and they explained to him that a great event would occur in the world. Philemon, the high priest, spoke. He was their leader, and he lived constantly in the presence of the king; he was the priest of Amsūs, a city of ancient Egypt. He said: "No doubt the vision of a king is a wonder because the dreams of royal personages can be neither in vain nor misleading because of the greatness of their power and elevation of their rank. Allow me to share the king a dream that I had one year, which to date I have reported to no one." The king said, "Explain it to me, O Philemon." "I dreamed," he said, "that I sat with the king at the top of the lighthouse in Amsūs; the sky lowered down close enough to touch our heads, and it formed over us a dome that enveloped us. The king raised his hands toward heaven, and the stars came down to us in a multitude of different forms. Men implored the help of the king and gathered around his palace. The king raised his hands up to his face, and he ordered me to do the same; and both of us were in great distress. Then we saw a kind of opening in the sky from which came a light, and we saw that light rise above us—it was the sun. We saw him and implored him, and he spoke to us, telling us that the heavens would return to their starting point after three hundred and sixty orbits had been made. The sky descended almost to touch the ground and then returned to its proper place. Then I awoke, filled with terror."

The king commanded the priests to measure the altitude of the stars, and analyze what they portended. They made the calculations with great care, and they spoke first of a flood and then of a fire, which would burn the entire world. Then the king ordered the construction of the pyramids, and when they were completed according to his wise plan, he transported to them the wonders and treasures of his people and the bodies of ancient kings. He ordered the priests to deposit therein the secrets of their science and precepts of their wisdom. But the most famous of the descendants of Ham, the Copts and Indians, are the wise.

. . . . Surīd is the builder of the two pyramids that are attributed to Shaddād bin ʿĀd. The Copts deny that either the ʿĀdites or the Amalekites ever invaded their country because they say the Egyptians could defend themselves with their magic against any who attacked them. Al-Harabiun [sic for the Harranians—i.e., the Sabians] says the same.

Abū Maʿshar reported this opinion in his *Book of Thousands*: The reason Surīd built the pyramids was the vision that we have reported in its proper place. He confirms it in his *Book of Miraculous Dreams*, where he adds that he sent for his priests and astronomers and told them how he saw the sphere had descended to him in the guise of a woman, how the land with all its inhabitants had been overturned, and how the sun had been eclipsed. They then foretold to him the Deluge with all its circumstances.

This fact is told in a history book which was transmitted to the Copts by two brothers and found in a tomb on the chest of one of the corpses. The Copts say that these two men were the descendants of an Egyptian from ancient Egypt who escaped the rising deluge with Noah in the ark. He had believed the prophet, and he took his two sons with him. It is said

he was a son of Mizraim, son of Ham; he was an eminent and highly educated person. It is written in the book that King Sūrīd built three cities
in the Saʻid and placed there many wonders. Later we will have occasion
to speak again of these two brothers.

Thus, we read in this book that Sūrīd, son of Sahlūq, having had the
aforementioned vision, shared it with Philemon, the chief priest, and ordered the priests to consult the stars, to determine which events threatened the greatest part of the world. They immediately began their observations; they studied the sky very carefully and discovered a prodigy
coming down from heaven and up from the earth would consume almost
all men: this prodigy was to be a great flood, after which nothing would
remain. The king asked if this event would recur several times or if it
should be finished once and for all. They observed more and replied that
the human race with its empires and all things on earth would reappear
as they were before. Then the king ordered the construction of temples
and great monuments, for himself and his family, in order to safeguard
their bodies and all their riches, which they would deposit within. He
inscribed on the ceilings, on the roofs, on the walls, and on columns, all
the secrets of science, in which the Egyptians excelled more than any
other nation; and he had painted a picture of the great stars and lesser
stars, with signs that permitted their recognition. He also engraved the
names of plants and their properties, how to construct talismans, their
descriptions, and the rules of mathematics and geometry. All who know
the books and the language of Egypt can make use of these images and
inscriptions.

The priests told the king that when the following events took place,
they would occur over the whole world except for a very small part, and
the time of their realization would be when the heart of the Lion would
be in the first minute of the head of Cancer, with the planets occupying
the following positions: the moon in conjunction with the sun would be
in the first minute of Aries; Zaus [*Zeus*], that is to say, Jupiter, would be at
29° of Pisces; Mars 28° 5′ of the same constellation; Aphrodite or Venus at
29° 3′; Hermes or Mercury at 27°; Saturn in Libra; and the apogee of the
moon at 5° and a few minutes of Leo. The King, having heard the report,
said to the priests, "Now look to see whether after this event there will
come another from heaven onto the earth that will be the opposite of it,

I mean to say, the destruction of the world by fire." They informed him that it would be so. "Look then," he said, "to see when this will happen." They resumed their observations and found that this deluge of fire would take place when the Heart of the Lion would be in the final minute of 10° of Leo; the Sun would be in the same minute in conjunction with Saturn and in trine compared to the Head; Mars would be in Leo in an oblique passage; and Mercury in the same minute as he; Siline [*Selene; i.e., the Moon*] in Aquarius, in conjunction with the Tail, in twelve parts; Venus opposite her on a straight path; and Mars in Leo on a straight path. At that moment the sun will cover the earth in a manner heretofore unknown. The priests brought all this to the king and said: When the Heart of the Lion will have completed two-thirds of a revolution, there will be no living animal on earth that will not be stricken and die, and when it will have completed a full revolution, the system of the spheres will be destroyed.

The king ordered the construction of tall monuments, the cleaving of huge slabs, the extraction of lead from the land of the West, and the rolling in of stones from the region of Aswan; these great black rocks were drawn on chariots. He laid the foundations of the three pyramids, Eastern, Western and Colored; the last of these was entirely made of white and black colored stones. It is said that the builders had palm wood sheets covered in writing, and after having extracted every stone and having it cut, they placed over each stone one of these sheets; they then gave a blow to the stone, and it traveled far beyond the reach of sight. They came back close to it and did the same again until they had led it to its assigned place. Craftsmen then carved each slab so as to affix in the middle an iron rod; they placed over it another slab with a hole in its center, and the rod entered the hole. They then poured lead around the slab and into the hole so that the adjustment was perfect.

They decorated the pyramids with paintings, inscriptions, and figures capable of confounding the imagination [*see fig. 5.1*]. The doors were placed forty cubits underground, in subterranean passages made of lead and stone; the length of each underground passage was one hundred fifty cubits. The door of the eastern pyramid was on its east side, a distance of one hundred cubits from the middle of the face. The door of the western pyramid was on its west side, also at the distance of one hundred cubits

**Figure 5.1.** The elaborately decorated tombs of later times inspired legends that the Giza pyramids were originally inscribed with scientific secrets. *Library of Congress Prints and Photographs Division, LC-DIG-stereo-1s21900.*

from the middle of the face; it corresponded with the door of the subterranean passage. The door to the colored pyramid, in stones of two colors, was on its north side, one hundred cubits from the middle of its face; they dug until they reached the door of the corresponding subterranean passage and thus passed into the door of the pyramid. The height of each of the pyramids was a hundred royal cubits, equivalent to five hundred cubits today. The length of each side was a hundred cubits; the faces rose perpendicularly up to forty cubits, and they then bowed inward so as to form sharp edges which joined at the top. They began construction in a time of happiness; people gathered to see them and were amazed. When they were finished, they covered them in gaudy silk from top to bottom, and they declared a feast in their honor which all persons in the empire were required to attend.

Then the king commanded the construction of storehouses in stones of flint of various colors. He filled the western pyramid with emerald objects, images made with the substances of [*i.e., associated with*] the stars, wonderful talismans, iron tools of outstanding quality, weapons that cannot rust, glass objects that can bend without breaking, all types of drugs (simple and compounded), deadly poisons, and a host of other things too numerous to describe. Into the eastern pyramid, he transported the idols of the stars, representations of the heavens, wonders built by his ancestors, incense to offer to the idols, books containing the history of ancient Egypt, an account of the lives of the kings and the dates of all the events that had transpired, still other books comprising a proclamation of all that would happen in Egypt until the end of time, with a description of the paths of the fixed stars and their influence at every moment. He also placed vessels containing drugs and other similar things. In the third pyramid, he deposited the bodies of the priests in black flint coffins, and with nearly every priest he placed books which recounted all that he had done and the story of his life.

The priests were then ranked in order. The first order was that of the Nazarites, that is to say, the priests who had served the seven stars for seven years each. The word Nazir signified, among them, one who had mastered the totality of science. The second class consisted of priests who had served six stars, the third those who had served five, and so on; and each of these seven orders had a name. The king placed the coffins of the priests down the sides of the pyramid according to their rank, and near their bodies he placed the books they had written on gold leaf in which they had recorded the past and the future and a record of the wonders performed by each of them. On the walls he placed idols who were seen to perform all of the various arts, arranging them according to their rank and power. He wrote a description of their operations, how to accomplish them, and the utility of what had been drawn. Through engravings and images, he described the nature of all things, the science of law and the laws of all the sciences. Then he filled the pyramids with the treasures of the stars, all of the gifts that had been offered to their idols, and the treasures of the priests; the amount of wealth simply cannot be calculated.

Finally he assigned a guard to each pyramid [see fig. 5.2]. The guardian of the eastern pyramid was an idol striped white and black, with two open and flashing eyes. This idol was sitting on a throne and held a kind of spear. When a man looked at him, he uttered a terrible cry, which made him lose consciousness; he would fall to the ground unconscious and could no longer get up, dying on the spot. The guardian of the western pyramid was a striped flint idol: he was standing, held a kind of spear, and wore a snake on his head. If a man approached him, the snake would jump on him, entwine around his neck and choke him before

**Figure 5.2.** Statues of the pharaohs and the gods, like these from the Seventh Dynasty, inspired medieval legends that they would come to life to guard pyramids and tombs. *Library of Congress Prints and Photographs Division, LC-M31- 848.*

returning to the head of the idol. The guardian of the colored pyramid was a small idol of an eagle standing on a pedestal. He attracted everyone who looked at him, and left them to die at his feet. When all these things had been established, King Sūrīd entrusted surveillance to the invisible spirits and offered them sacrifices, so they would turn down anyone who would want to approach without providing the agreed-upon offerings and without performing the established rites in their honor.

The Copts say that the pyramids bear a painted inscription in Arabic whose interpretation is this: "I, Sūrīd, the king, built these pyramids at such and such a time. I completed the building in six years. Let anyone who would come after me and believe himself a king as great as I destroy them in six years, for all know that it is easier to destroy than to build. I also covered the pyramids in silk: Let those who come after me cover them in turn." For a very long period these monuments remained intact. As for covering them in silk, no king could do so without overspending and without possessing true madness. . . .

It is said in some books of the Copts that King Sūrīd, after hearing the priests tell him that a fire would come from beyond the sign of Leo and burn up the world, made underground passageways in the pyramids in preparation; the Nile could be brought into these underground passages and discharged from there at several points in the western territory and in the land of Sa'id. The King filled these channels with wonders, talismans, and idols.

Some Copts say that King Sūrīd, having heard the report of astronomers, said, "See if yet some other disaster will threaten this country." They made observations and said, "A deluge will threaten to submerge the majority of the country, which will be devastated for several years, after which its prosperity will be reborn." "What," asked the king, "will be the cause of this devastation?" They said, "A king will massacre his own people and take their wealth." "And then?" he asked. "The country's prosperity will be reborn from the murder of the king." "And then?" "Monstrous men will come along the side of the Nile will invade and occupy the greatest part of the land." "And then?" "They will cross the Nile, and they will take the people into captivity." Sūrīd ordered their predictions inscribed on the pyramids, on monuments, and on stones.

## COMPARING THE THREE VERSIONS

The accounts in the *Akhbār al-zamān*, Murtaḍā ibn al-ʿAfīf, and Ibrāhīm ibn Waṣīf Shāh are almost word-for-word identical, but there are a few differences. The *Akhbār*'s narrative contains some copyist errors (e.g., calling Amsūs *"Ashmūn"* by mistake) and is disrupted because the author has taken the story and broken it into two parts, placing the dream narrative in a section on Egyptian priests and the rest in the chapter on kings. The other two authors don't do that, and the lost original version was probably a single narrative. As a result, the *Akhbār* has what looks like a copyist error in the reference to Abū Maʿshar, attaching it to the Shaddād bin ʿĀd claim, probably because it sat on the seam where the author moved the dream narrative and forgot to move the reference with it. Murtaḍā gives what looks like the better reading, so I have used his above. Ibrāhīm ibn Waṣīf Shāh omits the claim that the information was found in an ancient book from before the flood as well as the reference to Abū Maʿshar by name and all the astrological calculations derived from Abū Maʿshar's *The Thousands*. It is impossible to say which version came first, though logic would suggest that references to Abū Maʿshar were added later to give scholarly credibility to the story.

## LEGENDS OF ISLAMIC PYRAMID EXPLORATION AND EXPLOITATION

All three narratives go on to discuss legends that sprang up about the Caliph al-Maʾmūn and the treasures he was imagined to have found in the pyramid. They speak also of the various grotesque monsters and ghosts that guard the temples and pyramids and how they keep treasure hunters away but can be bribed with the right offerings and rituals to give access to the treasures within. The authors give, too, the story of twenty men who explored imaginary subterranean chambers beneath the pyramid. These men watched the floor open up and swallow one of their companions, crushing him to death. His ghost warned them not to seek the pyramids' treasure any longer. A similar story found men traveling through a mazelike set of passages beneath Giza, discovering a statue of Hermes, fabulous treasures, and frightening spirits. Yet another story, told of both the Great Pyramid and the temple at Akhmim, held that the ghost of a slave beat some men who brought a boy to the pyramid or temple for sex until they ran away. Another sex story said that a man and woman who tried copulating in the pyramid suffered seizures until they died. The authors seemingly wanted to discourage sex in the pyramid, which was apparently a problem in those days, perhaps because the poets called Khufu's and Khafre's pyramids earth's bosom and rhapsodized over their breast-like appearance.

Philemon, by the way, went on to have his own adventure. According to our authors, he lived for another three or four hundred years, long enough to have a falling out with the last pharaoh before the Great Flood. Having received a divine vision, Philemon decamped to Babylon, where Far'ān tried to have him killed remotely, by letter. He befriended Noah, and his family joined Noah on the Ark, where his daughter married Noah's grandson Mizraim. After the flood, Philemon returned to Egypt and helped Mizraim discover the ancient wisdom he and Sūrīd had kept safe, interpreting the antediluvian inscriptions and rebuilding Egyptian civilization.

Obviously, there are a lot of things going on in this story. Let's talk a little about where they came from and what they mean.

# THE MEANING BEHIND THE MYTH

THE STORY OF SŪRĪD AND THE PYRAMIDS PRESENTED IN chapter 5 isn't just a colorful legend. It would gradually grow into the dominant myth associated with the Giza pyramids and a story that heavily influenced pop culture depictions of the pyramids' true purpose. It's not much of an exaggeration to say that without the Sūrīd story, there would be no *Mummy* movies, no *Ancient Aliens* TV show, and no effort to find supernatural secrets in the pyramids. Since so much of what pop culture thinks it knows about Egypt comes directly or indirectly from the Sūrīd story, this chapter will help us better understand the legend by looking at the meaning behind it and how it came together from a constellation of ancient and medieval ideas.

## THE SPURIOUS HISTORY OF THE SŪRĪD STORY

In many cases, medieval tales about Egypt are relatively easy to trace to their source. Other stories are harder to analyze. From the very first, those who read the myth of Sūrīd tried to find out what it really meant. The account of the two Copts who found the story in an old book that had escaped the flood in the Ark formed the core of a different and quite elaborate story attached to the Sūrīd myth. About fifty years after the *Akhbār al-zamān* had started circulating, we find that Muḥammad ibn Salāma al-Quḍāʿī, writing around 1050 CE, had an elaborate version of the Copts' book-hunting exploits, which he claimed to have inherited from a string of previous authorities. He wrote that the story of Sūrīd had been found in a rotten manuscript on the chest of a mummy buried at Abu Hermes. This was the monastery of Abu Jeremias near Saqqara that the Arabs wrongly associated with Hermes Trismegistus—they had misheard its name and incorrectly associated it with the nearby temple of Imhotep, also identified with Hermes. Unable to read the writing, the Copts traveled to a distant monastery to the last monk able to read Egyptian writing. "This book," the monk said, "was written in the first year of

## Hermes and the Source of the Nile

Some stories' antecedents are much easier to trace. In chapter 5, we heard that Hermes Trismegistus excavated two lakes and a canal and erected statues to feed water into them to control the Nile floods, a story later amended to refer to the Noachian deluge. This story's antecedent seems pretty clear: In Diodorus's *Library* 1.52, written between 60 and 30 BCE, he discusses the achievements of the most ancient King Moeris, who, long before the Trojan War, excavated Lake Moeris near Memphis and a canal and used them to regulate the Nile. (This is mostly true, done by Amenemhat III, also known as Moeris.) Beside it he built the Two Pyramids of Giza and topped them with great statues. (This was not true, but the statues atop the pyramids show up in other in Arabic legends.) The Arabic story merely relocates the tale to the more logical source of the Nile, probably after the historical basis of the original tale was lost following the abandonment of the waterworks in 230 BCE. The Arabic account adds further details about the source of the Nile drawn from Ptolemy's geography.

the Emperor Diocletian and was copied from a book copied itself in the first year of Emperor Philip [*i.e., Alexander the Great's father, Philip*]. This emperor had made this copy from a gold tablet, written letter by letter." In this version, the two brothers were copyists of the text in Philip's day, and their names were Ilwa and Yertsa.

The account presents the story of Philemon and his vision from God of the coming flood, though it does not name Philemon, and it presents Abū Ma'shar's calculations for the flood and the conflagration. From there, the tale proceeds as we read in chapter 5. But more interesting is the way that al-Quḍāʿī tries to tease meaning from the story by elaborating promiscuously on the *Akhbār*'s offhand mention of an ancient manuscript, emphasizing a quasi-historical origin that foregrounded concrete—but fake—details about textual transmission and translation to give the story a plausible origin deep in the ancient past.

Al-Quḍāʿī might be the oldest effort to investigate the deeper meaning of the Sūrīd story, but he was far from the last. He did, however, inaugurate the school that sought to historicize the story and investigate it as a true account of real events. Similar attempts to literalize the story can be found in other writers of the medieval period. Abu Jafar al-Idrisi (1173–1251) wrote the longest treatise on the pyramids of his era, covering their construction and purpose. He devoted a quarter of his book to evaluating whether they were built before or after the flood, for which a majority of his authorities saw evidence for a preflood origin. Al-Idrisi tried to follow Abū Ma'shar and use astronomical alignments and astrology to date the pyramids. He concluded that they were more than twenty thousand years old. His friend al-Halabi went farther and said that the pyramids were the work of a pre-Adamite race, a separate creation from the time before the first human. Another text, of fourteenth-century provenance, alleged that the Great Sphinx had once sat atop the Great Pyramid until the flood washed it down. But such stories were far less common than that of Sūrīd, whose component parts we will now explore.

## THE DISCOVERY OF THE BOOK

The idea of secret ancient texts has a long history. Our imaginary ancient Greek text supposedly translated under Diocletian from an earlier copy

**Figure 6.1.** The story of Sūrīd was allegedly found in a book buried at Abu Jeremias near Saqqara. The monastery itself remained buried near Saqqara until the twentieth century. *Library of Congress Prints and Photographs Division, LC-DIG-stereo-1s21784.*

made by Philip from an Egyptian original bears close similarities to late antique stories circulating around the literature of Hermeticism, alchemy, and magic. The opening to the *Kyranides*, a fourth-century hodgepodge of ancient magical texts, claims to be a Greek copy of a Syriac original engraved on iron pillars by Hermes. The *Book of the Secrets of Creation and the Art of Nature* attributed (falsely) to Apollonius of Tyana (Balīnūs) perhaps dates back to a fifth-century Greek original, but the surviving Arabic text, the *Kitāb sirr al-Ḥalīqa*, claims that its author descended underneath a statue of Hermes in Tyana and discovered another statue of Hermes enthroned with an emerald tablet on which was written the secrets of creation. Sheik Sadiq Muhammad ibn Umayl's *Silver Water and Starry Earth*, circa 950 CE, describes descending into a subterranean chamber beneath an Egyptian temple known as the "Prison of Joseph" in Memphis and finding a statue of Hermes (actually, Imhotep) holding a book covered in hieroglyphics that he interpreted as occult secrets, about which he wrote a long poem. There was, in short, a lengthy tradition of claiming contemporary texts to have originated from conveniently inaccessible ancient places. These stories, in turn, had actual Egyptian antecedents, as we saw with the occult book hidden in a sarcophagus in "The Story of Setna," which seems to have formed the model for the Hermetic hidden book legends.

The story appended to the Sūrīd legend about the discovery of a statue of a teacher and his students beneath the pyramid quite obviously reflects the story of Hermes's underground statues. Indeed, according to the scholar A. Fodor, into the twentieth century, locals near Giza still claimed that a hidden chamber beneath the pyramid held a statue of a king with a globe, though in modern stories Hermes gave way to the more historically accurate Khufu.

The choice of Abu Jeremias as the location for the book is self-explanatory since the site bore in Arabic the name of Abu Hirmis, or the House of Hermes. Indeed, not only did it share its name with the pyramids, often known in Arabic as Abu Hirmis, but inscriptions at the monastery speak of a monk, Enoch, whose name was the alter ego of Hermes, and a fresco found there depicts Jeremias holding an open book, just as Imhotep (conflated with Hermes) did (see fig. 6.1).

### SŪRĪD AND PHILEMON

Scholars are not entirely sure how the character of Sūrīd came to inhabit his role. Some suggest that his name reflects that of Idris, the Islamic prophet identified with Hermes and Enoch, since Sūrīd's name in written Arabic (which lacks vowels) is S-R-D, the opposite of Idris, or D-R-S. Others suggest that Sūrīd's name descends from the Suphis of Manetho, his name for Khufu, after undergoing many corruptions and changes. This argument may be the stronger; there are several possible paths from Suphis to Sūrīd. One is a direct corruption of the Greek, while another posits that Sūrīd was originally Sōrīd, from the Greek for "son of Soris," referring to Suphis's predecessor on Manetho's list, Soris. The complicating factor, of course, is that Ibn Wahshiyya knew of Sūrīd as a philosopher but not a king, suggesting that the Idris connection may be more appropriate. It is also possible that Sūrīd is a composite, a name that persisted because it echoed both Suphis and Idris. However he was named, the composite figure absorbed stories associated with the real Suphis—that is, Khufu—including his association with magic and the occult and his imagined authorship of sacred books of wisdom. In this, the Sūrīd character has genuine roots that reach back to the later years of ancient Egypt.

The character of Philemon is more challenging to explore because no clear antecedent exists, although the story told of him echoes Hermes, Enoch, and Joseph—all recipients of dream visions. Ibn Wahshiyya wrote of a Philaos, who knew of magic and astrology and built treasure chambers in the pyramids to guard them. That story looks a lot like the one attributed to Philemon, the executor of Sūrīd's plans, and the name Philaos seems just close enough to Philemon that the characters could be one and the same. Perhaps in support of this view, the *Picatrix*, a medieval Arabic book of alchemy from around the time of the *Akhbār*

## The Many Faces of Philemon

Because of the vagaries of Arabic transcription of Greek names, Philemon may not be the name behind the Arabic Filāmūn, for historical figures named Polemon and Palaemon also passed under some variant of the same transcription. The variations are exhausting: Aclīmūn, Afilāmūn, Aflīmūn, Iflīmūn, Falīmūn, Fīlamūn, Fīlāmūn, Filīmūn, Qlīmūn, and more. I can't help but wonder if Philemon wasn't named for Ovid's myth of Baucis and Philemon, itself also related in some sense to the Great Flood. In that story, told in *Metamorphoses* 8.621–696, a disguised Jupiter (Zeus) and Mercury (Hermes) visit Philemon and his wife, who show them hospitality, unlike all the other people of the town. Jupiter warns them to flee, and he destroys the town by flood, leaving Philemon and his wife to gain immortality by changing into a tree beside their house, which becomes a temple. The idea of a temple guardian with foreknowledge of the flood and an association with a tree (which equals wood for the Ark?) seems too close to be coincidental. The story was well-known to Christians, as evidenced from Acts 14:11–12, where Paul and Barnabas are hailed as the disguised Zeus and Hermes.

*al-zamān*, knows of a philosopher called Iflīmūn who is apparently our Philemon.

## KINGS AND GIANTS

However the characters of Sūrīd and Philemon came to be, their characteristics in the medieval account of the pyramid offer important insights into the legend. According to the earliest forms of the story, particularly the *Akhbār al-zamān*, these men were giants, born of the race of Cain after the sons of Seth had mated with the daughters of men.

Abū Ma'shar had known the Watchers as the sons of Seth who fell from grace, and the *Akhbār al-zamān* must be founded on the same story, albeit in a somewhat rationalized form, for it tells how the sons of Seth and Cain were at war, and it calls the seventy leaders among the Sethites *nuqabā'*—literally, "Watchers." It ascribes most of the deeds of the evil angels to djinn but does state that the death of the Watchers led to corruption and idolatry. The *Akhbār* also describes—albeit incidentally— the first king of Egypt as a giant and a descendant of Cain, as were all the antediluvian kings who followed him. They were the Nephilim, the mighty men of old. In the text, the author chooses to make this quite clear, explicitly calling the kings both giants and sons of Cain. Over time, as Islam evolved away from popular Judeo-Christian mythology, the giants, always more popular among Christians than Muslims, gradually vanished from accounts of the pyramid story. Murtaḍā ibn al-'Afīf, who copied from a near-original source, repeated the identification with giants, but Ibrāhīm ibn Waṣīf Shāh, much more censorious than the other authors, cut out every mention of giants, referring to the old kings only as "mighty" and eliminating mention of their heritage as descendants of Cain. This version dominated later centuries. Jalāl al-Dīn al-Suyūṭi, writing the era's last great Islamic treatise on the pyramids around 1500, remained silent on giants.

## THE ORIGIN OF SACRED KNOWLEDGE

The change from giants to human kings kept the legend in line with evolving Islamic views, but it made the story confusing. If the kings of

Egypt weren't Nephilim, then the source of their wisdom becomes un-clear. According to ibn Waṣīf Shāh, the first king had learned only a part of what his great-grandfather, Dūai or Dāwil, had in turn learned from Adam. By contrast, the earlier *Akhbār* more logically claimed that the first king of Egypt had learned *all* of the knowledge the angel Darābīl had taught to his thrice-great-grandfather, Adam, directly from Adam and added to it the evil wisdom of the djinn. The parallel texts make plain that Ibn Waṣīf Shāh substituted Dāwil for Darābīl and rewrote the sentence to ensure that the Egyptians' knowledge did not have a divine origin but was rather the earthly learning of Adam.

According to the *Akhbār*, God revealed to Seth sheets of paper on which were written the secrets of the universe, supplementing those given to Adam. These revelations, passed down in corrupt form through the line of Cain, became the foundation of Egyptian magic. Idris, who was also Enoch and Hermes, preached to the Cainites and brought some of them to the one true faith. According to the *Akhbār*, Cainites in Baby-lon, not just in Egypt, inscribed their sciences on stone walls because Noah's father, Lamech, also received a vision of the flood and the con-flagration. This motif—drawn from the Jewish "Prophecy of Adam"—helped inspire the dream visions of Sūrīd and Philemon.

### THE DREAM VISION

Very few scholars have examined the story of Sūrīd in detail. A. Fodor's 1970 article "The Origins of the Arabic Legends of the Pyramids" from the *Acta Orientalia Academiae Scientiarum Hungaricae* is probably the best known. Fodor assumes that Coptic Christians wrote the underlying text of the Sūrīd story around the fourth century CE, based on a some-what older Gnostic or Sabean original featuring Hermes. He speculates that late antique Hermeticism and Gnosticism, under pressure from Orthodox Christianity, developed the myth as a way of explaining how their ancient wisdom could be coequal in antiquity with or even older than the Judeo-Christian scriptures and have survived the flood that otherwise destroyed everything. The apocalyptic writings of Enoch and/or the Watchers, preserved in legend on pillars and tablets, provided the answer once Enoch could be identified with Hermes Trismegistus.

## Other Potential Parallels

Fodor believes that the dream vision preserves ancient Egyptian iconography, albeit filtered through a Judeo-Christian lens. For him, the moon is Isis, as interpreted by the Greeks, who mistook her for a moon goddess. The birds he sees as the Egyptian *ba*, a soul in the shape of a bird. He suggests that the mountains are those of the Pyramid Texts, which come together to close off the Nile at the end of time. It is interesting speculation, but the imagery is too generically Judeo-Christian to prove specific ancient Egyptian connections.

His analysis helps make sense of the strange dream visions of Sūrīd and Philemon, with their phantasmagorical imagery and apocalyptic predictions. Philemon's role standing in for Hermes and Enoch seems to find confirmation in his dream visions, both his own and the dream vision of Sūrīd, the latter of which seems to have been originally part of Philemon's story before the flood until someone relocated it to the construction of pyramids three hundred years earlier. As Fodor and Mark Pettigrew both explained, the dream vision appears to be an adaptation of a Hermetic original. It closely resembles a prophecy that Hermes delivered in a text called the *Asclepius*, written originally in Greek during the Roman period but preserved only in Latin. In it, Hermes prophesizes that "bad angels" will rule over Egypt and lead the people into sin, at which point God will wipe Egypt clean either by flood or by fire until all creation is destroyed. The story ends, as Philemon's dream does, with the claim that the heavens will return to their normal order.

There is a strange echo of these dreams in Enochian references in Jewish literature. The medieval *Book of Jasher*, which incorporates older Jewish lore, said that Enoch reigned over 130 princes for 243 years (*Jasher* 3:10), just as Philemon presided over 130 priests for the more or less 250 years from Sūrīd's vision to the flood. In 1 Enoch 26, Enoch has a dream

**Figure 6.2.** Christian concepts of the apocalypse, seen here in a sixteenth-century engraving by Jean Duvet, helped influence the development of Philemon's dream vision. *Library of Congress, Prints and Photographs Division, LC-USZ72-216.*

vision of two massive mountains and a smaller one between them, and there is a lush garden with a terrible valley in the center. The valley is the horrible place where the Watchers and Nephilim shall be punished. This dream vision closely parallels that of Sūrīd, who saw two mountains and white birds, likely symbolizing angels, depositing his countrymen, presumably corrupt Cainite Nephilim, in between, in the dread valley. Beyond that, the dream visions also reflect general Christian apocalyptic motifs (see fig. 6.2). The falling sky represents the reunification of earth and sky, which God had cleaved in the act of Creation. It is an act of un-creation. The angels beating people with rods and the birds gathering for the judgment are a close parallel to Revelation 19, where the Son of Man on his white horse smites the unbelievers with an iron rod and an angel, speaking as the sun, calls the birds together to feast on their corpses.

Philemon's receipt of such dreams and his role as a vizier to an Egyptian king, of course, recall Joseph, who seems to be the direct model for Philemon's office. Indeed, the connection is made quite clear when we discover that Sūrīd's capital at Amsūs was probably Memphis (though some think Cairo), where the "Prison of Joseph" stood—the same "Prison of Joseph" that Sheik Sadiq Muhammad ibn Umayl visited when he mistook a statue of Imhotep for one of Hermes Trismegistus. Ptolemaic Greek texts from the same area speak of an oracle of Hermes Trismegistus in the same place, one known for its dream visions.

## THE ASTROLOGICAL READINGS

Sūrīd gathers the priests of Egypt and has them calculate the date of the coming flood. They give the exact calculation Abū Ma'shar made, but it is interesting that the text provides the astrological reading in poorly transcribed Greek—so poor, in fact, that al-Maqrīzī's copy made nonsense of several names. This suggests that Abū Ma'shar was working from a Greek text, possibly directly from calculations made by Annianus. Elsewhere in the *Akhbār* are Greek words and phrases, often in distorted form, from what seems to be underlying Greek texts. The copyists clearly did not understand the Greek, and Ibn Waṣīf Shāh cut out much of it altogether.

According to the legend, the flood would not occur for three hundred years from the time that Sūrīd had his dream. Because the Arabs imagined absurd lengths for the reigns of the pharaohs—as Nephilim giants, they lived for centuries, and Sūrīd reigned 107 years himself—it is difficult to know exactly how literally medieval people took the story. According to the calculations, Sūrīd built the pyramids of Giza around 3400 BCE, about a thousand years earlier than the real date of construction.

As the French scholar Gaston Maspero recognized more than a century ago, this part of the story cannot be Egyptian in origin or particularly ancient; it relies on the Greek version of Babylonian astrology, which was not used in ancient Egypt during Khufu's time. Indeed, this system of astrology developed only around 500 BCE, and it was introduced into Egypt during the Ptolemaic period. Herodotus, for example, writing around 440 BCE, makes only one mention of the stars in connection with Egypt, and that related only to the Egyptian calendar. Instead, the idea of the Egyptians as great astrologers is much later in origin, from the merging of growing beliefs about the power of Egyptian magic with the Greek belief that a *magus* followed the Babylonian model combining magical powers with astrological skills.

Nevertheless, the connection forged in this story between the pyramids and astrology would forever color how Western thinkers—particularly of occult inclination—would imagine the true history of the pyramids.

## THE BUILDING OF THE PYRAMIDS

The narrative given by the Arabic-language authors offers a surprising account of the building of the pyramids, namely, that workers touched a papyrus containing a magic spell to stones cut at Aswan and the stones simply flew into place upon being touched! The granite for the King's Chamber in the Great Pyramid did indeed come from Aswan, but most of the other blocks came from elsewhere. So far as I could find, no one has traced this story, and its origins are unclear. One might speculate that it is founded on a fanciful reading of Egyptian tomb paintings depicting overseers directing the placement of large blocks, similar to those still extant in the tombs of architects. But this is only speculation.

This odd story, however, seems to be a placeholder. Al-Mas'udi, writing at about the same time as the *Akhbār al-zamān*, doesn't know of this story. Instead, he quotes a native Copt to the effect that the pyramid stones were stacked in layers one at a time. He mentions no magic. But two other stories would seem to have bearing on the question. One relates to the alternative pyramid myth in which Shaddād bin 'Ād was the builder of the pyramids. He and the other 'Ādites were giants and were able to lift the massive blocks because of their size. Similarly, the *Akhbar* states that after the flood, two fallen angels taught black magic to the pharaoh 'Adīm. He was a giant and ordered the quarrying of rocks for a new pyramid at Dahshur, completed by his son Shaddāt. But as we have seen, these characters are duplicates, Coptic revisions of 'Ād and Shaddād bin 'Ād, with the story relocated from the original Giza to the less important Dahshur.

This tells us that the older form of the story involved fallen angels—likely the Watchers—and the giants building the pyramids. But stories of Watchers and giants were not consistent with medieval Islamic views, where even in the *Akhbār al-zamān*, giants are more symbolic than an actively evil presence, as in Jewish and Christian legends. So later writers minimized and eventually replaced them. Indeed, when Ibrāhīm ibn Waṣīf Shāh repeats the story, he adds a new wrinkle, stating that the Copts claim the "angels" were really demons in disguise. By his time, angels weren't believed to be capable of sin, so the story had to change.

In favor of this view is the fact that the two fallen angels were Harut and Marut, who in the Qur'an (2:102) are angels sent to test mankind by teaching the art of magic. But in early Islamic lore they were identified as fallen angels who sinned by copulating with a mortal woman and spreading occult arts. Later Islamic scholars denied that they were angels at all, in keeping with the view that angels cannot sin. Their story, however, is extremely similar to the medieval Jewish legend of Azael and Shemyaza, who are obvious adaptations of the Azazel and Semjaza from the Book of Enoch. They similarly fell from heaven, sinned with women, and taught occult sciences. Scholars are divided on how the two tales are related, but their connection here to the act of building pyramids provides evidence that there was once a now-lost version involving the Watchers and giants building the pyramids. The last surviving remnants of the original are 'Adīm's consultation with the angels and Surīd's status as a member of the family of Nephilim giants who ruled Egypt.

The legend next tells of the various rooms and underground chambers that Surīd constructed in and beneath the pyramids. These are understandable as fanciful exaggerations of the real interior chambers of the pyramids, along with the honeycomb of chambers and tombs in and around the Giza Plateau. Similarly, the treasures deposited in the three Giza pyramids reflect both genuine Egyptian funereal treasures and also Greek and Islamic ideas of what constituted scientific and magical wonders. Although, notably, none of the descriptions matches the interiors of the Giza pyramids in any way—their chambers, for example, are far too small to house so many sarcophagi and treasures!—they do resemble the labyrinthine tombs of later Egyptian history, which the Arabs would have opened and explored at the time the myth developed. Descriptions of desiccated corpses in sarcophagi wrapped in bandages and holding books need no explanation. They are obviously accounts of actual mummies, probably seen in tombs outside the pyramids, since most scholars believe the Giza pyramids to have been robbed in antiquity.

The guardian spirits of the pyramids—a seated man, a standing man, and an eagle—appear to describe Egyptian statues of the pharaohs, often depicted enthroned or standing, and the hawk of Horus, a common royal symbol.

## THE INSCRIPTIONS

That leaves the inscriptions, the most confounding part of the pyramid legend. The story as we have it tells us that the Giza pyramids were filled inside and out with thousands of pages' worth of scientific knowledge, all inscribed on their stones. The interior inscriptions are obviously a fantasy, one likely inspired by the inscriptions appearing inside Sixth Dynasty pyramids, where the Pyramid Texts can be found, and on the walls of temples and tombs. The Giza pyramids, however, have no interior inscriptions.

But the exterior inscriptions are a much more challenging question. Herodotus was the first to report that the pyramids' exteriors had inscriptions (or, more specifically, one—about vegetables), and many travelers and writers down to the Middle Ages, just before the removal of the casing stones, report seeing inscriptions across the whole of the pyramids. And yet none of the surviving casing stones on the pyramids has an inscription, and so far as I know, none of the blocks taken from the Great Pyramid for use in the building of Cairo has one either. Perhaps the solution can be found in the writings of Wilhelm von Boldensele and Ludolf von Sudheim in the 1330s, both of whom describe seeing different inscriptions on each side of the Great Pyramid, in Latin, Greek, Hebrew, and an unknown tongue. Obviously, at least three of these had to postdate the pyramids by thousands of years. This doesn't explain Herodotus's observations, except perhaps that there was a narrow band of writing that was lost when the casing stones were removed but which did not completely cover the surface. This was certainly supplemented in later times with travelers' graffiti and later additions around the base.

The specific inscription attributed to Surīd challenging any future pretender to his power to destroy the pyramids was part of a preexisting legend not originally connected to the pyramid myth. Ibn Khuradadhbeh, who lived around the time of Abū Maʻshar, already gave a version of the inscription a century before the Surīd story was first recorded, but his version did not mention Surīd. Instead, he said that the Giza pyramids were inscribed with all the secrets of magic and these words: "I am the one who built these. Let him who proclaims himself a powerful king destroy them, for to destroy is easier than to build!" This inscription became part of the Surīd story as older material was folded into new stories. The inscription is probably fictitious since a similar statement appears in al-Masʻudi in reference to the Caliph al-Rashīd's eighth-century efforts to tear down a Persian structure to prove the power of Islam.

Both, in turn, are also similar to an account found in Diodorus. The boast of the primordial pyramid builder Surīd challenging any to surpass the pyramids is clearly modeled on that of Ozymandias—better known as Ramesses the Great—whom Diodorus quotes thusly from an inscription on the Colossi of Memnon at the Ramesseum: "I am Ozymandias, king of kings; if any would know how great I am, and where I lie, let him excel me in any of my works" (1.47.4, translated by G. Booth). Surīd's words are suspiciously similar. A. Fodor suggests that the additional claim in the *Akhbār al-zamān* that Sūrīd said he had covered the pyramids in silk was added in imitation of the Kaaba in Mecca, which is covered in silk, implicitly identifying the pyramids as sacred parts of salvation history. The description of Sūrīd's furnishings of the pyramids, from the astrological inscriptions to their library of science books to their ancestral statues, matches fairly well with Diodorus's description of Ozymandias's tomb in *Library* 1.49, with a little medieval exaggeration. There was, as they say, precedent.

## THE AFTERMATH

Sūrīd's death places the throne into the hands of his son Harjīt or Hūjīb and his son Menāūs, Karūras, or Afrūbin. They built the second and third pyramids of Giza. Despite valiant efforts from scholars like A. Fodor to liken the first set of these names to those of Khafre or Khufu's son Hordjedef (Djedefhor) and the second set to Menkaure, any such connection remains speculative. After two more kings, the final ruler before the flood was Far'ān (Pharaoh), who usurped the throne from his cousin with the help of a sorceress. Corrupt, venal, violent, and cowardly, he is depicted like the sinful Nephilim who precipitated the flood by incurring God's wrath. Importantly, he is seen as an illegitimate king because he usurped the throne from the legitimate possessors of wisdom and magic, as Mark Pettigrew pointed out. For Muslims, *Pharaoh* was a title born by wicked Egyptian kings.

Philemon was the only Egyptian to escape the flood, and he did so by becoming a believer in the God of Abraham. The moral lesson is obvious.

Aside from a few additional references to postdiluvian pharaohs building small pyramids, and one king who spent his reign sitting atop one of the Giza pyramids, this is the last word on the pyramids in the Hermetic history of Egypt.

# 7

# THE TRANSLATION OF PYRAMID LEGENDS

ONCE THE SŪRĪD PYRAMID LEGEND HAD TAKEN SHAPE, IT provided the template for pop culture's ideas about the Giza pyramids, and even ancient Egypt as a whole, for the next thousand years. The reasons this particular story became so influential are a grab bag of coincidences and happenstance, but the result was a persistent belief across the Western world that the Egyptian pyramids contained deep occult secrets inseparable from Noah's flood and the perceived magic of the antediluvian world. This chapter will explore how this process got started, looking at the translation of the Arabic-language pyramid legends from the Islamic world to Europe and how European thinkers treated such stories as secret sources of hidden wisdom.

## BIBLICAL SPECULATION IN THE MIDDLE AGES AND RENAISSANCE

In the Byzantine lands, Greek learning never truly faded away, and Herodotus and Manetho remained current into the Middle Ages. On the Western extreme, Alfonso X of Spain's *General Estoria* was silent on the pyramids, though his writers spoke of Nephilim and Hermes

Trismegistus and had the lost second book of Ibrāhīm ibn Waṣīf Shāh, whom he identified by the name Alguazif. This second book, parallel to the second book of Murtaḍā ibn al-'Afīf, covered Egypt from Moses to the Middle Ages. But Alfonso lacked the first book, and he seems to have known nothing of Sūrīd, instead following Greek sources for the early history of Egypt, which he centers on the life of Busiris (i.e., Osiris), one of the first kings of Egypt in Greek myth. On the other hand, Petrus Comestor and Ranulf Higden, in their influential world histories written in the twelfth and fourteenth centuries, respectively, both claimed that Egypt had been home to the postflood giants, the Anakim.

In time, this began to change as Europeans encountered Islamic writings due to the Crusades in the Near East and the *Reconquista* in Spain. At first, Hermetic writings piqued the interest of Europeans, particularly writings about alchemy. Through these, Western writers discovered that Hermes Trismegistus (or one of the other two men of that name) was also Enoch and reigned as king in Egypt. In such guise, he begins to

### Chinese Legends of Egypt

The fame of the Egyptian pyramids and the legend of Sūrīd spread across the Islamic world, from Spain in the West to the subcontinent in the East. But until the Renaissance, Islamic accounts were largely unknown outside the Muslim world, even among the lands that touched it. In the East, the Chinese geographers did not speak of the pyramids, despite knowing the work of Islamic writers. The *Zhu Fan Zhi* geographical treatise of Zhao Rukuo, written in the Song Dynasty in the thirteenth century, knows, in a distorted way, of Joseph and his granaries, but not the pyramids. Zhao focuses his description of Egypt on the Nile and tells an unusual legend, of uncertain origin, that an old man lived in the river and rose up once every two or three years to laugh or frown to predict whether the next year would be happy.

appear in twelfth-century alchemical texts. The hunt for more alchemical and Hermetic texts eventually led to the discovery of Arabic accounts of ancient Egypt, though it took a surprisingly long time.

Through the Middle Ages, Western Europe knew Egyptian history primarily through Latin authors' summaries of Greek history and myth. So, Petrus Comestor and Ranulf Higden attributed the origins of Egypt to the Greek mythological character Aegyptus and imagined Egyptian history through biblical stories and pious legends attached to Bible stories. Their vision of Egypt ultimately rested on the efforts of churchmen like Eusebius (known from Jerome's Latin translation) to marry Greek and biblical histories. This lasted down to the Renaissance, when new information from the East started to challenge the limited Latin inheritance of the West. Travelers' reports had made clear the pyramids could not have been granaries, so scholars began to fall back on the second-best biblical option: the claim in Josephus's *Antiquities* that the pharaohs had forced the Jews to build the pyramids while slaves before the Exodus. The French cleric Henri Spondanus and the Dutch classicist Perizonius supported this position in the seventeenth century, though Oxford astronomer John Greaves and the traveler George Sandys had noted in the same century that the story did not accord well with biblical claims in Exodus 5 that the Israelites worked with brick for the Egyptians, not stone.

## ISLAMIC LEGENDS COME TO EUROPE

Another effort to remake the pyramids in biblical image surrounded the claim, popular in the sixteenth and seventeenth centuries, that the King's Chamber in the Great Pyramid was intended as the burial place of Pharaoh, who drowned when Moses parted the Red Sea. Some European travelers, such as Sandys, brought back the story that the pyramids were the work of Queen Daluka after the Exodus, with its quasi-biblical pedigree. At the same time, however, the late Arab legend, current in Egypt in those days, that the Giza pyramids and the Sphinx were guardians against the Nile flood (a bastardization of the older Noachian Flood version), found its way into European travelogues and scientific treatises.

The Arabic myth of Sūrīd or Hermes as the builder of the Great Pyramid appeared almost simultaneously in three different parts of Europe during the brief seventeenth-century explosion of European interest in Arabic material—and it was no coincidence. In Britain, John Greaves included the story in the first Western scientific investigation of the pyramids, which he produced in 1646. In Italy not long after, Athanasius Kircher, a German Jesuit scholar, investigated Arabic sources for Egyptian history as part of a series of works laying the foundation for Egyptology. In France, the scholar Pierre Vattier made a translation of Murtaḍā ibn al-ʿAfīf in 1666, which was itself translated into English in 1672, to great curiosity and interest. All three scholars knew one another and were working toward similar aims. Taken together, these scholarly sources helped inject the Sūrīd/Hermes story into a cultural mainstream still defined by alchemy and the occult and not yet by the full embrace of what we would consider modern science. It was a time, after all, when Isaac Newton could be both the greatest scientist of his day and an occultist with strange ideas about hidden truths encoded in the stars. As a result, when European scholarly interest in Arabic material declined in the eighteenth century, the Sūrīd story would linger on the edges of respectable history, an Eastern curiosity of greatest interest to artists and occultists.

## JOHN GREAVES AND THE SCIENCE OF THE PYRAMIDS

Travelers to Egypt in the Middle Ages brought back reports of the pyramids and the country's wonders, but they rarely went much beyond describing the pyramids as Joseph's granaries and the hieroglyphs as mysterious writing or magical formulae. With the Renaissance, however, scholars began to question the received wisdom about Egypt and started to investigate it in a more objective and rigorous way, albeit from a distance. Pierio Valeriano Bolzani was one of the first in the West to attempt to decipher the hieroglyphs, inspired by the rediscovery and publication of Horapollo's discussion of hieroglyphs. Working from Italy, he studied Egyptian artifacts in Rome, and he developed an allegorical interpretation of the hieroglyphs from Horapollo's speculative ideas. Despite its inaccuracies, it was an important step in the development of a scientific discipline of Egyptology.

John Greaves, an Oxford University mathematician, astronomer, and antiquary, was not initially interested in the hieroglyphs or the mysteries of occult Egypt. Instead, he had a practical purpose in mind when he set off from England in 1637 to visit Egypt as part of a grand tour of the East, ostensibly to obtain rare books and manuscripts, particularly in Arabic. Greaves hoped to investigate Ptolemy's *Almagest*, an ancient Greek book of astronomy that survived only in Arabic, by discovering the exact spot in Alexandria where Ptolemy had taken his measurements. En route, Greaves stopped at Rome, where he met with Athanasius Kircher, who had not yet written his great books on Egypt. (Some believe they actually met on Greaves's trip home.) Kircher had just discovered a century-old Arabic treatise on the pyramids by Jalāl al-Dīn al-Suyūṭi, whom he called Gelaldinus, which Abraham Ecchellensis had obtained in the early 1630s and brought to Rome in 1636. It is possible that Kircher and Greaves discussed its account of the many Arabic myths about who built the pyramids. Greaves and Kircher hit it off, and Greaves planned to dedicate a book to him, writing out a draft dedication that he never published. He sought after Greek texts in Constantinople and spent nearly five months at Alexandria. While there, he twice visited Cairo, made a scientific survey of the Giza pyramids, and engraved his name in one of the chambers. His measurements were the most accurate that had yet been made and served as the start of the scientific study of Giza. He also collected a large number of manuscripts in Greek, Arabic, and Persian before returning to England and setting to work writing up his account of the pyramids, known as *Pyramidographia*, which he published in 1646 and later revised after readers found some mathematical errors. The book was translated into French, where it helped spark the interest of French scholars in the mysteries of Egypt. The French translator Melchisédech Thévenot was a friend of Pierre Vattier, who translated Murtaḍā ibn al-'Afīf for Louis XIV.

But for the moment our interest lies with Greaves. Most of his *Pyramidographia* is devoted to description, measurements, and scientific investigation of the Giza pyramids, which is beyond our interest. But in his first chapter, he relates ancient legends of the Giza pyramids from the standard Greco-Roman sources and follows this with Arabic legends

## John Greaves and al-Hakam

Greaves gives the story of Sūrīd much as the *Akhbār al-zamān* does, including some of the tales of al-Ma'mūn appended to it. As we have seen, al-Hakam did not know the Sūrīd story, which had yet to be written, and he lived too close in time to al-Ma'mūn to have known the legends that arose around him a century after his death, so Greaves either possessed a manuscript of al-Hakam's history of Egypt that had been edited to add a later story, or he had a copy of a book like the *Akhbār al-zamān* wrongly attributed to al-Hakam. He speaks of al-Hakam twice. The first time, he provides what begins as a genuine quotation from al-Hakam about there being nothing known for certain about the pyramids, but it goes on to talk about Sūrīd with words that do not appear in any extant text of al-Hakam. Greaves's version is closest to that of Ibrāhīm ibn Waṣīf Shāh in its details, but it is much condensed, and his direct source remains unknown to me.

that would have been news to his readers. He gives a summary of the many different Arab legends found in al-Jawzī's *Mir'āt al-zamān*. Then he relates the Sūrīd story in the form we know it from what he says is a work by Ibn 'Abd al-Hakam, though this is almost certainly wrong. The attribution to al-Hakam, however, has caused great trouble over the years because it has led many to wrongly conclude that the Sūrīd story dates back to the eighth or ninth century. As for Greaves, he considered the story to be a fanciful romance, so encrusted with Eastern extravagance as to be wholly divorced from truth. He gave no credence to myths, though he inadvertently helped pass them on to the West.

But Greaves also introduced a new legend of the pyramids in his book with fateful consequence. Greaves had read in the Arabic manuscripts that the pyramids had been associated with the worship of the stars. He concluded that this must have been a reference to astronomy. In the

**Figure 7.1.** The summit of the Great Pyramid, where John Greaves believed that ancient Egyptian priests would climb to make celestial observations. *Library of Congress, Prints and Photographs Division, LC-DIG-matpc-01499.*

*Pyramidographia,* Greaves wrote that the fifth-century Greek neoplatonist philosopher Proclus had claimed in his commentary on Plato's *Timaeus* that the Great Pyramid of Egypt had a flat top from which the priests of Egypt observed the stars and recorded the rising and setting of the star Sirius (see fig. 7.1). Greaves's language was ambiguous in its seventeenth-century idiom. He had meant to say that he himself had speculated that the flat top of Egypt's Great Pyramid was the observation platform where the Egyptians had made the measurements Proclus described. But due to his ornate sentence construction, he made it sound as though Proclus had declared the pyramids to be celestial observatories. For the next three centuries, almost no one would check to see if Proclus really said that even as speculators developed increasingly elaborate fantasies about the pyramids serving as intermediaries to the stars.

Greaves wrote that he believed that obelisks, pillars tapering to a pyramid-shaped peak, were "but lesser models of the Pyramids," and he recalled the Arabic tradition that all sciences are inscribed in the pyramids, though his own firsthand observations of the Giza pyramids' blank interiors contradicted the point. Since the hieroglyphs still remained undeciphered and unreadable, it remained possible that the mysteries of science really were inscribed on the obelisks, a point that Greaves's friend Athanasius Kircher would find compelling.

## ATHANASIUS KIRCHER AND THE
## SECRET OF THE HIEROGLYPHS

In Rome, the eccentric Renaissance polymath Athanasius Kircher presented himself as something of a universal genius, a man who knew everything, including the oddest and most unusual claims in human history. He investigated reports of giant human skeletons, among other oddities; devoted time to investigating Atlantis, which he placed in the middle of the Atlantic Ocean in a famous map; and he wrote long books about the mysteries of the subterranean world and the wonders of ancient Egypt—the latter before ever visiting the country (see fig. 7.2). Kircher wrote three major works of Egyptology, *Historia Obelisci Pamphilii* (1650), *Oedipus Aegyptiacus* (1652–1655), and *Sphinx Mystagoga* (1676), in which he became one of the first Western writers to make use of Arabic treatises to help understand the history of ancient Egypt. He drew on the hieroglyphic treatises of Ibn Wahshiyya and Abenephius, and he presented Arabic literature in the original Arabic (or as close as his faulty transcriptions allowed) with Latin translation.

In the Western world of the Renaissance, the problem of the hieroglyphs had been a knotty one. Those with knowledge of Latin literature inclined toward Ammianus Marcellinus's view that they were religious instructions kept safe from the flood. Neoplatonic scholars, such as Marsilio Ficino, who had a growing knowledge of Greek literature, especially Horapollo, speculated that the hieroglyphs were symbols intended to represent Platonic philosophy and had been created by crafty priests to keep ancient philosophical truths hidden in plain sight. Ficino, in particular, had claimed that Plato himself had gained his knowledge from an Egyptian tradition stretching back to Hermes Trismegistus, the very character Kircher thought had built the pyramids and obelisks of Egypt as a treasury of ancient knowledge.

Kircher believed that he had cracked the secret of the hieroglyphs through recourse to texts like these and his own understanding of what

**Figure 7.2.** Athanasius Kircher studied hieroglyphics primarily by examining Egyptian antiquities that had been taken to Italy, such as the obelisk in front of Rome's Pantheon. *Library of Congress, Prints and Photographs Division, LC-USZ72-216.*

he called a secret Hermetic stream of wisdom that animated Egyptian religion. He correctly understood that the Coptic language of Egypt preserved elements of ancient Egyptian; he got basically everything else wrong. From the Arabic legends, he came to believe that the hieroglyphs contained all the secrets of Egyptian science and religion, secrets he believed were also shared by other pagan faiths. All of this, he believed, in keeping with the Arabic view of antediluvian history, were corruptions of an original monotheistic faith that decayed in the centuries after the flood, just as the *Akhbār al-zamān* reported that the monotheistic rulers of Egypt had succumbed to idol worship under the tutelage of demons and djinn.

For Kircher, the pyramids were part of a divine plan, symbolizing God's secret wisdom. From his reading of Eastern texts, Kircher adopted the belief that the angels had given Adam perfect wisdom, which was preserved from the flood by Noah's sons. Ham, the evil son, who was also Osiris, corrupted the divine wisdom with black magic and superstition

## Dating the Hermetic Texts in the Renaissance

Ficino came to his conclusions about Plato being an heir to the wisdom of Hermes after translating the *Corpus Hermeticum* in the late 1400s and assuming, wrongly, that the newly obtained Greek texts had actually been written by Hermes at the dawn of history. In 1614, Isaac Casaubon proved that the Hermetic texts were no older than the early Christian era, signaling the beginning of the end for scholarly pursuit of Hermetic lore (which lived on among occultists). Kircher rejected this conclusion and believed Hermes had actually lived and had invented Egypt's hieroglyphs.

until Hermes Trismegistus—who was also Enoch—recovered the perfect antediluvian wisdom and preserved it on obelisks through the hieroglyphs. This was for him the second Hermes, for the first Hermes lived, as in Abū Ma'shar's formulation, before the flood, where he invented pyramids as a way to preserve knowledge from the deluge. Unfortunately, just as in Arabic tradition, the second Hermes's successors corrupted the perfect line of wisdom with black magic and idolatry, which is why Egypt was both a land of admirable wisdom and also biblical evil. The story he told, so surprising to Western Europeans, was completely familiar to the Islamic world. Kircher, in his elaborate and labyrinthine weaving of Eastern and Western sources, helped transmit Islamic ideas about Egypt to a Western audience.

Kircher was not terribly interested in the Sūrīd story; indeed, he references the king most directly in a chart of the Arabic version of the list of kings of Egypt, where he wrongly ascribes the pyramids to Sūrīd's grandfather, Sarbaq. In another place, quoting a different Arabic-language author's king list, he correctly labels Sūrīd (spelled "Surit") as a pyramid builder. He wrongly states that the Arabs give no length to the kings' reigns. He gained his knowledge of Arabic pyramid myths from al-Suyūṭī's treatise, where Kircher learned of the myth that Hermes built the pyramids. He would also have read of Sūrīd, even if he ignored it, since the story appears in the exact same paragraph from which Kircher derived his knowledge of Hermes's pyramid building. Other tales were more interesting to him. He quotes the story of Daluka, for example, and is much more interested in the version of the story that makes Hermes into the primary figure in the construction of pyramids and obelisks—the latter of which Kircher considered more important. Kircher's emphasis on Hermes—a minor point in al-Suyūṭi's treatise—is obviously due to Kircher's interest in Hermeticism and occult philosophy.

For this reason, he also extensively quoted from the manuscript of Abenephius, in whose writings Hermes is identified as the originator of obelisks and the possessor of ancient wisdom. In his work, the Suphis of Manetho appears to have been revised as "Sothis," referring to the star Sirius by its Greek name. This helped solidify the idea that the pyramids and the stars were intimately connected. Relying on Arabic accounts of hieroglyphs on the Giza pyramids, Kircher argued that hieroglyphs were mystical clues to the Adamic wisdom of the antediluvian world and, therefore, the pyramids had to have a sacred function since they were inscribed with this ancient scientific wisdom. Hermes, who was Enoch, was the builder of the pyramids and obelisks in Arabic legend and buried within the Great Pyramid. He therefore confirmed in spectacular fashion the divine purpose of the pyramids.

Kircher's claim would give a mystical sheen to the pyramids that they would never again shake among occultists, pseudoscientists, and history's discontents.

PIERRE VATTIER AND THE MYTHOLOGY OF EGYPT

The French scholar Melchisédech Thévenot—scientist, traveler, diplomat—was familiar with the work of John Greaves and Athanasius Kircher. When he sought to create an anthology of travelogues of voyages to the East, he translated Greaves's *Pyramidographia* because of its firsthand account of Egypt. This French translation helped inspire interest in Egyptology in France. Thévenot showed a copy to his friend Pierre Vattier, a doctor and professor of Arabic to Louis XIV. Vattier had developed a reputation as an accomplished translator of Arabic literature, a reputation due more to the dearth of Arabic translations into French than any particular skill of the learned doctor. Vattier was apparently intrigued.

In the 1660s, Pierre Vattier primarily focused his work on Arabic treatises on philosophy from the Islamic period. He freely admitted that when he came across the Egyptian history of Murtaḍā ibn al-'Afīf, he dismissed the text practically sight unseen, for the manuscript copy in the library of Cardinal Mazarin bore a handwritten title in Italian identifying it as *On Necromancy and the Origins of the Necromancers*, a grimoire of no interest to him. He later claimed that he went back to read the book only because the manuscript was so beautifully written and decorated, though it is hard not to think that Vattier wanted to make a contribution to the discourse on the Arabic literature about the pyramids then so prominent in the scholarly world. He had hoped to translate, as well, two massive volumes of Egyptian history from the Arabic, but when he died in 1667, he had only read and translated Murtaḍā ibn al-'Afīf, the shortest of the books—and only partially at that. He translated the whole of Murtaḍā's first book, about early Egyptian history, but merely summarized the second half, about late Egyptian history and the Islamic period. More's the pity because the Arabic original disappeared sometime after Vattier translated it, and his French text is all that remains of Murtaḍā's work.

After years of working with Arabic philosophy, Vattier wrote that he found himself shocked to discover fanciful Arabic storytelling that rivaled the classics of Greek and Roman mythology. He was acutely taken with one story in particular, the fatal romance of Gebir and Charoba. An old version of the story, told in the *Akhbār al-zaman*, features Jirūn and Queen Hūriā of Egypt, with Jirūn being a Canaanite general who has betrayed his usurping Egyptian king for love of the queen only to fall before her ruthless defense of Egyptian independence. Ibrāhīm ibn Waṣīf Shāh, always more censorious, assigns the story to the queen Zalfa banūt Mamūn, but instead of a grand narrative, he merely states that she killed herself when faced with the overwhelming power of the usurping king and his Amalekite general.

As Murtaḍā told the story, mixing together parallel but originally competing tales of Jirūn and the legendary Amalekite conqueror Al-Wālīd,

Gebir (or Gebirus—as Vattier transliterated his name) is a giant descended from the 'Ādites who brought four thousand stones from afar to dam up the Nile, but Charoba, a queen of Egypt in the time of Abraham, who gave Hagar to Abraham after befriending Sarah, used her womanly wiles to stop him. Charoba came to power by poisoning her father and was blackmailed into contracting a marriage with Gebir. (Despite early scholarly efforts to tie Gebir's name to the biblical toponyms Ben-Gebir and Eziongaber, the name is probably from the Arabic *j-b-r*, meaning "to force," reflecting his role as potential rapist of Charoba and Egypt in the narrative.) She convinced him to use the stones he brought to build a great city where Alexandria would later stand on the promise that she would marry him when it was done. He built and built until he and his men were exhausted, but demons came up out of the sea and took the stones away while they slept. A nymph told him how to defeat the demons by sending artists to the bottom of the sea in glass diving bells so they might observe the demons and return to make statues of them. These statues would fool the demons into thinking Gebirus's men were like them and thus would leave the city be.

When Gebirus finished the city, Charoba concocted a second ruse. She asked Gebirus to send to her a third of his army at a time that she might reward them. She set before them a great feast and poisoned them all. She then visited Gebirus in his palace, presented him with a poisoned robe, and slashed him to death with a knife. He cursed her with his dying words, lamenting that he had been felled by a mere woman. She had his severed head displayed in her capital at Memphis. Within a year, the curse was fulfilled. While sailing beside the Giza pyramids, she stopped to urinate and stepped on a snake, which killed her. She died crying out that Gebirus's curse had been fulfilled.

To be entirely fair, Murtaḍā's version of the death of Jirūn/Gebirus doesn't make as much dramatic sense as the older and clearer version in the *Akhbār al-zamān*, though it retains more color than the dismissive version in ibn Waṣīf Shāh. For one thing, Murtaḍā's version speaks as though Gebirus cursed Charoba, but he doesn't actually offer a curse. In the *Akhbār*, Hūriā kills Jirūn while proclaiming that men think they have conquered women, but now a woman is the conqueror. And unlike the misogynist conclusion of Murtaḍā's story (taken to its logical conclusion by ibn Waṣīf Shāh), the older version allows the queen an unalloyed victory, a long life, and a dignified death.

The three versions reflected changing attitudes toward women over the centuries. Naturally, the version that gained wide currency was the one that conformed to patriarchal values. Through Vattier's translation, it spread, as we shall see, to the Gothic novelists and poets of England. Vattier himself thought that story to be the equivalent of the grand romances of ancient literature: Orpheus and Eurydice, Menelaus and Helen, and Odysseus and Penelope. I think he rather exaggerated.

In 1672, the Welsh translator and anti-royal Republican John Davies rendered Vattier's French text into English on account, he said, of the colorful and strange stories contained therein, thereby making the myths and legends available to English-speaking audiences for the first time.

## LATER TRAVELERS AND THEIR STRANGE IDEAS

The English traveler George Sandys ventured to Egypt in 1610 and marveled at the wonders of Giza. He correctly dismissed the popular belief that the pyramids were Joseph's granaries, but when he viewed the Great Sphinx on the Giza Plateau, he could not help but be taken in by the occult speculation that had swirled around ancient Egypt. He wrote that the human-headed leonine statue represented the constellations of Virgo, the virgin maiden, and Leo, the lion, and concluded that the statue symbolized the time when the sun rose in Leo and Virgo, which he linked to the Nile flood. He added that the ancient Egyptians used a sphinx in their hieroglyphs to represent a prostitute, luring men in with a beautiful face and then pouncing on them like a ravenous lion.

Under the influence of the Greco-Roman classics, Sandys imagined the Sphinx to be a woman and also the tomb of Armais, though the locals around Cairo claimed it to be the tomb of Atrīb, as Arab historians recorded. The claim that the Sphinx was associated with the constellations of Leo and Virgo is a strange one, but it seems to be amplified from a tradition recorded by the late Roman poet Ausonius, whose poems were weirdly influential in the medieval period. He had said that a sphinx—the Greco-Roman mythic figure, not the Egyptian one—was a mixture of three animals: "*volucris, Leo, virgo, triformis Sphinx*" ("bird, Lion, maiden, the three-form Sphinx") (*Riddle of the Number Three*, 40–41). While he was describing the mythic sphinx of Greco-Roman lore, European travelers saw the Egyptian statue as female and brought with them the associations of the Latin words *leo* and *virgo*. (The statue lacks wings and therefore was not associated with birds.) Thus, the Latin words, shared with the names of the constellations, helped give the Sphinx a new mythic history as a symbol of the stars, an association many still hold to be a genuine prehistoric belief even today.

The original source for Sandys's claim is, in a roundabout way, Horapollo's *Hieroglyphics*, as we saw in chapter 3, since Horapollo had connected the rising of the Nile to Leo under the influence of Greek astronomy. The connection to Virgo came about from the mistaken idea that the Sphinx was female, which shows the biases of European travelers, as the Egyptians had always recognized the statue as male.

Sandys's claim inspired another traveler, Thomas Shaw, who in 1738 published a book about his trip to Egypt and repeated Sandys's claims about the Sphinx representing an astronomical conjunction of the sun, Virgo, and Leo. However, Shaw had also read deeply of Athanasius Kircher's ideas and decided that John Greaves and the other learned men of science were wrong about the pyramids being the tombs of the Egyptian kings. The Great Pyramid specifically, he wrote, was simply too complex, too perfect, and too massive to have been a mere tomb. Instead, it had to have "some nobler purpose," which was to be a physical manifestation of the perfection of the Judeo-Christian God and to serve as His temple. Therefore, for Shaw, the pyramids served to demonstrate God's glory, while the Sphinx connected heaven and earth by symbolizing the heavens on the ground. The pagan mysteries of Egypt could therefore be revealed as nothing less than a memorial of God's divine plan.

But these men were not alone in their travels. In 1737 and 1738, Danish naval captain Frederic Louis Norden traveled through Egypt and Nubia to make a report of these regions for King Christian VI, though neither man would live to see the publication of the resulting French-language volume, *Voyage d'Egypte et de Nubie*, in 1755. The volume is famous for depicting the Sphinx for the first time without its nose and in a realistic style. Perhaps most interesting is that Norden preserves what seems to be the last gasp of the old medieval Arabic pyramid myth: Norden reported that the locals he met attributed the construction of the pyramids and the temples to giants, just as the old Arabic myth identified the builders as giants. Norden dismissed this out of hand, noting that if true, then the doors to Egyptian buildings would have been bigger.

Norden specifically wrote against the account of John Greaves, criticizing him for counting three major pyramids at Giza. He claimed that there was a fourth, darker (*"plus noire"*) than the others, terminating in a cube and surrounded by a "great heap" of rubble. He excused Greaves for missing it, saying it was hard to see the pyramid because it was quite a ways from the other three. Due to an ambiguity in the French, the pyramid was often translated into English as the *Black Pyramid* rather than merely a *darker* pyramid.

However, Norden had apparently mistaken one of Menkaure's satellite pyramids, the westernmost, for a fourth Great Pyramid. The ruined satellite pyramid, in the form of a step pyramid, ends in a cube, while the easternmost one (opposite Menkaure's northeast-facing corner) could be said to resemble rubble, the "great heap" Norden describes. Given that he was also pretty bad at estimating heights, to judge by his estimates of known objects, so closely does this hypothesis fit that it seems unlikely that any other solution would work as well. Nevertheless, his claim would linger on across the centuries, with a fourth Great Pyramid appearing in various engravings and references to the Black Pyramid of Giza occurring in occult and conspiracy literature down to the present.

# **8**

# THE ROMANCE OF THE PYRAMIDS

RENAISSANCE SCHOLARS TRIED TO UNDERSTAND THE EGYP-
tian pyramids and the ancient history of Egypt scientifically, but their
efforts were halting and incomplete. Nevertheless, their speculative attempts to evaluate many different sources of evidence for the pyramids'
true purpose, including Arabic texts not previously known in Europe,
helped spark a number of fantasies about the awe and mystery of the pyramids. In this chapter, we will examine the tension between the gradual
growth of scientific knowledge about the pyramids and the flourishing
romantic visions of Egypt that often stood in direct contrast to what
science had come to understand. By the nineteenth century, this resulted in a decisive split between "official" academic histories of Egypt
and the paranormal, supernatural, and romantic Egypt of literature and
the occult.

## MURTAḌĀ AND THE ROMANTICS

Of all the Arabic writers on the pyramids, the least famous in his own
time, Murtaḍā ibn al-'Afif, whose name was so forgotten that he wasn't
successfully identified until the 1970s, became the most influential of all.

For more than a century after his book's publication in English in 1672, it was the only English-language edition of Arab pyramid myths in circulation, aside from the short translation provided by Greaves. When John Davies translated the text from French as *The Egyptian History*, but with internal headings identifying the book as *The Prodigies of Egypt*, he did so as part of a series of translations of heretical and Hermetic works that fit in with the antiestablishment ideology of the ex-Republican who opposed the monarchical status quo. As such, Murtaḍā's work was widely read among reformers and early English Enlightenment figures, who sought alternative perspectives beyond those of Christian tradition.

Its greatest influence, though, came at the end of the 1700s, when the Gothic novelist Clara Reeve read Murtaḍā's work, likely in Vattier's French edition, and was inspired by the story of Charoba. Reeve took the outline of this story and turned it into the novella *The History of the Charoba* (1785), appended to her *Progress of Romance*. Reeve's novella, in turn, sparked the fancy of the adolescent W. S. Landor, who reworked the story into the epic Romantic poem *Gebir* (1798). In and of itself, the poem is no great shakes and would likely have been forgotten except for its influence on the Romantics. Samuel Taylor Coleridge, Charles Lamb, Sir Walter Scott, Percy Bysshe Shelley, Robert Southey, and other stars of the Romantic firmament were overly taken with Landor's poem, and they produced their own works inspired by and in imitation of it. Southey took *Gebir* with him as one of the few volumes he carried on his travels.

Of all the Romantics, Shelley was the most taken by *Gebir*. According to his friends, he would spend whole days reading and rereading the poem, to the point that one friend grabbed the book from him and threw it out the window to stop his ceaseless reading of it. Shelley, for his part, went outside and retrieved it. The poem helped develop within Shelley a fascination with Arabic lore and Egypt. (It helped that this occurred while Napoleon was sparking Egyptomania in Europe.) This would eventually manifest, in faint echo, in Shelley's famous poem "Ozymandias" (1817), which places in verse a passage on Egypt from Diodorus Siculus recounting Ramesses the Great's challenge for any rival to best his works (see chap. 6). Shelley reframed the boast—which paralleled that of Sūrīd—as a mournful reflection on the transience of greatness. Not all the Romantics agreed, however. Sir Walter Scott found the pyramids to be "disagreeable" and said that if any tyrant today were to attempt such a "waste of labour," the public would rightly treat them with derision and scorn.

Murtaḍā's book had been forgotten by his countrymen, and its only surviving Arabic copy disappeared, leaving only an imperfect French translation to mark its passing. It fascinates me that the whims of fate chanced it so that a single copy of one medieval text survived to influence the direction of the Romantics.

## ROMANTICISM AND HERMETICISM

Murtaḍā ibn al-'Afīf had yet another legacy for the future, albeit one he didn't intend. For the Romantics, the Islamic world represented a counterpoint to the oppressive culture of the West, especially in the seemingly heretical (from a Christian perspective) way Islam interpreted familiar biblical stories and traced the ancient history and wisdom traditions of the world. It isn't entirely possible to separate the fluorescence of interest in Arabic legends of the pyramids from the growing influence of Hermetic, alchemical, occult, and Masonic mythologies in Western Europe in the seventeenth and eighteenth centuries. Although much of the alchemical and Hermetic material is beyond our scope, these occult pursuits sought to find hidden wisdom in Arabic texts. In searching for the secret teachings of Hermes Trismegistus, investigators encountered Arabic ideas about Egypt and incorporated them into occult teachings. In the original Arabic texts, Hermes was typically associated with Egyptian temples, but Pierre Vattier made a mistake in his translation of Murtaḍā ibn al-'Afīf that transformed European legends about Egypt. Vattier wrongly believed that the Arabic word *berba*, which referred to Egyptian temples, actually referred to the pyramids. As a result, those who came after him more often than not transposed Hermetic myths about Egyptian temples to the pyramids, making them even more a center of wisdom and occult secrets than even the Arab-Egyptians had intended.

This conflation would eventually lead to an explosion of bizarre ideas about the pyramids and temples of Egypt. One of the strangest is also

## Hermes and the Tarot

The origins of the claim Hermes created golden tarot cards are found in tarot mysticism, specifically the work of Court de Gébelin and the Comte de Mellet in 1781, where the latter identified the tarot as "the science of Hermes" and implied that it was coded to a Kabbalistic interpretation of the mystical meaning of Hebrew letters. This directly inspired Jean-Baptiste Alliette, writing under the name Etteilla, to imagine the tarot as a golden encyclopedia of antediluvian wisdom, as well as a system for foretelling the future. In *Manière de se ré créer avec le Jeu de Cartes nommées Tarots* (1783), he wrote of how Hermes Trismegistus and sixteen other wise men worked to inscribe seventy-eight golden tablets at the Temple of Fire three leagues east of Memphis 171 years after the flood. He argued that the these became the tarot deck, called by him the *Book of Thoth*, which he was able to use Kabbala to decode from Egyptian symbols he identified as "hieroglyphs." In reality, though, they were mostly Hellenistic Greek symbols.

among the earliest: the claim that Hermes Trismegistus invented tarot cards and hid the golden originals in a temple or pyramid somewhere in Egypt. This claim from the 1780s would eventually lead a Victorian-era occult fraternity, the Hermetic Brotherhood of Luxor, to assert that Hermes hid the golden originals of the tarot in "one of the pyramids," in which form later occultists would cite the manufactured legend.

Similarly, the Freemasons had begun making use of Egyptian motifs in their rituals. From the earliest days of Freemasonry, the secret society had worked with forms of the Enochian Pillars of Wisdom story. An old Masonic text from the late 1400s, known as the Matthew Cooke manuscript, refers to the antediluvian pillars and to Hermes Trismegistus, following standard medieval legends. It and other old so-called Gothic Constitutions referred to Enoch and his pillars and imagined that Enoch

**Figure 8.1.** The reverse of the Great Seal of the United States features an Egyptian-style pyramid with a Masonic-style all-seeing eye. *Library of Congress Prints and Photographs Division, LC-USZ62-45509.*

had created a subterranean temple housing a tablet of divine mystery, just like Hermes's Emerald Tablet in Islamic lore. In every case, early Masonic texts traced the origins of the craft to Egypt. In some versions, it originated after the flood and was passed on to the Israelites before

the Exodus; in others, it originated with Euclid while the Greek mathematician was in Egypt. In the 1700s, when Freemasonry emerged from
Masonic guilds into the form we know it today, it did so in the context
of a culture where Egyptian mysteries held a particular cultural cachet
that rivaled the biblical. It is no surprise that when the old constitutions
were revised into a more formal (and fictitious) history of Freemasonry,
Egypt played a major role and that many Masonic lodges used Egyptian
motifs in their architecture. Specific rites of Masonry, such as the rites
of Misraim and Memphis, founded in the late 1700s (the former by the
infamous occultist Cagliostro), were dedicated to Egyptian and Hermetic themes. Under the influence of Freemasonry, the United States
placed an Egyptian-style pyramid on the reverse of the country's Great
Seal, with the all-seeing eye of God, a Masonic symbol, hovering over
the pyramid (see fig. 8.1).

## SCIENCE VS. PYRAMIDS MYTHS

These occult uses of Egyptian motifs and legends reached their peak
right before Napoleon invaded Egypt in 1798 and launched his great
project to document and explore Egypt in scientific detail. During
Napoleon's three years in Egypt, more than 150 scientists and scholars
combed the country, learning about it in ways that Western science had
not previously encountered. Dominique-Vivant Denon, a diplomat who
headed up the investigation into ancient Egypt, was among the first to
report on the temples of Egypt to the West. Like his Arab predecessors,
he described them as repositories of the arts and sciences. Napoleon's
men eventually produced the famous *Description de l'Égypte*, which
both celebrated ancient Egypt in all its real-life glory and also stripped
away some—though certainly not all—medieval myths and legends by
plainly showing the facts on the ground, which often failed to match the
myths. That massive study's editor, Edme-François Jomard, accepted
that the pyramids were tombs, but he cited medieval Arabic legends,
claiming on their authority that the Great Pyramid had been covered
in inscriptions in unknown tongues, for example. He created a compendium of ancient and modern accounts of the pyramids, including many

of the Arab authors we have discussed. More importantly, Champollion's decipherment of the hieroglyphs a few years later revealed a history of Egypt that had little to do with the accounts descended from medieval myth that circulated in the occult world.

The divergence didn't begin all at once, of course. As late as 1845, Jean Gilbert Victor Fialin, Duc de Persigny, was still advocating for the medieval folktale, reported by al-Maqrīzī, that the Sphinx was constructed as a magical talisman to hold back the desert sands.

Nevertheless, science and superstition had crashed into one another. Suddenly the scientific view of Egypt began to diverge markedly from the occult history of the country, which remained mired in medieval myth and legend even as mainstream scholarship—by fits and starts—moved on. To that end, one early effort to reimagine the pyramids in scientific form came from L. Vernon Harcourt, who imagined that the pyramids had nothing to do with the sacred or the occult but declared instead that they were giant filters that cleaned Nile river water. His efforts to completely secularize the pyramids and remove them from the biblical worldview ran into stiff opposition from those who wanted to see them as a bulwark against the encroachments that science had made into religion. The Reformation and the Enlightenment had begun to divorce the scientific worldview from religious faith, and Charles Lyell's *Principles of Geology* had shaken the foundations of belief in the literal truth of the Noachian Flood narrative. Perhaps, some thought, the pyramids could be used as proof of the Noachian Flood—and the Bible—against the threat of scientific evidence.

The Reverend Thomas Gabb accepted the myth that the pyramids were antediluvian, and in his 1806 book *Finis Pyramidis*, he claimed that they were the work of the Nephilim, who had built them not, as the Arabs thought, to preserve science, but rather to please their wives, who wanted them built to reflect their vanity. Similarly, the orientalist Thomas Yeates imagined himself to be writing a scientific treatise on the pyramids in 1833 when he declared that, scientifically speaking, the Great Pyramid was probably a copy of the Tower of Babel and that both the pyramid and the tower had taken their measurements from Noah's Ark. Such claims traced back to late antique speculation and would not have been out of place in the religious writings of Clement and Philo. The architect George H. Wathen claimed that they were built *after* the Great Flood, but they were still biblical. They were, he said, meant to hold the Queen of Sheba's treasure.

In 1833, the lawyer and literary scholar James Crossley spoofed both the occult and biblical views of the pyramids when he hoaxed a text on mummies by the seventeenth-century occultist Thomas Browne that had Browne declaring the pyramids "Satan's abodes." The brief text refers to Mizraim, Hermes Trismegistus, and even the fallen angels in a phantasmagorical fantasy where Satan uses Egyptian mummies to preserve warriors for the battle coming before the Last Judgment. For five decades, learned men accepted Crossley's hoax and dutifully recorded that a legend held the pyramids to be the work of Satan. The irony, of course, is that the actual medieval Eastern story of the antediluvian Egyptian kings being giant offspring of the fallen angels wasn't really that far from Crossley's fantasy.

## COLONEL VYSE AND THE POPULARIZATION OF PYRAMID LEGENDS

Nevertheless, most scholars recognized the pyramids as the tombs of the Egyptian kings. Men like Benoît de Maillet, James Fergusson, Joseph Gwilt, Christian Charles Josias von Bunsen, and more endorsed the idea in the late-eighteenth and early-nineteenth centuries and represented the scientific mainstream in their views, which went on to dominate the highest levels of scholarship. Our interest isn't with the facts of the pyramids but with the legends, so the gradual accumulation of evidence supporting the pyramids' sepulchral function is not of concern to us here. With the decipherment of the hieroglyphs and the growing knowledge that they told a story more in line with the ancient fragments of Manetho than with that of the Hermetic occult, it seemed that in time the scientific view would inevitably dominate the biblical and medieval stew of legends that were still passing for history in much of the West. But then something strange happened, almost by accident. The medieval legends found a new niche.

And it all happened for what seemed to be scientific reasons.

Those reasons revolved around the expedition launched by Col. Richard William Howard Vyse, a former member of the British Parliament who traveled to Egypt in the 1830s and infamously used gunpowder to blow his way into the internal chambers of the Giza pyramids. After his expedition, in 1840, he published his two-volume study, *Operations Carried On at the Great Pyramids of Gizeh in 1837*, in which he presented his findings and discussed the construction, measurements, and purpose of the various structures on the Giza Plateau. Among his discoveries was a cartouche of the pharaoh Khufu in a small, closed-off chamber above the Great Pyramid's burial chamber, which confirmed for the first time that Herodotus and Manetho were correct in ascribing the building of the structure to that pharaoh. While the fact seems commonplace today, it was a tremendous revelation in its day and forever transformed how science viewed the myths, legends, and stories that had swirled around the pyramid. Now it was impossible to argue that Hermes, Shaddād bin 'Ād, or Joseph had built the Great Pyramid. At a stroke, millennia of speculation had been washed away. Surīd, however, hung on by a thread so long as it was possible to identify him with Manetho's Suphis and thus Khufu.

As part of his review of the history of investigations into the Giza pyramids, Vyse had chosen to present a compendium of testimonia about the pyramids going back to the earliest of days. However, crucially, he asked a "Dr. Sprenger," who must have been Aloys Sprenger, later the translator of the first volume of al-Mas'udi's *Meadows of Gold* into English, to translate for him as many Arabic accounts of the pyramids as he could gather, creating the first such compendium of medieval Arabic accounts of Egypt in the English language and one that remained unrivaled for more than a century and a half. Vyse was careful to disclaim that these stories were nothing but lies and that "ignorance and superstition have so completely disguised tradition and facts, that it is scarcely possible to ascertain the foundations upon which they rest."

The second volume of Vyse's *Operations* presented several different Arabic pyramid myths, including those involving Hermes and Surīd. Sprenger and Vyse acknowledged the versions of the Surīd story Greaves and Vattier had given, but they chose only to reference them in passing

## Dr. Sprenger and the *Akhbār al-zamān*

Dr. Sprenger describes translating the Sūrīd story from the Bodleian Library MS. 9973, which as I understand it is today MS. Bruce 28. This manuscript title he gave as *Akbar Ezzeman*, but today it is transliterated as the *Akhbār al-zamān*. Sprenger explained that in consulting the manuscript, he discovered that it was damaged quite heavily, so he restored the story from the parallel text in al-Maqrīzī, having determined that much of the material was nearly word-for-word identical. Today, we know that text as a quotation from ibn Waṣīf Shāh and that it is not *quite* identical. Nevertheless, the resulting translation was the first in English from the *Akhbār al-zamān*.

and instead presented the Sūrīd story from the *Akhbār al-zamān*, with restorations from supplementary manuscripts to fill gaps in his copy. Though Sprenger chose to translate some sections and summarize others, it was an important contribution to the understanding of medieval pyramid myths in the anglophone world.

So far, so good. But then things took a turn. Sprenger knew that in the *Meadows of Gold*, al-Masʿudi had made reference to another work of his, a universal history of time called the *Akhbār al-zamān*, a work of thirty volumes. Sprenger assumed that the short manuscript he consulted was either a part of the same or an abridgement of it by another hand. Therefore, he attributed the "restored" texts to al-Masʿudi, whose name appears on some of the manuscripts of the book. This incorrect attribution is how it shows up in the partial English translation in *Operations*. It is from this edition that nearly all English-language writers learned of and reported on the story for more than a century, which is why down to the 1960s and beyond, one still finds al-Masʿudi cited as the author of the Sūrīd story.

## THE DIVINE PYRAMIDS

Vyse's collection of medieval testimonia became one of the most influential documents on the pyramids of the nineteenth century. Despite Vyse's careful conclusion that such stories had little practical value to science, they caused a sensation among pyramid speculators, who began putting out an enormous number of books making any number of wild claims about the divine mystery of the pyramids—stories that, ultimately, traced their origins to late antique and medieval efforts to work the pyramids into the history of Noah's flood. His work did for medieval legends in English what Vattier had done for them in French. On both sides of the English Channel, and both sides of the Atlantic Ocean, the conviction that the Giza pyramids had a divine purpose and were intimately connected to secret advanced science dominated popular accounts of the pyramids. Egyptologists such as Giovanni Battista Caviglia imagined that the pyramids held mystical secrets from the depths of time, while others sought more prosaic but nonetheless fantastical ways of imagining knowledge encoded in them.

One of the most important arguments of the nineteenth century revolved around the question of whether the Great Pyramid contained astronomically or terrestrially important measurements and if such measurements pointed to a lost civilization or to divine intervention.

This question emerged from a rather conventional inquiry with a scientific answer. Scholars wanted to know if the Giza pyramids had been built using a particular standard measurement, such as the royal cubit known to have been favored by the pharaohs. However, in investigating this question, unusual ideas began to creep in. If there were a standard measurement, would that mean, they asked, that it was somehow a perfect measurement tied to the cosmos or the divine? In 1780, Alexis-Jean-Pierre Paucton—who was partly inspired by Arabian legends he read in Kircher's books—concluded that each side of the base of the Great Pyramid represented one five-hundredth of a degree of longitude as measured at the equator and therefore the Egyptians understood astronomy and the size of the earth better than anyone until modern times. Unfortunately, the measurement he used for the base of the Great

Pyramid was far too small. In 1850, John James Wild, then just twenty-six, concluded that the Giza pyramids were constructed using a standard cubit of twenty inches and that this cubit was astronomically defined, suggesting—after Greaves—that the Egyptians had studied the stars in more detail than records would suggest.

A. Dufeu, a French member of the Egyptian Institute, published a book speculating that the Great Pyramid represented an advanced science characterized by an "extreme precision" that modern nineteenth-century science simply could not duplicate. To that end, he argued that the Great Pyramid encoded within itself its own longitude. Although his book was couched in scientific terminology and pretended to mathematical certainty, he cited medieval reports for support, which he knew secondhand, from Jomard's work. Although Dufeu was not directly inspired

## A. Dufeu's Bizarre Numbers Games

A. Dufeu's methodology was bizarre. He imagined that the Egyptian cubit—the ancient unit of measurement used at the pyramids—could be divided into 360 parts. These could then be used to measure the subterranean chamber beneath the Great Pyramid in light of numbers derived from the Nile floods in order to determine that the chamber encoded a measurement of 152°38' and 20" from Giza along the 44° line of north latitude. Thus, he concluded that the Egyptians had visited the future United States, because Oregon is 152° from Giza. He also agreed with some of the medieval estimates of the pyramid's date, placing its construction around 4800 BCE, though he proposed this number from his estimate of when Khufu lived based on the presumed date of Menes's reign, which he based on some numerical calculations made from Manetho's lists, the Sothic cycle, and a lot of assumptions. Needless to say, his speculative number play was fanciful and wrong.

by medieval stories, his ideas developed indirectly from the foundations laid by earlier quasi-scientific speculation based upon medieval legends.

## PIAZZI SMYTH AND GOD'S PYRAMID PLAN

Dufeu's idea that the Great Pyramid represented an ancient and perfect form of science presaged the more famous version presented by the Scottish astronomer Charles Piazzi Smyth, who was the Astronomer Royal of Scotland from 1846 to 1888. Piazzi Smyth had absorbed the claim popularized by Athanasius Kircher that the Great Pyramid was built to divine specifications, and he believed that the Great Pyramid's measurements were the key to understanding God's plan. He reported the results of his investigations in the influential *Our Inheritance in the Great Pyramid* in 1864, a book heavily influenced by *The Great Pyramid: Why Was It Built? & Who Built It?*, an 1859 book by the publisher and essayist John Taylor, which had done the Arabs one better. Unlike them, Taylor placed the pyramid after the flood, but he outdid them when he said it was a building designed by Noah himself and built by the sons of Joktan from the line of Shem, using the knowledge given by the sons of God, who were the sons of Seth. He claimed that the pyramid contained deliberate references to the numbers pi and phi so that these mathematical values would signal the pyramid's divine origins. He argued that ancient references to an unreadable inscription on the pyramid were probably an account of the circumference of the earth or, he said, the diameter of the preflood earth before God destroyed it. He claimed that the pyramid likely memorialized the antediluvian world. Taylor drew heavily on Colonel Vyse's book and arguably would not have developed his ideas without it.

Piazzi Smyth, who became the most famous pyramid theorist of his time, drew on Taylor's work (and dedicated his own to him). He similarly believed that the structure had been constructed using what he called the "pyramid inch," a measurement he borrowed from Taylor, who had calculated it to be one one-thousandth of an Anglo-American inch longer than a standard Anglo-American inch. This number, when used to measure the pyramid, could reveal supposed relationships between the

**Figure 8.2.** Khufu's granite coffer was carved to hold his sarcophagus, but many have imagined that it served a magical, symbolic, or scientific purpose. *Library of Congress Prints and Photographs Division, LC-DIG-stereo-1s21351.*

pyramid and the measurements of the earth and even to the years of creation. In short, he said that the pyramid was a "Monument of Inspiration" from God, just as the Bible was a "Book of Inspiration."

Piazzi Smyth also made the claim that the pyramid stands at the center of the earth's landmass. He claimed (wrongly) that the latitude and longitude lines passing through the pyramid cross more land and less sea than any others on earth. This isn't true; a line at 70° west would cross more land. But whatever. Beyond this, he also alleged that the Great Pyramid, as God's divine seat on earth, symbolized the Ark of the Covenant in Khufu's sarcophagus where archaeologists assumed Khufu had been buried since their measurements were exactly in concordance, though he did not think that the Ark rested in the coffer, as they had different shapes (see fig. 8.2).

The granite coffer in the Great Pyramid has interior measurements of 77.83 inches (1977 millimeters) in length by 26.65 inches (677 millimeters) in width and 34.33 inches (872 millimeters) in depth. The Ark of the Covenant is a bit harder to pin down since its measurements are less exact: "Have them make an ark of acacia wood—two and a half cubits long, a cubit and a half wide, and a cubit and a half high" (Exodus 25:10). The exact size of a cubit is disputable, but most scholars claim the size of the Ark at forty-five inches in length by twenty-seven inches in width and height on the standard conversion of one cubit to eighteen Anglo-American inches. However, another cubit, the so-called long cubit of approximately twenty inches, also existed, which would make the measurements fifty inches by thirty inches by thirty inches. Since the exact length of a cubit, to the millimeter, is unknown, we just can't be more exact.

To make this work, Piazzi Smyth rejected standard measurements, preferring instead to adopt a conversion of one cubit to 12.5 "pyramid" inches, which are ever-so-slightly longer than an imperial inch. Thus, Piazzi Smyth calculated that the Ark was 62.5 by 37.5 by 37.5 pyramid inches, roughly the same in Anglo-American inches. From this, he tried to deduce the maximum and minimum volume of the Ark by imagining how thick the gold-covered wood used to build it could have been. This yielded a range (wholly arbitrary) of between 1.75 and 1.8 inches. Thus, he imagined an interior volume of between 71,213 and 71,282 cubic pyramid inches. He therefore compared this favorably to the 71,250 cubic pyramid inches calculated for the Great Pyramid coffer. We could go on, but you get the idea: the divine "perfection" of the pyramid lay more in the imagination of the observer than the facts built in stone.

He also claimed that the coffer was a scale model of Noah's Ark! Thus, the 71,250 (approximate) cubic inches of the coffer (using Smyth's pyramid inches) are proportional to the 7,125,000,000 cubic pyramid inches of Noah's Ark—if you agree with Smyth that we can choose particular numbers for converting cubits to pyramid inches and you are OK with doing as Smyth did and adding nearly ninety-four million extra cubic pyramid inches to account for the Ark's roof and its window.

## MATHEMATICAL MYSTERIES

All of this, however, had an ulterior motive. Piazzi Smyth, like Taylor before him, opposed the metric system as artificial, French, and anti-British. Their arguments for the divine perfection of the pyramid inch, so close to the British inch, were intended to support the British imperial system of measurements over the Continental metric system—invented by atheists during the French Revolution—by stamping it with the approval of Almighty God.

In adapting Kircher's idea of a divine pyramid, taken over from medieval myths of the pyramids as arks in stone, inspired by divine dreams, Piazzi Smyth spawned a new type of pyramid legend, one related to the mathematical mysteries of holy numbers. Piazzi Smyth had claimed that the boxes had similar *cubic volume* despite having different dimensions. In less than twenty years, however, writers had already mangled this from *similar* to *exactly equal* cubic volumes. Later claimants, mathematically illiterate and much less subtle than Piazzi Smyth, confused *cubic volume* with dimensions and, despite the plain evidence of Exodus and Piazzi Smyth himself, have made the Ark of the Covenant into the secret contents of the Great Pyramid coffer!

Piazzi Smyth also introduced a new wrinkle into pyramid legends. In the formative years of Egyptology, the unusual and the mainstream sat side by side, and scholars of immense learning might advocate the strangest of ideas. But by the middle nineteenth century, the most extreme hypotheses had come to be recognized as fictitious, remnants of mythological or occult ideas. Piazzi Smyth spoke out against what he called "academic archaeology," dismissing the scholarly consensus that Egypt's pyramids were the tombs of the pharaohs as "mystical mythology" designed to deny the antiquity and exceptionalism of the Great Pyramid as God's monument on earth. In so doing, he created a new myth: archaeologists as an occupying force working to hide the truth about the pyramids. Sadly, it would be the most fruitful addition to the mythology of the pyramids in modern times.

## MULTIPLICATION OF MYSTERIES

Piazzi Smyth's book was published in 1864. By the time the second edition went to press more than a decade later, the number of speculative ideas about the Great Pyramid's true purpose had exploded. Claims circulated that the pyramid was really a model of the Northern Hemisphere, a tool for calculating Earth's density, a coded reference to the distance from Earth to the sun, a calendar, a representation of the law of gravity, a scale model of the solar system, a tool for calculating astronomical events prominent and obscure, an embodiment of mathematical principles, and an ungodly number of claims for its various Christian, Jewish, and pagan religious purposes past, present, and future, from symbolizing creation to predicting the End of Days. One claim made it into an early meeting place for Freemasons. In 1844, the Reverend George Oliver even claimed that Freemasons had built the Great Pyramid to symbolize the penis of Nimrod, through which he believed Masons were initiated into Masonry. By the end of the century, Charles Taze Russell was using Piazzi Smyth's pyramid prophecy claims to predict the Second Coming of Christ, and his movement survived to become the Jehovah's Witnesses.

In 1877, James Bonwick, a British writer and educator residing in Australia, set for himself the task of cataloging all the different claims made for who built the Great Pyramid and why. His list, published in *Pyramid Facts and Fancies*, ran to forty-seven different solutions (many of which I drew upon in this chapter), and that was before the French got into the act by developing a new legend of the pyramids based on medieval Arab myths and an important archaeological mistake.

# 9

# THE GREAT MISTAKE

THE LEGENDS ASSOCIATED WITH THE GIZA PYRAMIDS HAD remained fairly stable from the time of Athanasius Kircher down to the late nineteenth century. There were, of course, slight differences between the Victorian versions of pyramid myths and their medieval and late antique counterparts, but the general outlines had remained the same. Ancient and modern legends both assigned the pyramids to various biblical or quasi-biblical figures, placed them either immediately before or after the flood, and assumed that they stored, encoded, or displayed remnants of the special sciences that the antediluvians were imagined to have possessed. By the end of the nineteenth century, a newly developed set of legends did not alter this set of beliefs significantly, but the new stories attempted to give the patina of scientific truth to arguments that had previously been made on mythological, philosophical, or numerological grounds. These stories developed because of an accidental turn of the spade on the Giza Plateau in 1858.

## THE INVENTORY STELA

The author of that accident was Auguste Mariette, the French archaeologist and Egyptologist who founded the organization that later became

142

Egypt's Supreme Council on Antiquities. In 1858, Mariette began excavations near the Sphinx, and he uncovered a temple to the goddess Isis, within which he found an inscribed stela. When he read the hieroglyphic inscription, he was shocked by what it said. The inscription stated that Khufu had discovered the ruins of this temple of Isis beside the Sphinx and built his pyramid near it before restoring the temple to its former glory. Believing that Khufu had ordered the carving of the stela, Mariette saw in this inscription proof that the Sphinx was older than dynastic Egypt, implying the existence of a predynastic culture capable of monumental sculpture. He argued, too, that a building called the Valley Temple next to the Sphinx, which he believed dated to the same time as the Sphinx due to similar erosion patterns, was a monument to Osiris from predynastic times. Mariette's prestige and influence in the francophone world led other French scholars to embrace his ideas, such as his mentee and successor Gaston Maspero and the geologist François Lenormant. Both attributed the Sphinx to a tribe of spiritually advanced wandering mystics called the Followers of Horus, or *Shemsu Hor*.

But Mariette had made a fatal error.

The Inventory Stela was not a record from the reign of Khufu around 2450 BCE. Instead, it was a pious fraud, a fake story carved in the 600s BCE, during the Twenty-Sixth Dynasty, to give a grander history to the small temple of Isis that was much younger than the pyramids. Mariette had taken it at face value, as did his French colleagues. But those outside France immediately recognized that anachronisms and errors in the text indicated a much more recent date.

We see this rejection of French views in no less prominent a source than Charles Piazzi Smyth's classic of nutty pyramidology, *Our Inheritance in the Great Pyramid*. In that book, Smyth reports quite correctly that the Inventory Stela is nothing but "a rigmarole by certain revivifiers of the ancient Egyptian idolatry, with additions, under the 26th dynasty." This opinion, Piazzi Smyth said, was supported by the English Egyptologist William Osburn and none other than Heinrich Karl Brugsch, the great German Egyptologist, who condemned the stone as of a "late date" and of no value in understanding the ancient history of Giza.

The careful reader will notice that there is a bit of a nationalist undercurrent here. Supporters of the Inventory Stela's antiquity, and thus that of the Sphinx, were largely French: Mariette, Maspero, Lenormant. Those who opposed its antiquity were not: Piazzi Smyth, a Scot; Brugsch, a German; Osburn, an Englishman. This was not a universal view in the North, of course: Flinders Petrie and E. A. Wallis Budge both though the Sphinx to be early dynastic or late predynastic, for the same reasons. But I found almost no dissent in French sources of the era, though admittedly my reading of them is much sparser. Despite the flimsy evidence for the French position, it seems to have maintained an unusual staying power in the francophone world for decades while the Northern European world gradually rejected it. The French, who wanted to maintain primacy in Egyptology, had an interest in continuously finding the oldest and most important evidence of high civilization.

## THE RISE OF THE FOLLOWERS OF HORUS

Now, you would think that the recognition of the French error would be the end of the story, but it is not. The story of the Followers of Horus was simply too potent for writers the world over to reject merely because the factual foundation for it was phony. Lenormant gives us the fullest account from the Victorian era of the predynastic Sphinx and the cult of the Followers of Horus, but it was not through him alone most writers on the occult and the mysterious got their information. It turns out that it was Maspero who was just as responsible for delivering the false facts to a receptive audience. Those who consumed his work in English might have wondered why. The French text of Maspero's 1875 book *The Ancient History of the Peoples of the East* discussed the claim of a predynastic Sphinx, but the English translator omitted it from the English version. The claim made it through the translation process in 1894, when M. L. McClure translated Maspero's *Dawn of Civilization* and let it appear in three footnotes. But for the most part, the writers influenced by Maspero and Lenormant drew from the French originals and thus introduced the idea to English-speaking audiences, sometimes in corrupt or exaggerated ways.

Maspero did not actually have much to say about the Followers of Horus. He imagined them as a "half-savage" tribesman who started the work of founding city-states along the Nile and were later remembered as the original gods of Egypt. But Lenormant had already expanded this brief description to encompass the whole of Egyptian culture, assigning the Followers of Horus the work of inventing hieroglyphics, building cities, establishing the major temples of Egypt, developing the Egyptian priesthood and religion, and creating megalithic monuments and tombs. Neither man was entirely unjustified in his conclusions. Both were describing what scholars today call the Predynastic Period, when the rudiments of Egyptian culture came into being. But they erred in overstating the achievements of this period, especially in assigning to them monumental sculpture and stone architecture not seen for centuries after.

Such a description resonated too strongly to let stand on its own. Spiritualist philosopher Léon Denis, citing Lenormant for his information, declared the Followers of Horus to be Atlanteans, nor would he be the only one. The Ancient and Mystical Order Rosæ Crucis, a Rosicrucian group founded in San Jose in 1915, similarly believed that the pyramids had been built by people from Atlantis and for decades in the twentieth century ran advertisements in American magazines proclaiming the fact. The occultist Helena Blavatsky, one of the founders of Theosophy, alleged that the Atlanteans had a secret brotherhood invested with the secrets of magic that survived the sinking of Atlantis and spread its wisdom worldwide. It took no great imagination for her successors to link this occult brotherhood to the Shemsu Hor. Blavatsky further claimed that the wise men of lost races from ages past made their homes in subterranean chambers beneath pyramids, like Hermes in Arabic lore.

### THE RETURN OF HERMES TRISMEGISTUS

While François Lenormant sought a lost race of predynastic Egyptians, his contemporary Louis Figuier, one of the most racist scientists of his era, tried to remove the Arabs and other non-Whites from the story altogether. He created a new myth that Alexander the Great had uncovered one of the most famous pieces of occult literature, the Emerald Tablet of Hermes Trismegistus, inside the Great Pyramid. This tablet is supposed to be the original of the one we discussed in chapter 6, and its famous text describing the Hermetic view of the world as an intimate bond between earth and sky was widely copied in medieval Hermetic lore. It was twice translated into Latin in the Middle Ages from an Arabic text, and most scholars believe it originated in the eighth or ninth century, perhaps from a preexisting late antique Greek original.

The idea that Alexander was the discoverer of the Emerald Tablet is today quite popular in modern occult circles because Carl Jung and several other writers have referred to it. The claim was popularized in the mid-1800s when the occult writer Éliphas Lévi—the creator of the infamous goat-headed image of Baphomet—made mention of it in his *History of Magic*, but he copied it from Figuier. In his *Alchemy and the Alchemists* (1854), Figuier wrote that "tradition reports that this piece was found by Alexander the Great in the tomb of Hermes, hidden by the care of Egyptian priests, in the depths of the Great Pyramid of Giza. The piece was called the Emerald Tablet, because it was said that it had been engraved by Hermes' hand on an immense emerald slab with the point of a diamond."

What's odd about it is that this isn't really the tradition, although parts of it are clearly copied from Arabic texts about Egypt and Hermes. Originally, the story featured Apollonius of Tyana—that is, the Arabic Balīnūs—as we saw in chapter 6. The great alchemist Albertus Magnus, writing around 1200, swapped out Alexander for Apollonius but made no mention of the pyramid in relating the story. He placed it in some unknown, anonymous location, all the better to preserve the mystery. Most versions that substitute Alexander for the original Apollonius of Tyana place the tale in Hebron, which was the traditional location of Adam's tomb. I've been unable to trace Figuier's source back farther, and it seems that he conflated Albertus Magnus's account with what he (correctly) knew to be an Arab-Egyptian tradition that the Great Pyramid was Hermes's tomb. If that is the case, then Figuier's error spawned a strange sidelight in occult studies that made Alexander into the first raider of Khufu's treasures.

This, however, was simply the last in a long effort to try to wedge pyramid and Hermetic legends born of faith into a more secular historical understanding of Egyptian history.

## The Emerald Tablet

(Translated by Henry Carrington Bolton and Thomas Thomson)

1. I speak not of fictitious things but of that which is most certain and true.
2. Whatsoever is below is like that which is above, and that which is above is similar to that which is below to accomplish the miracles of one thing.
3. And as all things were produced by the meditation of one Being, so all things were produced from this one thing by adaptation.
4. Its father is Sol, its mother Luna; the wind carried it in its belly, the earth is its nurse.
5. It is the cause of all perfection throughout the whole earth.
6. Its power is perfect, if it be changed into earth.
7. Separate the earth from the fire the subtile from the gross, acting prudently and with judgment.
8. Ascend with the greatest sagacity from the earth to heaven, and then again descend to the earth, and unite together the powers of things superior and things inferior.
9. Thus you will possess the glory of the whole world, and all obscurity will fly far away from you.
10. This thing has more fortitude than fortitude itself, because it will overcome every subtile thing and penetrate every solid thing.
11. By it this world was formed.
12. Hence proceed wonderful things which in this wise were established.
13. For this reason I am called Hermes Trismegistus, because I possess three parts of the philosophy of the whole world.
14. What I had to say about the operation of Sol is completed.

## BIBLICAL PYRAMID LEGENDS REDUX

While mainstream scholarship steadily moved to place the pyramids in an Egyptian cultural context, the occult tradition sought to restore the pyramids' medieval role in the Abrahamic narrative of faith, if not always in ways mainstream Christians, Muslims, and Jews might recognize as theologically correct. Blavatsky, for example, accurately noted that the Giza pyramids were older than the written texts of the Bible, which meant that Piazzi Smyth must certainly be wrong to conclude that the pyramids represented God's word in stone. Instead, she said that any similarities between the pyramids and the Torah had to be from the "servile copying on the part of the Jews," who plagiarized the Bible from the measurements of Khufu's pyramid! Blavatsky drew on Eastern lore to declare the pyramids deeply connected to the constellations, particularly Draco, which sat at the north celestial pole when Noah's flood was presumed to have occurred. She imagined that the primeval Egyptians envisioned the heavens acting out a cosmic play symbolizing the flood that submerged Atlantis as the constellations rose and fell over the horizon and that the pyramids were observatories for watching this cosmic allegory unfold.

Blavatsky was certainly not the first to associate the pyramids with the stars. Many writers had done so before her, but perhaps none so bizarrely as Carl von Rikart, the pen name of an unknown German, who in 1869 published a book called *Menes and Cheops Identified in History under Different Names*. In that book, von Rikart attempted to argue that Egyptologists were blinkered by their small-minded anti-Bible stance and therefore did not recognize that the pharaohs of Egypt were the characters of the Bible. For example, he equated both Menes and Khufu with Noah's son Shem and claimed that Abraham convinced Shem to build the Great Pyramid to symbolize God's covenant. Contemporary reviewers noted that his work was full of errors, including places where he mistook typos for facts in his sources and his seeming belief that the historian al-Mas'udi was a fictitious character named Masondi. One critic called him "wild and incoherent," while another pronounced him "wholly unfit" to write about history.

## Von Rikart's Numbers Games

Carl von Rikart was an eclectic and inconsistent biblical literalist. He, for example, was so convinced that the Bible must be literally true that he proposed that the waters that rained down in the flood must have fallen "90,000,000 miles" to Earth because the Bible said the water came from the firmament, which biblically is beyond the sun! Yet he is so permissive an interpreter that he believed the forty days of rain to have been forty years, on account of forty days being insufficient to enact the entire flood drama.

But I especially want to discuss von Rikart's one stroke of originality, in which he anticipates later developments in historical mythmaking in impressive ways. He claimed that Noah and the denizens of the Ark survived the flood because they were put into stasis and hibernated, and he believed this undergirds the story of Rip Van Winkle. He finds proof of his assertion in the *Akhbār al-zamān*, with its story of Sūrīd and the prophecy of an evil star causing the flood. And like any good fantasist writing of pyramids, he must connect them to the myth of the Watchers because, really, how can you speculate about the pyramids without them? After rehearsing the medieval myth of Sūrīd and the flood, von Rikart correctly recognizes that it is closely tied to the stories of Hermes, Seth, and/or Enoch building two pillars before the flood to preserve all knowledge. But von Rikart follows a different thread. He knows that Sūrīd allegedly inscribed texts full of scientific knowledge, and he equates these (correctly enough) with the "sacred book(s)" that the Egyptians had long ascribed to the pharaoh Khufu, the builder of the Great Pyramid. He therefore follows the *Akhbār al-zamān* (which he cites from Colonel Vyse's *Operations*) in identifying the content of the sacred books as being astrological material.

Von Rikart wasn't content, though, to leave it at that. He identified the content of the books as the wisdom possessed by the Magi, who he thought traveled to Judea following the Star of Bethlehem because of prophecies contained in Sūrīd's books, where, to top it off, the Star of Bethlehem was allegedly identified as a periodic comet returning on a fixed schedule.

## THE PYRAMIDS AND THE STARS

Despite the wild speculation and bizarre ideas, von Rikart hit upon one idea that would soon find its way into the pages of respectable journals. From Greaves's ideas about pyramids as observatories and their amplification by his successors, such as the orientalist Thomas Maurice, he proposed that the Grand Gallery of the Great Pyramid and its other internal shafts were meant as observation points to watch the passage of the stars, comparing them to telescopes and imagining priests watching the stars through them.

The notion that the pyramids served as observatories found a fierce advocate in Richard Anthony Proctor, an English astronomer who imagined that the Great Pyramid had served as a telescope for making observations of the planets and the stars. He was influenced by the claims circulating among writers on history, and he noticed that John Greaves had made a rather unusual claim about the flat platform atop the Great Pyramid, which Proctor thought Greaves had attributed to Proclus, and Proctor happily repeated the claim. However, Proctor had misread Greaves—though to be fair, so, too, did most writers down to the present—and failed to realize that the opinion belonged to Greaves, not Proclus.

But even Proctor understood that Greaves's claim was illogical. The platform was too small, for one thing, and there was no logical way to climb up to it when the pyramids were new and their sides bore casing stones nearly as smooth as glass. Instead, Proctor proposed that the *interior* chambers of the Great Pyramid, particularly the long, straight Grand Gallery, had served as a telescope while the pyramid was under construction, back "when the grand gallery of the Great Pyramid opened out on a large square platform, where priests could be stationed in order

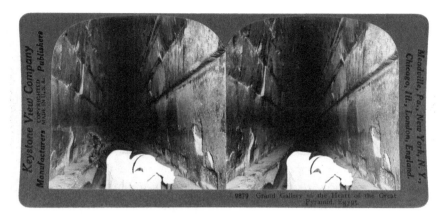

**Figure 9.1.** The long, straight Grand Gallery in the Great Pyramid inspired speculation that it had served as a telescope or some other mechanical purpose. *Library of Congress Prints and Photographs Division, LC-DIG-stereo-1s21383.*

to observe and record observations" (see fig. 9.1). By reinterpreting the pyramid's architecture this way and imagining the Queen's Chamber as a onetime outdoor platform, Proctor could save what he thought was Proclus's ancient opinion without endorsing the ridiculous.

Proctor was no pyramid fantasist. He firmly believed that his claims were scientific and represented the best explanation for what he mistook for ancient records. Proctor was notably skeptical of the extreme claims of Piazzi Smyth and his ilk. In the pages of the journal *Knowledge,* for example, Proctor attacked Piazzi Smyth's ideas and demonstrated with logic and reason that the correspondences Piazzi Smyth had seen between measurements of the pyramid and the measurements of the earth and the heavens were simply coincidence. He cited a *New York Tribune* parody of Piazzi Smyth pointing out that the same types of coincidence could be found in the *Tribune*'s headquarters, which must therefore also be a divine structure. Proctor had founded *Knowledge* in part to help push the public away from pyramid fantasies, but he soon discovered that his gentle efforts to expose faulty logic were falling on deaf ears, as readers preferred myths and conspiracy theories to scientific truths. As David Gage explained in his 2013 book about Egyptology in British culture, *Dialogues with the Dead*, Proctor found himself railing against pyramid quackery with a ferocious intensity, and he was increasingly

frustrated by the purveyors of pyramid myths and a public all too will-
ing to eat them up.

## THE PYRAMIDS AND ATLANTIS

Imagine, then Proctor's consternation when one of the biggest bestsellers of the 1880s turned out to be a book alleging that the pyramids were
the result of Atlanteans visiting Egypt and teaching the benighted people
there how to build super-structures to honor the sunken continent. That
was the premise of *Atlantis: The Antediluvian World*, an 1882 volume written by a former congressman from Minnesota named Ignatius Donnelly.
Donnelly had lost a congressional election due to election fraud on the
part of his opponent. When he failed to convince the House of Representatives to reinstate him in office, he decided to try to make some extra
money by writing a bestseller. The result was a massive tome tracing what
he considered to be the fingerprints of the lost civilization of Atlantis
on ancient cultures around the world, especially Egypt (see fig. 9.2). As
the subtitle of his book suggests, Donnelly viewed Atlantis as a biblical
civilization from before Noah's flood, headed by wise monotheistic kings
that the corrupt idolaters who followed later mistook for gods. Atlantis
itself was the Garden of Eden, the earthly paradise, with pyramids symbolizing the sacred mountain of Eden that connected earth and heaven,
like the mountain of purgatory described in Dante's *Purgatorio*. This
civilization had been laid low, Donnelly thought, by the corruption of
the giants, as told in the sixth book of Genesis, and therefore the sinking
of Atlantis and Noah's flood were one and the same event.

Donnelly proposed that the pyramid shape itself was indicative of
Atlantean architecture. As proof he cited the fact that pyramids could be
found in both the Old World and the New, with Mexican pyramids rival-
ing their Egyptian counterparts in size and shape. The tapering shape of
a pyramid was, of course, the only logical way to build a tall and stable
structure in the era before steel frame construction, but for Donnelly
the buildings had to have a common origin, halfway between them, on
Atlantis. How, he asked, could the human mind have chanced upon
such a unique shape? He had never, apparently, poured out a bucket of
sand to watch the formation of a spontaneous natural pyramid. He said

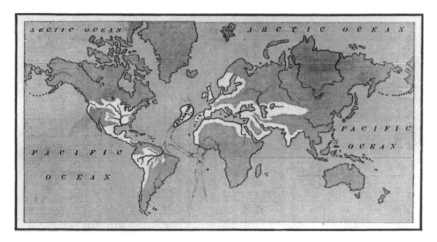

**Figure 9.2.** Ignatius Donnelly created this map to show what he believed to be the limits of Atlantis's empire, including Egypt. *Library of Congress Prints and Photographs Division, LC-USZ62-90566.*

that ancient texts proved that pyramids existed long before Egypt and therefore the Egyptians merely copied from the lost Atlantean originals. He professed to be incredulous that anyone could doubt the self-evident commonality of Mexican and Egyptian pyramids.

Donnelly had no trouble relying on Islamic myths and legends to help support his case for Atlantis's influence on Egypt. He spoke at times of the 'Ādites, the giants who supposedly built the pyramids, and claimed that they worshipped the sun from platforms atop the pyramids—reflecting, in an indirect and roundabout way born of copying from people copying from others—John Greaves's pyramid platform observatories. But, more directly, he copied Aloys Sprenger's translations of the Islamic pyramid myth and used that story to justify the fundamental premise of his book—that Atlantis was the biblical world before the flood. Since the Arabic legends of Hermes and Sūrīd clearly placed the pyramids prior to Noah's flood, did this not prove that Atlantis was the root of all pyramids?

But Donnelly would not go as far as others in assigning the Great Pyramid to the time before the flood. Instead, with the condescension of his era toward those of non-Western cultures, he assumed that the Muslims

## Ignatius Donnelly Imagines a Mexico-Egypt Connection

From *Atlantis: The Antediluvian World* (1882):

These two peoples, separated by the great ocean, were baptized alike in infancy with blessed water; they prayed alike to the gods; they worshipped together the sun, moon, and stars; they confessed their sins alike; they were instructed alike by an established priesthood; they were married in the same way and by the joining of hands; they armed themselves with the same weapons; when children came, the man, on both continents, went to bed and left his wife to do the honors of the household; they tattooed and painted themselves in the same fashion; they became intoxicated on kindred drinks; their dresses were alike; they cooked in the same manner; they used the same metals; they employed the same exorcisms and bleedings for disease; they believed alike in ghosts, demons, and fairies; they listened to the same stories; they played the same games; they used the same musical instruments; they danced the same dances, and when they died they were embalmed in the same way and buried sitting; while over them were erected, on both continents, the same mounds, pyramids, obelisks, and temples. And yet we are asked to believe that there was no relationship between them, and that they had never had any ante-Columbian intercourse with each other.

were possessed of a corrupt and confused story. He decided that the legend was a distorted memory of the building of an *Atlantean* pyramid to preserve knowledge. He went so far as to suggest that its destruction was also the origin of the legend of the Tower of Babel. He couldn't quite escape the myths he built upon, of course, for he accepted Maspero's and Lenormant's ideas about a predynastic civilization, which he traced to Atlantis. Therefore, following Plato, he claimed Egypt to have ten thousand years of civilization, stretching almost back to the fall of Atlantis in 9600 BCE.

In this, Donnelly followed the fantastical assumptions of Charles-Étienne Brasseur de Bourbourg, a French cleric who spent much of his life trying to prove that the antiquities of Mexico were the remains of Atlantis and that Atlantis gave rise to Egyptian culture. In his many works, including his last published article in 1873, but especially his 1868 book *Quatre Lettres sur le Mexique*, Brasseur de Bourbourg compared Mayan and Aztec cultures to Egyptian culture and made fanciful identifications between Mexican arts and sciences on one hand and Egyptian on the other. Just before his death in 1874, he had come to believe that somewhere between 9500 and 10,500 BCE, the earth's poles shifted, sending the continents tumbling and destroying Atlantis. He posited in *Quatre Lettres* that Mayan culture was the mother culture of Egypt, a position he altered a bit at the end of his life when he (wrongly) thought he had correctly translated a Mayan text to reveal the real fate of Atlantis in his imaged pole shift. The details are unimportant, however, since they stray far from our pyramid legends.

## MESOAMERICAN ORIGINS FOR EGYPT

Brasseur de Bourbourg's contemporaries did not know quite what to make of him. Among occultists, he enjoyed a reputation as a scholar of exceptional insight, for his ideas dovetailed all too well with the imaginary history of the world favored by those who practiced magic, spiritualism, and Theosophy. But among historians and archaeologists, he became known as something of a crank, albeit one who had done journeyman's labor preserving and publishing rare texts of extreme value. Augustus Le Plongeon, a photographer by trade, was overwhelmed with Brasseur de Bourbourg's ideas and quickly decided to expand upon them by inventing his own history of Atlantis, which he placed intermediately between the Maya and Egypt.

The lost continent was for him a waystation between the origins of civilization in the Mayan lands and their reception in the Old World in Egypt. He believed that Freemasonry was the connecting tissue tying these ancient cultures together and that Freemasonry had originated in Mexico, where its symbols could be found on the buildings of cities like

Chichen Itza. He and his wife, Alice Dixon Le Plongeon, invented a fabulous and romantic history for his ancient culture that drew, in part, on the works of Greek myth and history (or, more accurately, Greek stories about Egypt) to tell a new story. The upshot was that the Le Plongeons' work extended the myths and legends associated with Egyptian pyramids to those of the Maya and by extension to any pyramid anywhere in the world. The legends were no longer *Egyptian* so much as *pyramidal*, freeing medieval stories to be repurposed for new contexts.

In their telling, the most famous Mayan leader was Queen Moo, whose husband was the prince consort Coh, her brother. According to the story that Augustus and Alice Dixon Le Plongeon composed from their idiosyncratic reading of Mayan bas reliefs, Coh's brother Aac became homicidally angry that Moo had not chosen him, so he killed Coh, plunging Moo into a terrible grief. She fled to Atlantis, only to discover that it had been destroyed. She moved eastward to Egypt, where she established a new kingdom and constructed the Sphinx as a monument to her dead love, carving a lion statue in honor of Coh's nickname, Chacmool, which they said meant "Thundering Paw." The reflection of Queen Victoria's contemporaneous grief for her late husband, Albert, was hardly a coincidence. The outlines of the story, however, immediately recalled their direct source, the Egyptian myth of Isis and Osiris. The Le Plongeons had shamelessly borrowed from it to create the story of Moo, but with equal shamelessness they also claimed that their story was the original and that Egyptian religion was a false worship of Moo and Coh. When scientists and laymen alike objected, Augustus Le Plongeon sulked, and his last years were marked by claims of a vast conspiracy of scholars to discredit him and bitterness that his ideas had failed.

Just before Donnelly published his *Atlantis*, Le Plongeon had published *Vestiges of the Maya*, in which he attempted to prove, using similar evidence, that ancient Mexico and ancient Egypt had been in prolonged communication with one another thousands of years before Columbus. Scholars were not impressed and dismissed the story as so much fantasy. But Le Plongeon had two influential fans, Ignatius Donnelly and Helena Blavatsky, both of whom cited Le Plongeon in their works and incorporated his ideas into their own. Donnelly borrowed a bizarre claim that one-third of the Mayan language was Greek; Blavatsky relied on Le Plongeon to support the notion that the Egyptians and the Maya shared a single culture. She went so far as to use him to support the extreme idea that both used the exact same alphabet, though she overstated Le Plongeon's claim in *Vestiges of the Maya* (expanded in later books) that the two cultures shared certain hieroglyphs or characters that had a similar form and the same meaning—a claim later proved false when scholars fully deciphered Mayan hieroglyphs.

## MORMONS BRING EGYPT TO AMERICA

However, it was not just the spiritualists, Theosophists, and occultists who hoped to use the rapidly growing myth of Egyptians in America for spiritual purposes. The Church of Jesus Christ of Latter-Day Saints—the Mormons—had been founded in upstate New York on claims that its prophet, Joseph Smith Jr., had translated golden tablets from the Lost Tribes of Israel into English from "Reformed Egyptian," a fictitious script supposedly derived from that of Egypt and modified, as stated in the Book of Mormon, to describe Jewish wisdom in Egyptian words on the grounds that Egyptian supposedly took up less room than Hebrew (Mormon 9:32–33, 1 Nephi 1:2). Smith went on to acquire a set of Egyptian funerary papyri whose writing he claimed, wrongly, to be able to translate, revealing the autobiography of the patriarch Abraham.

In the Mormon belief system that Smith laid out, the Americas had been home to the Lost Tribes of Israel as well as an earlier occupation of prehistoric Jews. The Garden of Eden, he claimed, had been located in Missouri, and Jesus Christ had visited the future United States after he rose from the dead. The Lost Tribes, however, had fallen on hard times. Some, the Book of Mormon alleged, had sinned against God and had been punished with dark skin, with only those who repented regaining glorious Whiteness (Jacob 3:8; 3 Nephi 2:15). These sinners became Native Americans and viciously exterminated the God-fearing Jews, whose bodies filled the burial mounds of North America.

Because the early Mormon Church invested so heavily in the twin ideas that the Americas were first populated from the Mediterranean region rather than East Asia and that the first Americans were White, they sought out any claims—however absurd—that would seem to support the alternative history of America laid out in the Book of Mormon. To that end, the Mormon magazines and newspapers of the late 1800s did major business trumpeting the claim of Augustus Le Plongeon, Brasseur de Bourbourg, and the French traveler Claude-Joseph Désiré Charnay, the last of whom had asserted that some ancient Mexican antiquities reminded him heavily of Egyptian ones. The Mormons were particularly taken with Le Plongeon's claims that some Mayan glyphs resembled those of Egypt, a claim that one Mormon magazine flattened into a blanket statement that "ancient Egyptian inscriptions were made upon Maya structures ages ago," a phrase that went beyond even Le Plongeon's wild speculations. As Daymon Mickel Smith pointed out in a 2015 essay, claims like these remained current in Mormon culture for more than a century, taught as fact at Brigham Young University despite the widespread rejection of such claims by mainstream scholars.

### FAITH VS. SCIENCE

It was, however, symptomatic of the changing nature of communication in the Victorian world that bad ideas might be rejected by serious scholars yet find unending life among popular writers, occultists, and members of faith communities—groups who would become uncomfortable at the growing gulf between science and tradition. Since the publication of Charles Darwin's *On the Origin of Species* in 1859, the tension between secular views of history and science and traditional spiritual and mythical ideas had grown unbearable, and the break between them had become almost inevitable. To believe that the pyramids were ten thousand years old or the work of Atlanteans operating under divine command was to reject the discomforting authority of evolution and materialism.

By the end of the nineteenth century, the stories told about the Egyptian pyramids had escaped the bounds set by medieval legends and had grown and changed in seemingly fantastical ways. Each new development moved farther away from the traditional tales of the pyramids, but their origins in the medieval narratives of Sūrīd and his efforts to preserve sacred knowledge from Noah's flood remained recognizable beneath the trappings of Victorian science and the Belle Époque occult. The fingerprints of this medieval myth even left their mark on the defining vision of Egypt in modern pop culture: the vengeful mummy.

# 10

## THE CURSE OF KING TUT

EVERYONE KNOWS THE STORY OF THE PHARAOH'S CURSE AND the evil mummies that rise from Egyptian tombs to walk the earth. Hollywood, for one, can't get enough of them. The very first mummy movie was made in 1911 and featured a *Frankenstein*-style scene of a live electrical wire reanimating an Egyptian mummy. She attacks the man who purchased her sarcophagus and then marries an Egyptologist. The most famous mummy movie was, of course, made two decades later. Since Boris Karloff first climbed out of a sarcophagus in *The Mummy* in 1932, the story has been repeated time and again, not least in the four sequels between 1940 and 1944, the 1955 Abbot and Costello parody, and the two remakes of *The Mummy* in 1999 (with two sequels) and 2017. And this doesn't count the homages from Hammer Film Productions' horror movies and the B-movie knock-offs commissioned by rival studios. So common has the mummy motif become that it can be surprising to realize that the first entertainments about revived mummies date only from the nineteenth century, inspired by *Frankenstein* and its story of life made from death.

As scientists and even the occultists developed their histories of Egypt, the public became increasingly fascinated by everything Egyptian—and often wary of it as well. In the early 1800s, Napoleon's scientific triumph in Egypt—despite the ultimate failure of his empire—sparked a wave of Egyptomania that saw the fashionable people across Europe and America utilize Egyptian motifs in art, architecture, interior design, and literature. The Egyptian-style obelisk chosen for the Washington Monument was perhaps only the most famous example among many. The full range of Egyptomania is beyond our scope, so here we will focus on the theme of the living mummy and how it became conflated with the pyramids, giving rise to the common trope of a pyramid housing a vengeful mummy.

This modern tale developed in two stages, both of which took their influence in part from the medieval Islamic tales of Egypt that we have examined in this book. The first stage revolved around the first wave of Egyptomania launched by Napoleon and persisting deep into the nineteenth century. The second sprang up in the wake of the excavation of Tutankhamun's tomb and the subsequent deaths of several of the men involved in the operation. Both stages related to one another, however, since the latter built upon a foundation laid by the former.

### THE MUMMY ATTACKS

The first stage involved the creation of a myth of the vengeful mummy. Although today it seems like a common trope, it was actually quite rare prior to the nineteenth century. The Greeks and Romans had stories of people who came back from the dead, and medieval Europeans told tales of corpses that would return to life to suck the blood of the living, but these stories were not associated with Egyptian mummies. In the early seventeenth century, one of the first evil mummy stories began to circulate. A Polish prince named Mikołaj Krzysztof Radziwiłł wrote in his 1601 account of his *Ierosolymitana peregrinatio* (*Voyage to Jerusalem*) that in the late 1500s he had purchased two mummies in Alexandria, one male and one female. He cut the bodies up into small chunks, which he storied in separate boxes to fool Ottoman authorities (who then controlled Egypt) because the Turks were concerned that Europeans might use mummy parts in magic spells to harm the Ottoman Empire. He put the boxes on a ship, only to have the ship plagued by massive storms. Soon a

## Making More Mummies to Feed Demand

Demand for mummies to unwrap for entertainment was so high that fakery was not out of the question. King Edward VII had no idea that the mummy "discovered" during his visit to Egypt had been planted for his benefit, and according to Flinders Petrie, a tourist who purchased a mummy in Aswan was horrified to discover that it was no ancient artifact but instead the body of an English engineer who had died in the desert. The only good news was that no one had purposely murdered him to make a fake mummy. He had died of some unknown cause in the desert, where his body dried out, and unscrupulous locals didn't look too closely in their rush to sell. Petrie reported that many recently deceased became "mummies" that way.

priest on board had visions of ghostly figures he believed to be the spirits of the two mummies. Things got so bad that the mummies were thrown overboard, at which point the storms subsided and the visions stopped.

The vengeful mummy motif reemerged in the nineteenth century because of the very real fascination that Victorians had for the bandage-encased corpses of Egyptian nobles. In the nineteenth century, mummy "unwrapping" parties were strangely popular, with wealthy individuals importing Egyptian mummies to dissect either in private parties or in public events (see fig. 10.1). So common were unwrapping events that no less a luminary than Edgar Allan Poe wrote a comic story about one entitled "Some Words with a Mummy" in 1845. As Poe depicts, Victorians would gather at the homes of friends to unwrap mummies imported from Egypt to see what the Egyptians had hidden inside the corpses. Poe further satirizes the Victorians' claims to technological superiority by having his reanimated mummy, named Allamistakeo ("All a Mistake") discuss the wonders of his own age, an inkling of the school of pseudoscience that would claim all manner of astonishing accomplishments

**Figure 10.1.** The Victorians held mummy unwrapping parties, often in private homes, for the entertainment of guests. Bringing one's dog was optional. *Library of Congress Prints and Photographs Division, LC-DIG-pga-14310.*

for the Egyptians, including but not limited to free energy and flight. As Poe himself admits in his story, he drew on the same sources we have discussed throughout this book—Plutarch and Diodorus Siculus, among others—to concoct his somewhat fantastical comic history of Egypt. His mummy wasn't vengeful, just informative. His short tale bore a resemblance to the earliest known revived mummy tale, Jane Webb's 1827 novel *The Mummy: A Tale of the Twenty-Second Century,* which was set in 2126 and featured the Cheops of Herodotus being revived to critique the manners and mores of twenty-second-century Britain.

Unwrapping parties, however, produced a surfeit of wrappings. According to reports from the first half of the nineteenth century—which have never been confirmed by surviving examples—mummies were imported to America by the shipload to be stripped of their papyrus and linen wrappings to make paper. This may be a bit of a folktale, exaggerated from the real fact that American printers imported rags and linen fragments from Egypt and other countries to make newsprint. A similar story, however, appears in Mark Twain's *The Innocents Abroad* (1869) that mummies were so prevalent and worthless that the Egyptians burned them to fuel their trains: "I shall only say that the fuel they use for the locomotive is composed of mummies three thousand years old, purchased by the ton or by the graveyard for that purpose." Twain was joking, though many have thought him serious. Mummies *were* used, however, for medicines since the Middle Ages. Surprisingly, one could still buy ground-up mummies as medicine in the United States until 1910. Ground mummy was also used as a pigment for painters. No wonder some authors began to speculate that the mummies might not be terribly happy about becoming paper and paint.

At the same time, Western visitors to Egypt became familiar with, and published accounts of, Arab-Egyptian legends that djinn and other spirits guarded the Egyptian tombs, while archaeologists had begun to report that Egyptian tombs contained curses engraved upon them to keep visitors out. The journalist James Augustus St. John, for example, wrote in his popular 1844 travelogue *Egypt and Nubia* that the Arab-Egyptian residents of Cairo still believed that the tombs were inhabited by *ifrits*, a word sometimes used to describe a type of evil djinn and other times a ghost. Many of these accounts occurred in travelogues written by some of the leading luminaries of the day. Authors as diverse as Mark Twain, US Secretary of State William Seward, the Austrian Crown Prince Rudolf, and countless others wrote of their visits to the pyramids and popularized them as a tourist destination. This feat was made easier by the veiled Anglo-French colonial control in Egypt and the opening of the Suez Canal, which helped make Egypt more accessible, more comfortable, and safer for European and American tourists. Of course, not everyone was impressed. When the Austrian Emperor Franz Joseph climbed the Great Pyramid in 1869 at the opening of the Suez Canal, his only reaction was to tell his wife that he finally understood why so many Englishwomen wanted to climb the pyramid: the muscular young male guides didn't button their shirts (see fig. 10.2). In those days, however, it was easier to imagine the pyramids as alive with supernatural creatures. As the emperor's son Rudolf reported, jackals lived in nooks and crannies in the pyramids, and Egyptians and Europeans chased them about,

**Figure 10.2.** In the nineteenth and early twentieth centuries, climbing the pyramids was a popular attraction on any tour of Egypt. *Library of Congress Prints and Photographs Division, LC-M32-865.*

hunting them with shotguns and rifles across the rocky surfaces. "The Pyramids gave me, especially when men or animals were climbing upon them, the impression of being great artificially constructed mountains rather than architectural monuments," Rudolf wrote in the English edition of his travelogue. It was a far cry from the sterile presentation we see today.

## ANCIENT TEXTS, MODERN FICTION

Naturally, the authors of popular fiction fed into the fascination that these nonfiction accounts sparked, writing stories about mummies. Writers like Louisa May Alcott, Bram Stoker, Arthur Conan Doyle, and an estimated hundred others all tried their hands at uncanny stories about resurrected mummies and vengeful Egyptian spirits. Many of these suggested that supernatural retribution or a curse would fall on those who disturbed the dead. Théophile Gautier told an early tale of mummies and the supernatural when he wrote "The Mummy's Foot," published in 1840, in which a man buys a mummified princess's foot as a paperweight. Consider what that says about the nineteenth century that this was considered normal and plausible. Anyway, the owner of the foot takes him to Egypt to meet with the shades of the pharaohs, who thank him for returning the appendage to its owner. It wasn't exactly a curse narrative, but it was a step toward the modern genre. Of special note is that Gautier named the princess's father Xixouthros, whom you will instantly recognize as Xisuthros, the Babylonian flood hero from Berosus and one of the kings of the Cainites in late antique and medieval legends. Here, Gautier has folded the Babylonian and early Christian legends into Egyptian themes. And this was no accident. Gautier made quite plain that he envisioned Egyptian history as descending from the antediluvian world of the evil Cainites. Consider his hero's meeting with the pharaohs, as given in Lafcadio Hearn's 1908 translation: "All the Pharaohs were there—Cheops, Chephrenes, Psammetichus, Sesostris, Amenotaph—all the dark rulers of the pyramids and syrinxes. On yet higher thrones sat Chronos and Xixouthros, who was contemporary with the deluge, and Tubal Cain, who reigned before it." The themes of the pyramid, the flood, and the Watchers keep getting remixed in strange and unexpected places.

Louisa May Alcott told one of the first true mummy's curse stories in her 1869 tale "Lost in a Pyramid; or, the Mummy's Curse." It followed two other similar stories, an anonymous tale called "The Mummy's Soul" from 1862 and Jane G. Austen's "After Three Thousand Years" from 1868, both about female mummies taking revenge on men who aggressively violate their graves, an action that is often likened to rape. In the former story, an ancient bloodsucking insect is the means of the mummy's transference of her soul to the archaeologist's wife. An Arab-Egyptian character is present to relate supernatural happenings to Islamic legends of the *ifrits*, implying that the potency of Egyptian magic lives on under the cover of modern devils. The latter story imagined poisoned jewelry from an Egyptian tomb claiming the life of the modern woman who wore the purloined necklace.

Alcott, however, offered a version of the story much more in keeping with our theme. Her story placed the action in Khufu's pyramid and featured elements that reflected the Arab-Egyptian legends from the Middle Ages that had become familiar to the Victorians through their use in popular nonfiction accounts of Egypt, such as Vyse's *Operations*. Her story told of an expedition that uncovered the mummy of a sorceress within the pyramid and the cunning poison that led to her revenge on those who despoiled her corpse. Alcott had never been to Egypt, so she imagined the interior of the Great Pyramid as being a maze of passages, covered in hieroglyphs and stacked with shelves on which mummies had been housed like so much cordwood. Clearly, she had conflated the Great Pyramid with the later tombs where mummies were often interred en masse. Nonetheless, her conflation was far from atypical in the formative years of the "evil mummy" genre, and such stories began to shape the way the public thought about the interiors of the pyramids. The popular understanding of what a pyramid *should* look like inside became solidified a decade later when Gaston Maspero—yes, him again—discovered inscriptions on the interior walls of the small Fifth and Sixth Dynasty pyramids of Pepi I, Merenre I, and Unas, including the famous Pyramid Texts. Retroactively, their pyramids would influence how the public thought the older and larger Giza pyramids *should* look inside.

Conan Doyle tried his first mummy story in 1890, with "The Ring of Thoth," in which an Egyptian preserved through an immortality elixir waits centuries until he is released from his deathless mummified corpse by the titular ring while on display in a museum. Doyle's "Lot No. 249" from 1892 was one of the first to depict the now-stereotypical scene of a bandaged Egyptian mummy rising from its sarcophagus to exact vengeance. Doyle's story is something like *Frankenstein*, in which a college student reanimates the dead, and something like the legend of the golem, for he uses the shambling corpse to take revenge on his enemies.

Of special note is an 1897 story from *Argosy* magazine, "Pharaoh's Curse," by a mostly unknown writer named Lucian Sorrel. Combining the resurrected mummy trope with an Ann Radcliffe–style scientific mystery, Sorrel tells of a pharaoh's mummy that seemingly comes back to life and commits murder, in keeping with a curse that the king placed on his sarcophagus: "I, Pharaoh Ammon-Nekab, Lord of the Upper and Lower Lands, (give) warning to the strangers that follow. Know by the word of Osiris that I shall live again; and the death of the beast shall be to those that touch my body." In the end, it is revealed that the "murdered" man has actually died from a prick from a nail in the coffin that the pharaoh had caused to be impregnated with poison.

These are but a few of the stories of resurrected mummies and pharaonic poisons and curses that sprang up in Victorian and Edwardian literature, and those not mentioned here would prove an equally representative sample. In time, the tropes escaped Egypt altogether. H. Rider Haggard, for example, used the same conventions in *She* (1887), where the action occurs in a lost kingdom in Africa. H. P. Lovecraft recycled many of the standard chestnuts for "Out of the Aeons" (1935), a story he ghostwrote for Hazel Heald. It features a living mummy, a museum, and vengeance, but this time the mummy belongs to a man from the lost continent of Mu who had seen a space alien. It was not Lovecraft's first foray into the theme, as we have seen in his collaboration with Harry Houdini, which saw Houdini commune with the ancient gods of Egypt beneath the Giza Plateau. As it turns out, Lovecraft would take much more than just mummies and vengeful spirits from the legends of Egypt. And he owed it all to a romantic novelist who had developed an inexplicable love for Murtaḍā ibn al-'Afīf.

### THE BRITISH MUSEUM'S CURSED COFFIN LID

The novelist in question, however, did not write stories of vengeful mummies herself. Instead, she contributed to one of the most important developments in the modern legendry of Egypt, the curse of King Tut's tomb, which in turn fed back into fiction by giving new life (or unlife, in this case) to the mummy's curse genre. She did so because not all of the mummy's curse stories of the early twentieth century were presented as fiction. Prior to the unearthing of Tutankhamun's tomb in 1922 and the shocking death of the excavation's sponsor, Lord Carnarvon, allegedly at the hands of Tut's curse, the most important mummy's curse story was the supposedly true story of the ill-fated cursed coffin lid held in the British Museum.

It seems that a tabloid journalist and spiritualist named W. T. Stead was on the *Titanic*, and this gentleman had become associated with the sarcophagus lid of the so-called priestess of Amen-Ra housed in the

British Museum. It was reportedly the subject of his final conversation before the ship hit an iceberg. Stead had claimed that the sarcophagus lid was cursed and brought disaster on any who wrote of it, according to Stead's dinner companion Frederick Seward, speaking just after the *Titanic* sank. As early as 1912, a story had developed that the cursed sarcophagus was actually on board the ship, but the great Egyptologist E. A. Wallis Budge pointed out in a 1934 rebuttal that the sarcophagus cover remained where it had always been since 1889, "in the first room in the British Museum, bearing the number 22542." (It is on display in Room 62 now.)

### The Real Origins of Coffin Lid Curse

W. T. Stead's story was actually a retelling of a semifactual story that became popular after 1909. In 1907, a journalist named Bertram Fletcher Robinson died of influenza a full three years after writing a magazine article about the sarcophagus lid in the British Museum, known popularly as the "mummy board." Apparently, a certain Mrs. St. Hill had suggested at a 1909 lecture that the mummy board was to blame for Robinson's death. G. St. Russell in his article "The Mysterious Mummy" in *Pearson's Weekly* magazine that year expanded on the curse story and added Helena Blavatsky to it by having her declare the coffin lid to be "malignant." Blavatsky had died in 1891, but she was living in London in 1889 when the mummy board arrived at the museum. The article, however, was largely fictitious. In 1923, after Carnarvon's death, Conan Doyle had become convinced that the coffin lid was to blame for Robinson's death. I guess it seemed too much like his "Lot No. 249" to resist. Doyle, after all, believed in all manner of supernatural things and thought that Lord Carnarvon died from a psychically controlled "elemental" that carried out Tutankhamun's vengeance.

**Figure 10.3.** The fabulous treasures of Tutankhamun, such as his golden death mask, helped rekindle fascinations with Egypt and inspire stories about a curse protecting them. *Library of Congress Prints and Photographs Division, LC-M305- SL17-8920.*

Across many repeated accounts, the sarcophagus lid Stead described became a full sarcophagus and then a mummy. Modern accounts of the story—blatant fakery and ignorant misunderstandings, actually—have the mummy survive the sinking of *Titanic* only to cause the sinking of the *Empress of Ireland* and the *Lusitania*. None of that really happened.

## MURTAḌĀ IBN AL-ʿAFĪF AND KING TUT'S CURSE

The cursed coffin lid story served as precedent for the curse of King Tut. Our story proper begins with the real-life discovery of the tomb of Tutankhamun in 1922 (see fig. 10.3). According to legend, however, when Howard Carter broke into the tomb, he triggered an ancient curse, which read "Death comes on wings to he who enters the tomb of a Pharaoh." The particular wording of his curse is unusual, all the more so since it doesn't seem to appear in print until the end of the twentieth century, attributed to a bewildering array of sources. Sometimes it is said to come from a tablet found in Tut's tomb; other times it is just an Arabic proverb. Sometimes it is said to have been inscribed about the entrance to the tomb. Other times it is claimed that newspapers printed the curse either a month before or in the week after Lord Carnarvon died on April 3, 1923, from blood poisoning due to a mosquito bite. An alternative version of the imagined inscription on Tut's tomb reads that "Death shall come on swift wings to him that toucheth the tomb of the Pharaoh." That one goes back at least to a 1930 *New York Times* obituary for tomb excavator Howard Carter's secretary, whose suicide was attributed to the curse. The *Times* merely called it a "malediction" popular among modern Egyptians, though later it would describe it as inscribed on the wall of the tomb. Indeed, in 1936, an Egyptologist wrote to the *Times* to tell them that the sentence was completely made up, probably by one of their correspondents. Others concluded that newspaper correspondents misreported a spell from the ancient Egyptian *Book of the Dead* appearing on a statue in the tomb.

When Lord Carnarvon fell ill, journalists were quick to remember the stories of vengeful mummies that filled popular magazines and newspapers, and representatives of the *New York World* contacted celebrities with occult leanings for their views on the cause of his soon-to-be-fatal illness. Doyle, as mentioned, blamed a psychic entity. But the comment that struck a true nerve came from the pen of bestselling romantic novelist Marie Corelli.

Marie Corelli was born Mary Mackay, the daughter of Charles Mackay, the author of *Extraordinary Popular Delusions and the Madness of Crowds*. It is not without irony that Corelli grew up to become a popular novelist who actively promoted pseudo-history and psychical phenomena. Mark Twain hated her, but the public loved her novels, tinged with romance, science fiction, and fantasy. Different newspapers of the time gave various accounts of her statement on Lord Carnarvon falling ill, first published in March 1923, between the time of the mosquito bite and his April 3 death. The version below I have compiled from what I hope are the best readings of the several 1923 newspaper copies I was able to review:

> As one who has studied Egyptian mysticism all my life I may say that I am not surprised at an accident occurring to those daring explorers who seek to rifle the tombs of the dead monarchs of the land shadowing with wings. That is what the Bible calls it, a strange designation with a strange meaning behind it. According to a rare book I possess, which is not in the British Museum, entitled "The Egyptian History of the Pyramids" translated out of the original Arabic by Vattie, Arabic professor to Louis XVI of France, the most dire punishment follows any rash intruder into a sealed tomb. This book gives long and elaborate lists of the treasures buried with several of the Kings, and among these are named "divers secret potions enclosed in boxes in such wise that those who touch them shall know how they come to suffer." That is why I ask, Was it a mosquito bite that so seriously affected Lord Carnarvon? Could it be that he touched something poisonous among the garments or jewels of the entombed King? In any case I feel that intrusion of modern men into the 3,000 years' silence and death sleep of the Kings of Egypt is something of a desecration and sacrilege and that it will not and it cannot come to good.

The unusual title ascribed to the book has made it hard for later scholars to figure out what Corelli was referring to. Indeed, many concluded that her own romantic imagination made up the book altogether and through it, she "invented" the mummy's curse. While Corelli certainly helped develop the myth of the curse of King Tut, her citation is to a discoverable source: she is referring to the *History of Egypt* of Murtaḍā ibn al-'Afīf. As we have seen, the book was originally composed in Arabic around 1200 CE, but it survives only in a French translation made in 1666 by Pierre Vattier and then translated into English in 1672 by John Davies. This English translation appears to be the copy that Corelli owned. The odd title comes from her mistaken rendering of the title of the 1672 edition, which was *The Egyptian History, Treating of the Pyramids etc.* But you needn't take my word for it. In 1892, she cited the book by both name and author in her novel *The Soul of Lilith*. She got the name wrong there, too, calling it *The Egyptian Account of the Pyramids*. (Interestingly, using Corelli's mangled title, the chemists B. G. Lennon & Co. advertised for a copy of the book in 1898; I do not know if they found one—or what they hoped to do with it.) In a 1901 lecture published in her *Free Opinions, Freely Expressed* (1905), Corelli quoted from the book extensively in making some utterly oddball claims, namely that the ancient Egyptians had wireless telegraphy and the telephone, ideas she claimed that she was citing in direct quotation from Murtaḍā ibn al-ʿAfīf.

## MURTAḌĀ IBN AL-ʿAFĪF IN MARIE CORELLI'S CARELESS CITATIONS

The trouble is that Corelli wasn't actually quoting from Murtaḍā, but rather misremembering and conflating bits and pieces of Murtaḍā that she then claimed to be quotations. Presumably, she hadn't actually read the book since 1892 and the quotations were meant to be paraphrases. Her "telephone," for example, originated in a passage in which Murtaḍā said that a queen named Borsa would speak to visitors through a hole in her castle wall. Given this mangling, we can see how her allegation of poison in King Tut's tomb is misremembered from part of Murtaḍā's account of Sūrīd's stocking the Great Pyramid with treasure, including talismans, medicinal drugs, and both poisons and their antidotes. I suspect that Corelli—who had a long pattern of conflating and misremembering her sources—conflated passages like this with stories such as Sorrel's "Pharaoh's Curse." I can't prove that, of course, because I am not aware of evidence that Corelli was a subscriber to *Argosy* or that she had specifically read any of the hundred or so mummy's revenge stories published in Britain in the nineteenth and early twentieth centuries, but it seems unlikely that a bestselling novelist would have been unaware of *all* the stories. It is not strictly speaking necessary for Corelli to have known of Sorrel's specific tale to develop her own version—many others contain some of the elements—but the striking similarities, and the fact that the poisoned grave goods appear in Sorrel but not Murtaḍā and (to my knowledge) nowhere else leads me to suspect some transference. It's probably only coincidence that Corelli named a character in a 1906 novel "Lucy Sorrel," but, wow, what are the chances?

Even if she did not accidentally turn fiction into fact, the alternatives are not very encouraging. The long and short of it is that Corelli either quite confidently ascribed material to Murtaḍā ibn al-'Afīf for *decades* after reading the book without ever going back to check her source, or she maliciously misrepresented the material. The farther in time we move from when she read the book, the more inaccurate her published accounts of it become. This strongly implies that she relied on her memory without returning to check it against reality.

But ironically Murtaḍā, following earlier material from the *Akhbār al-zamān* or a closely related book, *actually did* allege that the kings of Egypt and the priests placed curses on the pyramids and tombs that promised death to those who attempted to enter and set up statues that would enforce the curse like ancient Terminators. Some have suggested that such stories were derived from the appearance of statues or carvings in the tombs that the Arabs opened. It is rather striking that the guardians of temples, tombs, and pyramids reflect, in a highly distorted way, the New Kingdom belief that the four walls of a burial chamber were each protected by a different supernatural guardian, whose aid was invoked, as given in the Theban version of the *Book of the Dead* (ch. 101a). At any rate, Corelli would have been aware of some or all of these various influences from her occult interests and research for her novels. Although her memory was faulty, or her intentions impure, Corelli rightly cited actual medieval legends that tomb robbers would be killed and thus helped give modern life to an old bit of pyramid lore as the curse of mummy's tomb.

## MURTAḌā IBN AL-'AFĪF AND THE *NECRONOMICON*

There was another unintended consequence of Corelli's letter to the *World*, and it concerned H. P. Lovecraft. Yes, *him* again. In September 1922, Lovecraft invented a dark grimoire for his story "The Hound," which he called "the forbidden *Necronomicon* of the mad Arab Abdul Alhazred." It was a book covering the dark history of the world and its magic: "We read much in Alhazred's *Necronomicon* about its properties, and about the relation of ghouls' souls to the objects it symbolised; and were disturbed by what we read." By 1927, Lovecraft had developed an elaborate history for his fictitious tome, from its origins as an Arabic volume called the *Al-Azif* in the eighth century, to its translation into Greek and Latin, the loss of the original Arabic, and an English version composed by the occultist John Dee at the court of Elizabeth I. In time, the book became less of a grimoire than a repository of the secret history of Earth, including its invasion by beings from other worlds. "Reading [it] leads to terrible consequences," Lovecraft wrote. The book went on to have an astonishing afterlife, inspiring efforts to write it into existence, such as the fake *Simon Necronomicon* cobbled together from Mesopotamian texts in the 1970s, as well as its use in many fictional contexts, including the *Evil Dead* franchise, where the cursed book brings doom to all who read it. Some who practice so-called magick use the fake versions

## The *Picatrix* and the *Akhbār al-zamān*

The Hermetic text known as the *Picatrix* is a Latin translation of an eleventh-century Arabic text called *Ghāyat al-Ḥakīm*. The book has an odd history, having been written sometime in the 1000s before being translated into a now-lost Spanish text by order of Alfonso X around 1256–1258 and then from Spanish to Latin sometime thereafter. As a result of its retranslation, the book acquired some odd readings. What is more interesting is that, like its near contemporary, the *Akhbār al-zamān*, it is not an original work so much as a composite of older material. The *Picatrix* is a textbook of the practice of magic and the occult rather than a pretended book of history like the *Akhbār al-zamān*. Despite the very different purposes of the two books, they share some of the same stories in common. The versions in the *Akhbār al-zamān* are more often than not the older and superior readings.

of the book to perform conjurings and spells. By some accounts, it is the most influential book never written.

The fine details of the *Necronomicon* are a synthesis of many influences. The moldy old book of forbidden lore is a stock element of Gothic literature, and Lovecraft was a longtime devotee of the fantastical tales of Arabic lore, notably the *Thousand and One Nights*, from which he gleaned his love for the wild and colorful legendry of the medieval Muslim world. Originally, the *Necronomicon* was a sort of analogue for a grimoire like the famous Latin version of the medieval Arabic book of Hermetic lore known as the *Picatrix*, but after 1923, its story grew more elaborate. As Jeb J. Card demonstrates in his 2018 book *Spooky Archaeology*, however, a good case is to be made that Lovecraft assembled bits and pieces of lore into a specific form because of the then-current discussion of the curse of King Tut, as mediated through Marie Corelli. Both the *Necronomicon* and Murtaḍā ibn al-ʿAfīf's book were Arabic texts of occult lore translated by European royal courtiers and passing through several intermediate versions before reaching Euro-American occultists. Card goes deeper, suggesting that the story of a dead king wreaking vengeance from his tomb with the help of a curse and a book of occult lore directly influenced the plot of Lovecraft's "Call of Cthulhu," a 1926 story about a titanic extraterrestrial entity that sleeps as though dead in an undersea tomb until he is resurrected when the stars reach the right position in the sky. Here, though, I will stick with the *Necronomicon*, and it is indeed interesting that Lovecraft's history of the book seems like a mirror of the complicated textual transmission of Murtaḍā's text. To the best of my knowledge, there is no direct evidence that Lovecraft read Corelli's letter, but it would have been surprising if he had not seen it; it was widely reprinted in the papers he was reading at the time and was referenced by many of the writers he is known to have read. As Card points out, Lovecraft was deeply involved in researching Egyptian mysteries in the mid-1920s, not least for Houdini's 1924 story, "Imprisoned with the Pharaohs."

Lovecraft seems to have taken inspiration from Corelli's reports about Murtaḍā ibn al-ʿAfīf's book, and Murtaḍā's book is a close copy of chunks of the *Akhbār al-zamān*. Weirdly enough, and unbeknownst to Lovecraft, who never read the French edition of the *Akhbār al-zamān*, the only version available in the West at the time, the book really is very much like the *Necronomicon* as he envisioned it. It covers the primeval history of the world, including the actions of godlike beings from the sky—the djinn—and the incredible antediluvian civilizations that once littered ancient Earth. It describes vast cycles of cosmic time and the puissant works and cyclopean architecture of the giants and monsters that reigned before the flood. It even has an evil monster, the antichrist, who is imprisoned on a mysterious island and will emerge from it "when the time is right," just like Cthulhu! It also describes the wonders of Arab and Egyptian magic at length, though not with specific spells.

In short, the *Akhbār al-zamān* is the closest we will come to the "real" *Necronomicon*. I translated the book into English for my website, and I lived to tell the tale. It is, frankly, a little disappointing. I sort of expected something cosmic to happen.

# 11

# MUMMIES IN OUTER SPACE

BY THE LATER TWENTIETH CENTURY, THE STORY OF THE MUM-
my's curse had become firmly embedded in pop culture. When TV pro-
ducer Alan Landsburg cast about for subjects to fill the first season of his
paranormal documentary series *In Search Of...*, he placed the imagined
curse of King Tut up front as the eighth episode. From the 1960s down to
the present, mass media such as television, mass-market publishing, and,
increasingly, the internet pushed legends about the Egyptian pyramids
and ancient Egyptian culture in ever more extreme directions. Although
these stories drew, often explicitly, on medieval tales, they increasingly
reflected the pseudoscientific, paranormal, and occult beliefs of the New
Age and the antigovernment paranoia the Cold War had fomented. They
also drew heavily on science fiction of the twentieth century as literature
and movies merged with an imaginary Egyptian history. This process
was already underway when the leader of the Soviet Union visited Egypt
in 1964.

## PARANOIA AND CONSPIRACY AT GIZA

In the spring of 1964, Soviet premier Nikita Khrushchev visited Egypt
to celebrate the construction of the Aswan High Dam, one of Egypt's

largest construction projects since the creation of the Suez Canal a century earlier and one that the Soviet Union had helped finance and complete. During his tour, the Egyptian president, Gamal Nasser, staged an elaborate show at the Giza pyramids in which thirty-seven-year-old Hefnawi Abdul Nabih, a "professional" pyramid climber, dressed like an ancient pharaoh, sprinted up the Great Pyramid in just five minutes, released pigeons from the summit, and then sprinted back down to hug the Soviet leader.

## William Randolph Hearst and Noah's Pyramid

To an extent, the application of medieval stories in new ways was not unique to the middle twentieth century. Consider, for example, a splashy Sunday feature that ran in William Randolph Hearst's newspapers beginning on July 30, 1922, in the direct wake of the Tutankhamun sensation a few weeks earlier. Hearst's papers reported that "science identifies the Great Pyramid as the real Noah's Ark," and their writer confidently quoted a certain C. E. Getsinger, who might have been the man of the same name accused by the American Medical Association of running a patent medicine scam, to the effect that the pyramids were built for the survivors of the flood to take refuge within their chambers and preserve their secrets. The article even quotes Getsinger that that the high-water mark from the flood left a visible line near the top of the Great Pyramid—a patent absurdity since the pyramids were covered in casing stones until the Middle Ages, so the flood would not have left a mark deep within. It is less absurd once you realize Getsinger was pulling one over on a complicit Hearst journalist by spitting back the medieval Arab-Islamic pyramid story, apparently in the form given by al-Maqrīzī, without doing much to update the old ideas to fit modern facts. The story was a one-day wonder and did little more than amuse readers.

*Life* magazine reported the event by comparing the engineering of the Aswan Dam to the "secrets" of the pyramids, whose construction, editor Hugh Moffett wrote, was a mystery even to modern engineers. A decade later, the German writer Philipp Vandenberg apparently invented a new legend about this 1964 trip in his 1973 book *Der Fluch der Pharaonen* (*Curse of the Pharaohs*) to supplement the stories of King Tut's curse and other Egyptian mysteries he had collected from early-twentieth-century sources. He said Khrushchev had received an urgent cable from the KGB warning him against entering the Great Pyramid, so at the last minute he refused to tour its interior. Vandenberg speculated that the Soviet secret police wanted to protect Khrushchev from the alleged psychic damage Khufu's pyramid could cause those who entered. The *New York Times* gave Vandenberg's book a glowing review when it was translated into English a few years later, repeating the story of Khrushchev's pyramid misadventure for a readership of millions. Vandenberg cited no source for the story. If it really happened, it seems more likely that the KGB wanted to keep the premier out of a small, enclosed space where a radical hidden among the Egyptians might have done him harm. But psychic doom sounds better.

This small incident was typical of the twentieth-century approach to pyramid legends, applying old stories to new situations in unexpected and often confounding ways. But it also demonstrates the perniciousness of recently invented tales. Decades later, the respected Egyptian journalist Anis Mansour included Vandenberg's story in his own 1995 investigation of the so-called curse of the pharaohs.

It took the creation of a new modern myth to give the old pyramid legends one more twist that would help reinvigorate the ancient legend of the Watchers and the medieval stories of a preflood pyramid. That myth, of course, involved space aliens.

### UFOS OVER GIZA

In the 1930s, pulp fiction, particularly the variety known as weird fiction, began to play with the idea that space aliens had been involved in ancient history. H. P. Lovecraft was at the forefront of this artistic theme, writing a series of stories centering on extraterrestrial beings that came to Earth

in the distant past and served as humanity's first gods. He had himself
been inspired indirectly by Theosophy and directly by Victorian writers
who had taken their cues from Donnelly, Theosophy, Egyptomania, and
other key themes we've examined. In Lovecraft's stories, ancient ruins
and lost cities were their handiwork, and old idols and religious texts
were testaments to their presence. He was far from the only writer to use
the idea, but his stories influenced countless other writers to incorpo-
rate similar ideas into their own work. By the middle twentieth century,
the idea was so widespread in fiction that it could be found everywhere
from comic books to *Star Trek*. It was consequently no wonder that it
had begun to bleed into nonfiction. In one famous case, the editor of
*Amazing Stories*, Ray Palmer, actually promoted a series of novellas and
short stories by Richard Shaver about S&M-loving ancient underground
degenerates and their dealings with space aliens as though they were true
stories but lightly veiled behind the illusion of romance. Shaver claimed
that Egyptian myths, legends, and iconography were memories of the
fictitious cave-dwelling race and their amazing wonder weapons. The
pharaohs' distinctive crook-shaped staff was, he said, a "control-handle"
for a death ray. These stories ran from 1945 to 1948 and actually prompted
an FBI investigation when the bureau came to suspect that Palmer and
Shaver had conspired to invent the myth of flying saucers to promote
their stories.

This bleeding through the wall between fiction and nonfiction occurred in several places. The Soviets tried to use aliens as a substitute for
God in some midcentury propaganda aimed at Western audiences, for
example, with the apparent hope they could promote atheism and undermine confidence in Western science with the idea of aliens as ancient
gods. British UFO writers of the 1950s tried to relate flying saucers to old
stories of wonders in the sky and created a genre of ancient mysteries
books that flowered in full in the 1960s and 1970s. L. Ron Hubbard developed Scientology and its alien colonizers of Earth from the same stew
of influences. In Continental Europe, writers were even less concerned
than their Anglo-American counterparts about the divide between fact
and fiction. The Italian communist Peter Kolosimo tried to make the
case for Atlantis and space aliens in a 1968 book by heavily implying that
H. P. Lovecraft hid actual truths about aliens in his stories. He backed

up his views with recourse to the Arab-Islamic pyramid myth, which he knew only from secondhand sources. So confused was he that he thought the story came from a tome titled *La Murtadi*, taking Murtaḍā ibn al-'Afīf for a book rather than a person. For good measure, he threw in a bunch of material from Piazzi Smyth and a claim from Soviet propagandists that Egyptian obelisks were monuments to aliens' ballistic missiles. He added, like Donnelly and Blavatsky before him, that Egypt and the Americas were intimately linked, and he speculated that the Egyptian god Horus was a space alien. As ridiculous as all this sounds, the Italians gave Kolosimo one of their highest literary prizes for this book.

Kolosimo's volume, however, was merely a clown-car copy of a much more serious and influential—but just as wrong—book published in France in 1960 by the Russian émigré Jacques Bergier and the Franco-Belgian journalist Louis Pauwels. Entitled *The Morning of the Magicians*, the book promiscuously mixes ancient mysteries, space aliens, psychic powers, and Hitler into a confection that seems to promise profound New Age truths but in reality delivers warmed-over Theosophy updated for the Atom Age. The authors were huge fans of H. P. Lovecraft, whose works they would translate into French. Bergier even claimed, apparently falsely, to have corresponded with Lovecraft in his youth. Lovecraft hangs over their work, cited by name in *Morning* and explicitly taken for a prophet in Bergier's later solo work. In time, Pauwels would repent his New Age and neopagan beliefs, but in 1960, he and Bergier thought themselves heralds of a profound new way to understand the world by seeing the past as the playground of magic, the occult, and the psychical. Naturally, their book included old Victorian ideas about Egypt and the Giza pyramids, mostly from Piazzi Smyth, along with ideas about contact between Egypt and ancient Mexico, similar to Le Plongeon and Donnelly, as channeled through French writers of the twentieth century. They made reference to the medieval idea that Egypt gained its wisdom from the giants of old, a claim found in Arabic legends dating back a thousand years before the authors' "new" analysis, and they built on the old Islamic notion that magic spells made the blocks of the pyramid fly into place by suggesting that the ancients inherited a fabulous lost technology that modern scholars could only dream of understanding.

Although Egypt was not the focus of *The Morning of the Magicians*, the book opened the way for an entire generation of New Age writers and profiteers to resurrect Victorian speculation and repackage it for twentieth-century readers. Authors like Robert Charroux, Peter Tompkins, and Brad Steiger, as well as TV producers and personalities like Rod Serling, Leonard Nimoy, and Alan Landsburg, delivered the same old Victorian speculations about pyramid mysteries to audiences larger than any that the Victorians might have dreamed of reaching. When Landsburg and Serling broadcast *In Search of Ancient Astronauts* on NBC in January 1973, twenty-eight million people—one in eight Americans— watched the former *Twilight Zone* and *Night Gallery* star tell them about pyramid mysteries derived from Piazzi Smyth, an audience almost certainly larger than Piazzi Smyth's entire readership for the previous century. An earlier version of the show, released as a movie, was nominated for an Oscar for best documentary.

### CHARIOTS OF THE GODS? AND ALL THAT

All of this had been made possible due to the astonishing success of the book that *In Search of Ancient Astronauts* had been based upon, a 1968 German-language massive bestseller that had borrowed heavily from *The Morning of the Magicians* and transformed Pauwels's and Bergier's esoteric ideas into something so easily digestible that any hausfrau could now converse about aliens and archaeology.

Swiss hotelier Erich von Däniken's *Chariots of the Gods? Unsolved Mysteries of the Past* was published in February 1968 as *Erinnerungen an die Zukunft: Ungelöste Rätsel der Vergangenheit* (*Memories of the Future: Unsolved Mysteries of the Past*) and rapidly achieved bestseller status, selling more than two hundred thousand German-language copies in its first year of release and launching a wave of what German media called *Dänikitis*, or the obsessive desire to talk about ancient astronauts. An English translation by Michael Heron soon followed, released in Britain in 1969 and the United States in 1970, both as a book and as a serialization in the *National Enquirer*. Although the book was neither the first nor the best to discuss the ancient astronaut theory, its fortuitous timing, coming during the heyday of *2001: A Space Odyssey* and the Apollo moon missions, and careful revision by ex-Nazi propagandist and book editor Wilhelm Utermann, turned a book that even the publisher later conceded borrowed greatly from earlier authors like Jacques Bergier, Louis Pauwels, and Robert Charroux into a synonym for the ancient astronaut theory. Eventually, Pauwels's and Bergier's publisher threatened a lawsuit against von Däniken's, and the issue was settled with the inclusion of a citation for *The Morning of the Magicians* in *Chariots of the Gods?*

The details of von Däniken's views about space aliens and ancient history are beyond our scope, as is the majority of his fabricated and misrepresented evidence for alien contact in prehistoric times. However, in writing his book, he derived from earlier writers an appreciation for Victorian accounts of the pyramids and therefore dragged back into common circulation the claims that Piazzi Smyth had made a century before but had misunderstood. A polyglot Swiss for whom English was

## The Slipshod Scholarship of Ancient Astronauts

Across the massive game of linguistic telephone between the Victorians and *Chariots of the Gods?*, Piazzi Smyth's claims sometimes became unrecognizable. Piazzi Smyth had claimed (falsely) that the Great Pyramid stood at the meeting place of the lines of latitude and longitude that crossed the most land—the "center" of Earth's landmasses. Von Däniken, probably working from later Victorian summaries that (weirdly) claimed that ancient superscholars caused the Great Pyramid to weigh one one-billionth the weight of the whole earth as corrected for its specific gravity, mangled the claim and asserted that the pyramid stood at Earth's "center of gravity," a claim that made no real sense but was repeated countless times afterward. Von Däniken later told *Playboy* magazine that he didn't know what the claim meant either. He had simply copied it from a book and never bothered to check whether his understanding of the claim made any sense.

his third or fourth language, von Däniken's book was itself written in German and then translated into English by a translator who was not always careful about researching original sources.

This would be bad enough, but the justification von Däniken had for his resurrection of Victorian pyramid mysteries was both medieval and Victorian at the same time. It was, of course, the Sūrīd pyramid story, as given in Colonel Vyse's *Operations*. Because he was copying without doing any scholarly research, von Däniken made a number of errors and repeated false information that had been disproved long before. He attributed the Sūrīd story from the *Akhbār al-zamān*, for example, to al-Masʿudi because Aloys Sprenger had (wrongly) done so 130 years earlier. He wrongly identified the Arab Muslim historian al-Masʿudi as a Christian Copt because he misread Vyse's book. Von Däniken asserted from the Sūrīd story that Khufu had forged the evidence tying the Great Pyramid to him and that the building must have been built far longer ago, across many lifetimes. Mummies, he added, must have originated from the pharaohs' belief that space aliens would be able to revive the dead if their bodies still existed when they returned from outer space at some point thousands of years in the future.

This would not be the last time von Däniken would refer to the Sūrīd story to support claims about space alien contact thousands of years ago. In 1996, he wrote an entire book called *The Eyes of the Sphinx* devoted to interpreting myths and legends about Egypt, many of Victorian provenance, as evidence of space aliens. Apparently forgetting that he had ever read Colonel Vyse's translations of the story from the *Akhbār al-zamān* and al-Maqrīzī, he (re-)discovered al-Maqrīzī in German translation and became transfixed by the Sūrīd story anew. This time, though, he was much more interested in the identification of Hermes Trismegistus with Enoch and Idris, because he believed that when God carried Enoch off in Genesis 5:21–24, this was actually an alien abduction. In 1996, he merely (and correctly!) said that Sūrīd and Enoch had "parallels," but over time, this distinction faded for him. Purposely conflating the Sūrīd story with the version featuring Hermes, throughout the 2010s, he declared Sūrīd himself to be Enoch and once stated that Enoch hid secret "books" underneath the Great Pyramid. Bizarrely, he also thought that al-Maqrīzī wrote two thousand years ago or more instead of six hundred, a misconception he passed along in the early 2000s to his protégé, Giorgio A. Tsoukalos, after 2009 the face of the popular *Ancient Aliens* TV series, which, like *In Search of Ancient Astronauts*, originated as an adaptation of *Chariots of the Gods?* Tsoukalos would present von Däniken's mangled view of the Arabic legend of the pyramids both on cable TV and on social media, alleging that al-Maqrīzī was an ancient writer who had proven that space aliens assisted the Egyptians in building the Giza pyramids. Al-Maqrīzī had said no such thing, and Tsoukalos had apparently misunderstood part of von Däniken's *The Eyes of the Sphinx*, which is in and of itself a feat.

### ALIENS TELEPORT FROM PAGE TO SCREEN

Over the years, *Ancient Aliens* would present wildly distorted versions of Piazzi Smyth's ideas, as well as misunderstood versions of myths and legends from medieval Arabic texts. In one particularly egregious case from the 2017 episode "The Alien Frequency," the show falsely claimed that Herodotus had written that the Egyptians "were given knowledge from the Guardians of the Sky on how to float the massive limestone blocks with which they built the Great Pyramid." This very mixed-up claim, delivered to an audience of more than a million viewers, conflated Herodotus with the Abrahamic myth of the Watchers and the *Akhbār al-zamān* story that a papyrus written with a magic spell caused the stones of the Great Pyramid to slide into place. The "Guardians of the Sky" were just the Watchers from the Book of Enoch, but no one involved seemed to realize in borrowing the notion from von Däniken's books of the 1990s and 2000s that he was translating into English a German rendering of the Geʿez translation of the Aramaic original. So "Watchers" became "Watchmen" became "Guardians," and a new class of extraterrestrial sky being was born.

The same set of influences also gave rise to Roland Emmerich's 1994 movie *Stargate*, in which the pyramids of Egypt were revealed to be copies of alien spaceships piloted by extraterrestrials that had given Egypt its culture. Emmerich was a longtime fan of speculative history writers and incorporated their fringe ideas into his films. The star gate of the title was a portal that let Egyptians teleport to the aliens' world. Andre Norton's

1958 novel *Star Gate* includes a similar portal, which transports users to alternate worlds, a concept revisited in Pauline Gedge's 1982 novel *Stargate*, which was the very loose inspiration for—yes—the 1994 movie. So influential was this film (and the TV series derived from it) that *Ancient Aliens* and other advocates of the so-called ancient astronaut theory adopted it wholesale and began speaking of star gates and interdimensional portals as regular features of ancient Egyptian life. Emmerich went on to write and direct *10,000 BC* (2008), another movie based on speculative history, in which he depicted the Egyptian pyramids and Sphinx under construction during the Ice Age, just as the medieval Arab writers and Atlantis theorists had imagined them.

### THE ORION MISERY

So much of the modern legendry of the pyramids is little more than misunderstood and careless repackaging of Victorian and medieval ideas that it quickly becomes tiring to try to list all the thousands of variants now in circulation. But nothing quite shows the daisy chain of speculation as does the bizarre case of the so-called Orion mystery, which did more than anything else to keep medieval speculation at the forefront of modern popular understandings of the Great Pyramid and the Giza Plateau.

Remember Peter Kolosimo? Well, in his 1968 book, he reported on some (false) French and Soviet claims that an African tribe called the Dogon had secret knowledge of the Sirius star system gleaned from space aliens. Eight years later, Robert Temple, a young writer with occult leanings and an interest in Erich von Däniken and other ancient astronaut speculators, used the same claim as the starting point for *The Sirius Mystery*. The secret knowledge was little more than an error made by French anthropologists in the 1930s. A later study found that the anthropologists had overinterpreted myths and legends and had probably introduced the Sirius knowledge themselves accidentally since no trace of it could be found after they left. But Temple didn't know this, so he imagined a fantastical chain of events where the Dogon received their knowledge from Jason and the Argonauts, who, in turn, had gotten it from the Egyptians,

## Pharaoh's Pump

To give but one example of how Victorian ideas influenced modern speculation, in 1838, L. Vernon Harcourt proposed that the Great Pyramid was actually a water purifier, with Nile water passing through its various halls to become clean and safe. This was based, ultimately, on a false claim from Herodotus that a secret channel took water under the pyramid. In the 1990s, engineer Chris Dunn offered a variant that imagined the Great Pyramid as a water pump used for a gigantic power plant, where "vibrations" turned water into electricity. Eventually, he went beyond even his own original speculation and would conclude—without evidence—that the Egyptians filled the pyramid with hydrogen gas and used lasers to turn it into a proton energy beam.

citing the Egyptian priests in Plato's account of Atlantis. According to Temple, the Egyptians and the Greeks had positioned their cities in strategic places across the eastern Mediterranean to create a vast depiction of the constellation of Argo, in honor of Jason (who wasn't really Jason, but that's not relevant here) and space aliens, with each city standing for a star in the constellation. This work Temple ascribed to an ancient elite not unlike the Followers of Horus from French speculative histories of the nineteenth century. In later years, Temple would return to the subject of Egypt and propose that the Great Sphinx was originally meant to be the jackal god Anubis.

Despite the many shortcomings of *The Sirius Mystery*, it struck a nerve, even among some scholars outside of the fields of archaeology and anthropology, and it gained the reputation as the thinking person's ancient astronaut book. Three years later, the engineer Robert Bauval chanced across Temple's book in an airport bookshop and was transfixed. Temple's claims about star cities inspired him to look for similar star

**Figure 11.1.** When seen from the air, the three major pyramids of Giza roughly resemble the belt stars of the constellation Orion, prompting speculation this pattern was intentional. *Library of Congress Prints and Photographs Division, LC-M305-SL17-4479.*

correlations at a smaller level, among the pyramids. The result was *The Orion Mystery*, a 1994 book in which he proposed that the Giza pyramids had been laid out in the image of the three belt stars of the constellation Orion, with the Milky Way serving as a celestial Nile River to complete the tableau (see fig. 11.1).

But Bauval wasn't content to rest there. He had read a book by scientists Giorgio de Santillana and Hertha von Dechend called *Hamlet's Mill*, which had been published in 1969 and was one of the foundational texts of the alternative archaeology movement. Its writers mined global mythology to hunt out factors and multiples of seventy-two to claim that such numbers proved that world myths all encoded scientific data from a lost civilization about the precession of the equinoxes, in which the stars rotate backwards through the zodiac by one degree every 71.6 years, roughly seventy-two years to the nearest integer. Thus, numbers like 12, 36, 72, 432, 36,000, et cetera all become important "precessional numbers" suggesting remnants of this lost science. Bauval proposed that using this data, he could show that the pyramids had been arranged to "encode" an image of the sky as it was in 10,400 BC, a date later and more famously rounded to 10,500 BCE. But de Santillana and von Dechend had made a fundamental error. They weren't familiar with Abū Ma'shar and his synthesis of ancient astrologies, and when de Santillana and von Dechend looked across the Old World and saw what they perceived as "fragments" of a lost science, they were looking in the wrong direction. The use of multiples of twelve and thirty across the Old World wasn't the decay of a lost system of knowledge but rather the contributing factors toward Abū Ma'shar's unified system. The numbers themselves were easily explained—they derived from the months of the year, the twelve- and thirty-year cycles of Jupiter and Saturn, and Babylonian astrology. The cyclical planetary values also left their traces in non-Western cultures, who also could see the sky and needed no help from the Old World or Atlantis to count to twelve and thirty. (Of course, some in contact with the Islamic world borrowed Islamic astrology, too.) That these numbers all were reducible to multiples of twelve and thirty was harmonious but required no knowledge of axial precession. It was merely coincidence that the rate of drift for the stars was also close to a multiple of twelve, seventy-two years per degree. That is what allowed the authors of *Hamlet's Mill* to miss the actual facts behind the supposed secret connections and imagine a lost science that wasn't really there. But Bauval didn't know that, either.

Bauval's writing partner on *The Orion Mystery*, occultist Adrian Gilbert, was heavily into Hermetic lore. The two became convinced through *Hamlet's Mill*, the ancient astronaut theory, and Hermetic lore that the connection between heaven and earth laid out in Hermes's Emerald Tablet was literal, not metaphorical, and therefore the monuments of Egypt reflected on Earth the stars in the sky above. The connection was imperfect—the pyramids didn't quite match Orion's stars, for example, but in short order, Bauval partnered with a new writer, the British journalist Graham Hancock, to expand his claim exponentially.

## FINGERPRINTS OF MEDIEVAL STORIES

Hancock made his name attempting to recreate *Raiders of the Lost Ark* by hunting the Ark of the Covenant across Egypt and Ethiopia. In 1995, he published *Fingerprints of the Gods*, a lightly updated version of Donnelly's *Atlantis* (thanking its author by name) in which he attempted to trace the "fingerprints" of an Atlantis-like lost Ice Age civilization through Egypt and other ancient cultures. It was all old Victorian nonsense, but it played well as a more serious version of *Chariots of the Gods?*, replacing space aliens with Atlantis. In 1996's *Keeper of Genesis* (*The Message of the Sphinx* in the United States), he and Bauval began referring explicitly to the predynastic Followers of Horus as Gaston Maspero had imagined them (they cited his work specifically), as well as the idea of a cosmic "stargate" used by the pharaohs—just two years after the *Stargate* movie. (Whether this was *real* in a material sense they left vague, though Hancock would later link such claims with journeys to other dimensions undertaken through hallucinogenic drugs.) They updated the Victorians with a major claim, not quite original, which was unwarranted amplification of Victorian ideas masquerading as stunning new revelations. They declared the Great Sphinx to be a relic from a lost civilization from 10,500 BCE, a symbol of the constellation Leo, and also the marker of a specific point in time when Atlantis was destroyed.

None of this was exactly new. Maspero and François Lenormant had claimed the Sphinx to be predynastic, as we have seen, and an occult tradition identified it as a representation of Leo and Virgo. So, when Bauval and Hancock decided that the Sphinx represented the moment when the sun rose in Leo on the vernal equinox, and thus it dated to the "epoch of 10,500 BC," there was little new in the idea, but they married this old astrological speculation to "science" that was also Victorian in origin.

In 1992, the geologist Robert Schoch declared that the Sphinx had been weathered by water, not wind, and therefore was predynastic in origin (see fig. 11.2). Eventually, he would push this back to 10,500 BCE,

## The Occult Tradition of a Star-Linked Sphinx

Several Victorian and Edwardian writers had built on French claims of a predynastic Sphinx in light of medieval Islamic legends to suggest that the Sphinx itself wasn't just Leo but pointed in time to the era of the Sphinx's construction, which could be discovered through Theosophy, astrology, and the precession of the equinoxes. Theosophist and Hermetic Order of the Golden Dawn member Sidney G. P. Coryn used axial precession to date the Sphinx to as much as ten thousand years before he wrote in 1913. In 1909, an astrologer named John Kilduff drew on the same old ideas to declare the Sphinx to represent the moment when the sun rose exactly between Leo and Virgo on the vernal equinox, and thus he dated the Sphinx to 10,750 BCE.

and in 1993, he created a global sensation when he presented his claim on NBC in a special hosted by Charlton Heston. *The Mystery of the Sphinx* had thirty-three million viewers on its first broadcast and millions more when rerun on cable over the next decade. It won an Emmy award for research, despite being untrue. Mainstream scientists rejected Schoch's claims, but the public was transfixed. The claim inspired Hancock to write *Fingerprints of the Gods*. But unbeknownst to viewers who assumed Schoch was acting purely as scientist, he was heavily influenced by John Anthony West, a tour guide and speculative writer on Egypt. West, who also appeared in *Mystery of the Sphinx*, was himself deeply interested in the esoteric and the occult, and he had derived his ideas about a predynastic Sphinx from the occultist R. A. Schwaller de Lubicz, who had developed the water erosion hypothesis. Schwaller de Lubicz had read Maspero's *Dawn of Civilization* and adopted the idea of a predynastic origin of the Sphinx from Maspero, citing him directly in his book *Sacred Science* (1958/1961). It was in this book, and in attempting to justify Maspero's claims, that Schwaller de Lubicz invented the water erosion

**Figure 11.2.** Modern pseudohistorical speculators claim the erosion patterns on the Sphinx indicate it was carved twelve thousand years ago. *Library of Congress Prints and Photographs Division, LC-M32-8945.*

hypothesis of the Sphinx, the foundation for John Anthony West's and Robert Schoch's work.

## FAKE ARCHAEOLOGY'S AVENGERS ASSEMBLE

Frankly, it would all be too ridiculous to believe if it hadn't actually happened: ideas that originated in late antique and medieval efforts to marry Egyptian history to Noah's flood passed through early French archaeology to end up in the hands of occultists and were transferred to cable TV and the internet, where millions of people came to believe that archaeologists and Egyptologists were conspiring to hide the "truth" about an antediluvian civilization. Naturally, *Ancient Aliens* made Schoch, Bauval, and Hancock part of its stable of talking heads and repeatedly referred to all three men's ideas about Egypt. In 1998, Hancock and Bauval would join UFO believers in comparing the Great Sphinx to an eroded mesa in the Cydonia region of Mars, popularly called the "Face on Mars" due to its superficial resemblance to a human face wearing a helmet or headdress when photographed at low resolution. In 2015's *Magicians of the Gods*, Hancock brought it all together by embracing Charles Piazzi Smyth's claims about the Great Pyramid's myriad wonders and then supporting them with reference to the medieval Sūrīd legend. However, Hancock knew the story only from John Greaves—yes, from 1646!—and therefore misidentified the story as coming from the pen of Ibn 'Abd al-Hakam in the ninth century because he repeated the erroneous attribution found in Greaves. In 2019's *America Before*, Hancock speculated that Native Americans and ancient Egyptians grew out of the same civilization of Atlantis and shared the same religion and star lore.

The group of writers associated with Graham Hancock added one more revived legend to its tapestry of medieval and Victorian speculation. Since the mid-2010s, Hancock has claimed that his lost civilization was destroyed by a comet that struck the earth at the end of the last Ice Age, thus spawning a catastrophe remembered as Noah's flood. This claim was put forward many times in the past. Ignatius Donnelly made the same claim in his *Ragnarok* (1883), and the discoverer of Halley's Comet, Edmond Halley, had done the same in 1694 and suppressed his own work to prevent blasphemy charges. When Hancock tied the mysteries of the pyramids to the comet collision, he echoed not just the Victorian claims of Donnelly but also Sūrīd's and Philemon's dreams of the falling star and the medieval idea that the pyramid preserved knowledge from before the flood. The connection was no longer direct, but the long shadow of medieval influence had made these ideas so diffuse and so widespread that they appeared to be spontaneous conclusions drawn from fact rather than a system of legends invented centuries ago.

Hancock's books were bestsellers on both sides of the Atlantic, translated into more than two dozen languages, selling more than five million copies, and spawning television adaptations. Roland Emmerich claimed Hancock as the inspiration for *10,000 BC*. The ideas of Hancock and his colleagues may have been labeled *alternative archaeology*, but underneath it all, they were little more than medieval and Victorian legends masquerading as cutting-edge science.

# 12

## RACE AND RELIGION

FLYING SAUCERS OVER GIZA EVENTUALLY BECAME A JOKE, A visual shorthand for all the unusual ideas that surrounded the Egyptian pyramids. Art of UFOs hovering over the Great Pyramid appeared on T-shirts and coffee mugs and served as promotional artwork for cable shows such as *Ancient Aliens*. Even the cover of my first book, *The Cult of Alien Gods*, which examines the ancient astronaut theory from its origins to the twenty-first century, used a photo illustration of a stock image UFO superimposed over the Giza pyramids when it was published in 2005.

But the humor of imagining aliens buzzing the pyramids in their spaceships hides a darker truth: The wild stories we've looked at in this book aren't just funny, or strange, or wacky. Many groups have also used them to promote racism and religious extremism. This chapter will explore some of the consequences of believing in myths over reality.

### ABRAHAMIC RELIGIONS AND PYRAMID MYTHS

In the late summer of 2014, Egyptian heritage activist Amir Gamal made unsubstantiated claims that Israeli operatives were infiltrating archaeological teams across Egypt to fabricate evidence that the Jews built the pyramids before the Exodus. He believed that Israel was working with foreign governments to place Jews at the head of archaeological missions to undermine Egyptian history. According to Gamal, the Israeli government was also plotting to identify Pharaoh Sheshonq I with the biblical King Shishak (a rather common identification made long ago and supported by a stela at Megiddo) to claim the gold of Egypt as the temple treasure stolen by Shishak during his invasion of Judah (2 Chronicles 12:9). The ultimate aim, Gamal warned, was to strip Egypt of its heritage and vaunt the Jewish state over its Arab rival. That same year, Egyptian journalist Ahmad al-Gamal demanded that the government in Cairo sue Israel for the cost of the ten plagues that the Abrahamic faiths believe devastated Egypt during the New Kingdom. Nor was that the end of the reuse of old legends. In 2020, Egypt's former Grand Mufti Ali Gomaa appeared in a documentary televised across Egypt explaining that Idris taught Egyptians the art of pyramid building. He alleged that Idris invented mummification, and he said that the Sphinx was a statue of Idris, who was also Osiris. "There are presumptions that support this perception," Gomaa told an Egyptian TV journalist, according to an account in the *Egypt Independent* newspaper, "including the fact that the construction of the Sphinx preceded the building of the pyramids."

Nor were medieval myths confined to the Muslim world. In 2015, Dr. Ben Carson, a physician who was then the frontrunner for the 2016 Republican presidential nomination and later served as a cabinet secretary under President Donald Trump, faced a controversy when a 1998 video emerged showing him embracing the idea that the pyramids were Joseph's granaries. He called this his "belief" and supported the assertion with claims lifted directly from ancient astronaut books but revised for a religious worldview. Carson claimed that the pyramids had "hermetically sealed" chambers—a medieval Arab legend, but not a true one—and wrongly described popular ancient astronaut writers as "various scientists" who supported the idea that aliens built the pyramids. "You know, it doesn't require an alien being when God is with you," Carson said in support of the idea that God had designed and directed the building of the Giza pyramids. When challenged about the old claims on the campaign trail, Carson did not back down: "It's a plausible belief

## Pranking Christians at the Pyramids

Tensions between Jewish, Christian, and Islamic religious views of Egyptian history have simmered for almost as long as the cultures have been in contact, but sometimes these have been played for laughs. A 1909 edition of the *Brewer's Journal* reported that some Arab-Egyptians tried to fool Western scholars by placing dried grain inside the Great Pyramid for them to find, thus "confirming" that the building had been Joseph's granary. The find caused a brief sensation until the Egyptians took it too far and added American maize, which wasn't known in Egypt until after Columbus.

. . . because I believe in the Bible," he said. As we have seen, the Bible is silent on the pyramids, but by framing his claim as a religious belief, Carson drew a bright light between secular history and faith that would help redefine pyramid claims as cultural identifiers rather than scientific facts.

These claims sound ridiculous, but they exist at the nexus of Egyptian history, religion, and race, with various groups striving to win modern political, religious, and cultural wars by appealing to myths and legends about the past.

### AN ANCIENT EGYPTIAN WORLD TOUR

In the late eighteenth century, when scholars began to understand that many European and Asian languages were all part of the same Indo-European family, then known as Aryan languages, a theory arose that the origin of the Aryan race and language system occurred in India, and then a darker-skinned population eventually mixed with the White Aryans. Consequently, they traced all of the wonders of the world back to Vedic India, including those of the Egyptians, who scholars imagined for a time to be immigrants from Aryan India. Echoes of this myth survived for centuries. Eventually, the story found its way into a hoax article that ran in the *Arizona Gazette* in April 1909. The article contained a tall tale about the Smithsonian excavating the remains of a lost civilization in the Grand Canyon bearing elements of Egyptian and Tibetan cultures. The hoaxer relied on an eighteenth-century claim about Egyptians originating in India to give a spurious scholarship to his claim. More than eight decades later, the future *Ancient Aliens* talking head David Childress mistook the story for a true one and published articles and books referencing it, spreading the obscure newspaper story around the world. In time, cable TV shows such as *America Unearthed* would send their hosts in search of the Egyptians of the Grand Canyon, and a cottage industry arose to hawk books and videos in support of the claim.

Similar efforts to find Egyptian visitation in the ancient past occurred around the world. At several points in the 2000s, Australia's *Nexus* magazine claimed that Egyptian hieroglyphs had been found in Australia, and in 2012, *New Dawn*, another Australian magazine, alleged that Egyptian inscriptions proved a voyage from Egypt to Australia. Such claims aligned with Harvard zoologist Barry Fell's 1970s popular fantasy of an ancient Egyptian circumnavigation of the earth, but at the time of initial publication, experts who visited the site of the alleged Australian hieroglyphs, about an hour outside of Sydney, determined that they were modern graffiti. Other claims placed Egyptian travelers in Mexico, South Africa, the Pacific Ocean, and anywhere that Ignatius Donnelly might once have suggested people from Atlantis visited. The distinctive shape of reed boats used by the Inca on Lake Titicaca and by the ancient Egyptians even prompted claims that the Egyptians had colonized Peru. By the end of the 2010s, an entire mythology had arisen that saw the Egyptians as, basically, Donnelly's Atlanteans, substituting for their more fantastical counterparts.

## OF FAITH AND PHARAOHS

If such claims seem bizarre or even silly, they were nevertheless enormously popular for much of the past century. On the strength of the occult groups that had gained popularity in the late 1800s, many in the 1900s who were discontented with Christianity turned to ancient

Egypt—the great enemy of the Abrahamic faiths—as a source of wisdom and inspiration, using Egyptian themes and ideas to dress up their own search for a more satisfying spirituality. We see this in the Egyptian aesthetics of Freemasonry and the Rosicrucians, among other groups, and the serious thought given to the profundities of the Egyptian *Book of the Dead* upon its English translation. But it was Egypt's connection to Judaism, and by extension Christianity and Islam, that allowed yet another bizarre myth to take hold in the twentieth century.

In 1939, the psychoanalyst Sigmund Freud published *Moses and Monotheism*, a book that attempted to psychoanalyze Judaism to uncover the real psychodrama underlying the life of the biblical Moses. In the book, Freud applied his own unproven ideas about psychoanalysis to the biblical narrative to rediscover what he believed to be the true history of the Exodus. In his telling, Moses was not a Hebrew raised at the Egyptian court, as the Bible tells. Instead, Freud saw him as a native Egyptian who served at the court of the infamous Akhenaten, the so-called heretic pharaoh who began his reign as Amenhotep IV before adopting a new name and a new faith. This Eighteenth Dynasty pharaoh earned the ire of Egypt for closing the temples, moving the capital to a new city, and demanding that all Egyptians worship his chosen god, the sun disk known as the Aten, whom he upheld as the chief, or even the only, god (see fig. 12.1). His story had been lost to history until the remains of his capital of Akhetaten were rediscovered in the late 1800s. Interest in him grew in the 1920s and 1930s because he had been the father of Tutankhamun.

For Freud, Moses was a priest serving under Akhenaten, a true believer in the one true faith of the Aten. He claimed that Moses led a small group of friends and family out of Egypt after Akhenaten's death. This was the true Exodus, he said, and Moses fled Egypt to carry on the tradition of monotheism, which eventually gave rise to Judaism and the other Abrahamic faiths. The uncanny similarity between Akhenaten's Great Hymn to the Aten and the biblical Psalm 104 led some credence to this idea, though modern scholars discount any direct connection between the two texts. Freud's idea, however, sparked many imitators, some of whom were not as careful to separate Akhenaten from Moses. In the 1990s and 2000s, the Egyptian writer Ahmed Osman went so far as to claim that Akhenaten was himself Moses and that the patriarch Joseph (of the

**Figure 12.1.** Inscriptions depicting Akhenaten worshiping the sun disk, or Aten. Most such images were destroyed after the pharaoh's death to purge Egypt of his memory. *Library of Congress Prints and Photographs Division, LC-M31- 14564.*

pyramid granaries) had been Yuya, an official under Akhenaten's father. For good measure, he added that Christianity was originally an ancient Egyptian mystery cult dedicated to Tutankhamun, whom he believes to be the real Jesus, despite the 1,300-year time difference. Osman claimed that Egyptologists were too blinkered by their financial interests and careerism to accept his conclusions.

## AKHENATEN AND A SEARCH FOR GOD

The odd thing about Akhenaten—well, the odd thing about modern *ideas* of him, since he was a weird guy all on his own—is that he became an icon and prophet for so many disparate groups. We just saw him identified with Moses, but that was hardly all. The Rosicrucians of San Jose,

California—the Ancient and Mystical Order Rosæ Crucis, founded in 1915—ran an advertisement featuring a bust labeled "Amenhotep IV," which was Akhenaten's name before he changed it. Referring to Atlantis, the ad then asked, "Whence came the knowledge that built the Pyramids and the mighty Temples of the Pharaohs? . . . Did their knowledge come from a race now submerged beneath the sea, or were they touched with Infinite inspiration?" AMORC claimed that "Amenhotep IV, Leonardo da Vinci, Isaac Newton" and many others served among its illustrious ranks. It also says that "*Today it is known* that they discovered and learned to interpret *Secret Methods* for the development of the inner power of the mind" (emphasis in original). Like any good hustle, AMORC offered its membership *free* access to these secrets with a bit of pressure to become a paying member.

The AMORC myth—a concocted legend expanded and perpetuated by the Rosicrucian occultist Henry Spencer Lewis—claimed that the AMORC was a direct lineal descendant of an ancient Egyptian mystery school founded by the female pharaoh Hatshepsut. This seems to be a paganized gloss on Freemasonry's alleged ancient origins. (Both AMORC and Freemasonry are intertwined with European Rosicrucianism of the 1600s, which in turn took influence from Hermeticism and thus from Egypt and the myth of the Watchers. As you can see, if you tried to make a flow chart of these ideas, you'd end up with a pretzel.) Lewis, in his *Complete History of the Rosicrucian Order*, lays great weight on Akhenaten, "with whose history all Rosicrucians are greatly concerned. He was the last Great Master in the family of the founders and the one to whom we owe the really wonderful philosophies and writings used so universally in all Lodge work throughout the world." And lest you think this is the whole of Lewis's contribution to Akhenaten's fictitious occult history, there is more: he also declared Akhenaten "Aryan" and claimed he presided over 283 Rosicrucian brothers and 62 sisters. He specified that these Rosicrucian brothers wore linen outfits with cords around their waists and thus inspired all future monks.

Lewis admitted he derived his mythic version of Akhenaten from *The Life and Times of Akhnaton*, a 1910 book by Arthur Weigall, revised and reprinted in 1922. He follows it exactly, but interpolated into it a Rosicrucian cult and brotherhood, turning Weigall's sub-rosa narrative of how Akhenaten anticipated Christianity (a theme Freud redirected into his revision of Exodus) into one of how Akhenaten was actually a Rosicrucian.

## PSYCHICS, THE OCCULT, AND THE HALL OF RECORDS

The influence of Lewis on celebrity pseudohistory writers is profound. In *The Secret Chamber Revisited* (2014), Robert Bauval of *Orion Mystery* fame discusses Lewis's claims explicitly (though confusing him with a different occultist, Lewis Spence) and devotes part of the book to AMORC. Bauval further explains that he is friends with AMORC's current head, Christian Bernard, and gives talks to the organization about the Sphinx. Lewis had claimed to possess ancient maps showing the brotherhood's secret Hall of Records below Giza, a myth familiar from its parallel claim in the prophecies of the so-called "sleeping prophet" Edgar Cayce, a twentieth-century figure who alleged that he had visions of the past and

### Edgar Cayce and Occult Literature

Edgar Cayce, who prophesized in his sleep, openly admitted in his readings that he was borrowing his material directly from nineteenth-century occult literature. For example, in reading 364–1, Cayce discussed the sources for his ideas about Atlantis: "As we recognize, there has been considerable given respecting such a lost continent by those channels such as the writer of Two Planets, or Atlantis—or Poseida and Lemuria—that has been published through some of the Theosophical literature." Here he referenced Theosophical literature directly and explicitly cited the book *A Dweller on Two Planets* by Frederick Spencer Oliver, a supposed account of Atlantis and interplanetary exploration. Despite offering such explicit citations (in his sleep, supposedly!), believers insist Cayce's ideas were original.

the future in his dreams. Such tales originated in medieval legends that we discussed earlier in this book.

Lewis made his claim of a Hall of Records beneath the Sphinx in 1936, along with a diagram of the same, and Edgar Cayce miraculously came up with the same in 1939, much the way he miraculously dreamed dreams that reflected the occult literature he had just read and, in moments where he seemed to think he wouldn't be caught, explicitly cited that same literature by name in his prophecies. Cayce placed an imagined Hall of Records beneath the right paw of the Sphinx, but he also believed the pyramids to have been built in 10,490 BCE on orders from Ignatius Donnelly's Atlantis and Helena Blavatsky's Lemuria. In 1935, a psychic named H. C. Randall-Stevens published in *A Voice Out of Egypt* a very similar diagram of a chamber under the Sphinx, which Lewis seems to obliquely allude to as "mystical manuscripts that have been released in a limited manner in recent years." Lewis, for what it's worth, never offered evidence for his assertions, citing only "Rosicrucian archives" and the aforementioned "mystical manuscripts."

Randall-Stevens attempted to link Egypt and Atlantis with stories that closely paralleled the underground chambers and miraculous buildings found in medieval Arabic pyramid lore. He admitted that he modeled his claims on Masonic lore, which has the same origin point in the Enochian Pillars of Wisdom, and he may also have proposed an underground Sphinx temple in parallel to a Masonic myth known as the Secret Vault about an underground chamber built by Solomon on the site of Enoch's buried wisdom and the future temple. But since Randall-Stevens's and Lewis's claims seem to amplify, directly or indirectly, medieval Arabic legends of the Giza Plateau—which asserted that chambers and halls and "subterranean passages made of lead and stone" existed beneath the pyramids—it would not surprise me if these "archives" were little more than copies of medieval legends, repackaged with a showman's love of drama.

The evidence from Antoine Augustin Calmet's classic *Dictionary of the Holy Bible* shows a belief in chambers beneath the Sphinx was, if not exactly well-known in the 1700s and 1800s, at least easily accessible to even the least sophisticated psychic frauds. The dictionary quotes Richard Pococke's account of his Egyptian travels from 1743 in which he speaks of the Sphinx as having "apartments beneath." His claim derived from Pliny's report that the inhabitants of Giza believed that the Sphinx was hollow and the tomb of King Harmaïs or Armais, though he himself did not believe it. Based on such accounts, Giovanni Battista Caviglia, the Egyptologist, claimed that a secret network of tunnels would be found to connect all of the Giza pyramids, a claim copied by Vyse in his *Operations*, and his views were widely adopted in the early 1800s. Importantly, Charles Piazzi Smyth preserved such speculation in his *Life and Work at the Great Pyramid* (1867), recalling dismissively "all sorts of underground passages from the Sphinx to either the Great or Second Pyramid" that filled early modern Egyptology. William G. Clarke speculated in 1883 that perhaps a lucky turn of the spade would uncover "an interior vault" or a "subterranean passage" under the Sphinx itself. Theosophists spoke, from no good knowledge other than the preceding speculation, of the same passage: "According to tradition, a subterranean passage connects the interior of the Sphinx with that of the Pyramid." I would be remiss not to note that H. P. Lovecraft was familiar with all of this material and included the "legends of subterranean passages beneath the monstrous creature" in the story about the Sphinx he wrote for Harry Houdini, with which we began this book.

The idea was there for anyone to recycle, and it is no surprise that occultists did just that. The irony, of course, is that there actually *is* a chamber under the Sphinx—sort of. It just wasn't quite under the Sphinx, wasn't the Hall of Records that Edgar Cayce and Graham Hancock imagined, and wasn't all that old. An underground chamber containing a sarcophagus surrounded by water was identified controversially by Egyptologist Zahi Hawass as a cenotaph for the god Osiris. It is located beneath the causeway leading to the Sphinx. The shaft-tomb was explored in a live TV broadcast in 1999 with talk show host Maury Povich. Hawass organized it to combat what he claimed in a later article to be "New Age" beliefs that the so-called Osiris Shaft was the entrance to the underground complex of hidden chambers from medieval and Victorian legend. Hawass himself speculated from a different set of ancient texts that the shaft, which likely dates to the Sixth Dynasty, was nothing less than the underground tomb Herodotus described as being Khufu's burial place under the Great Pyramid.

Occult views of Giza and Egypt like those of Cayce and the Rosicrucians centered on the idea that seeking out physical evidence of Atlantis or some other lost civilization would somehow prove that the spiritual values embodied by occult and New Age groups were objectively true. It was a distinctly medieval view of faith, one not dissimilar to the trade in manufactured relics during the Middle Ages, when the joke went that there were enough pieces of the True Cross in European churches to make three of them. So, too, was it similar to Victorian efforts to find physical proof of God in the measurements of the Great Pyramid. Here, the search for the Hall of Records became a cudgel to be used against doubt, since the possibility that physical proof could be found removed the temptation to question the otherwise outlandish claims believers were asked to accept.

Our final group of legend hunters sought this same physical evidence for ideology, belief, and faith, but they sought it not in buildings and scrolls but in race and blood.

## NATIONALISM AND EGYPTIAN ORIGINS

Efforts to imagine Egypt in the image of modern nations, races, and cultures are very old. Turin, the capital of the old Kingdom of Piedmont and now one of Italy's major cities, developed a legend in the 1600s that it had been founded by the Greek mythic hero Phaethon, most famous for crashing the chariot of the sun god into the river Po. In Ovid's *Metamorphoses*, Phaethon was best friends with a guy named Epaphus, the son of Isis. He was a Greco-Roman version of the Apis bull. In a posthumous 1679 work, Emanuele Tesauro claimed that the real Phaethon was the (imaginary) pharaoh Pa Rahotep, who founded Turin and established the honors of the Apis bull there. This, he said, was why Turin was steeped in bull imagery. (In reality, the city took its name from a Roman misunderstanding of the indigenous word for mountain, which they thought sounded like the Latin word for bull.)

From the Middle Ages down to the present, the Scots have told a legend that their country was founded by a princess from Egypt named Scota, a daughter of the Pharaoh of Moses, who married a prince and fled her cruel father; everyone from antiquarians to spoon-bending celebrity Uri Geller has tried to find physical proof that the Scots were the progeny of an Egyptian royal and her Scythian husband.

The search for Scota is one of those eccentric quests that animate the antiquarians of the British Isles. It originates in a medieval confusion, in a time when Ireland and Scotland were both known as "Scotia," and the Christianized myths of the Celts tried to connect these lands back to the events of the Bible. Although the developed form of the Scota myth first occurs in the *Book of Leinster*, an Irish chronicle of the twelfth century, the earlier *Historia Brittonum* of Pseudo-Nennius makes reference to the Scota story (though in but one recension; the others speak only of a Scythian exile from Egypt and not his royal wife), demonstrating that it has a rather early medieval provenance. Scholars speculate that the story arose to support Scottish claims to independence, a countermyth to the more famous but equally false story of how Brutus of Troy, descendant of Aeneas, settled Britain and connected England back to the classical world and the founding family of the Roman Empire.

## Pseudo-Nennius's Sources

Medieval texts are rarely original. Most offer close copies of material from earlier sources, with small changes. If you are really interested, you'd probably like to know that the account of Pseudo-Nennius seems to derive from Henry of Huntingdon's *Historia Anglorum*, which in turn drew upon Bede's *Historia Ecclesiastica* and the Vatican recension of the *Historia Brittonum* (which predates the one referenced above), all of which traced the origins of the peoples of Ireland and/or Scotland back to "Scythia," though not always to Egypt. Across the texts, we see a gradual accretion of details as the myth became increasingly biblical, with each novel detail tacked on over the course of a century or two.

In 1301, Baldred Bisset rewrote Scottish history to downplay Irish involvement when he prepared the Scottish submission to the papal curia complaining about English aggression during the Wars of Independence. He rewrote the Scota myth to make her take the famed coronation stone of the British monarchs, the Stone of Scone, from Egypt with her during the Exodus, and Robert the Bruce made use of this as anti-English propaganda in 1323. It's all very interesting in an oddball sort of way, but aside from a few mythmakers (and a spoon bender), few took the story all that seriously after the Middle Ages. It was, however, precedent for a search for so-called White Egyptians.

## ARYANS AND ANCIENT EGYPT

The more that Europeans looked to ancient Egypt as a font for Western civilization, the more they felt the need to envision Egyptians in their own image. This was a departure from early modern Christian views, which saw the ancient Egyptians as evil, due to their antagonistic role in the Bible, and therefore as Black Africans. As Egypt's reputation became rehabilitated, the color Europeans imagined them to be changed as well. By the Victorian period, it was not uncommon for European and American scholars and writers to describe the Egyptians as a White Caucasian people who were overrun by swarthy hordes from the Arabian Peninsula after the coming of Islam. To do this subject justice would require a full book of its own, and here we can only touch on some of the ways that race and racism collided with science and myth.

In the late 1700s and early 1800s, scholars such as Arnold Hermann Ludwig Heeren argued that the Egyptians originated in India, which they saw as the homeland of the White Aryan race. As we have seen, they believed that Caucasian people came originally from India because they thought that Sanskrit was the primeval Aryan language, the ancestor of Latin and Greek. To these scholars, the original Aryans were corrupted, mixing with dark-skinned natives in India and Middle Eastern people in Egypt, surviving in their pure Whiteness only in northern Europe. Others, like the so-called father of scientific racism, phrenologist Samuel Morton, claimed that a study of ancient Egyptian skulls could prove

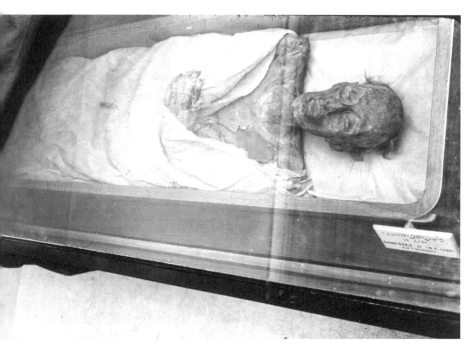

**Figure 12.2.** Scholars, speculators, and racists measured, observed, and probed mummies like that of Ramses II in the hope of discerning their racial characteristics. *Library of Congress Prints and Photographs Division, LC-M31- 14547.*

that they were White and superior to the "Negro" peoples they ruled over—that, in fact, White people were a different species altogether (see fig. 12.2). Later in the nineteenth century, as a growing understanding of the Indo-European family of languages gradually revealed that they originated in central Asia, not India, scholarly views of where Egypt got its White people consequently changed. Charles Piazzi Smyth reflected this transition in *Our Inheritance in the Great Pyramid* when he wrote that the Egyptians weren't Aryans from India but instead were "Caucasians" who descended from Siberia and the Caucasus—then believed to be the "White" homeland—into Egypt. The Atlantis theorist Ignatius Donnelly was even more explicit. He claimed that the first Egyptians were from Atlantis and that Atlantis had been populated by White people and Jews, the chosen races of God. "Atlantis was the original seat of the

Aryan or Indo-European family of nations," he wrote. The subtext was fairly obvious: the pyramids, the greatest wonders on earth, could only be the work of White people.

This view of Egypt as a country of White Aryans carried over into the twentieth century. The Nazis believed it, and Hollywood producers were quick to cast White actors as Egyptians, a practice that continues (and continues to generate controversy) down to the present, though less frequently today than in the middle twentieth century. A number of controversial books built on Ignatius Donnelly and his peers and sought out White founders for Egypt's wonders. One of the most popular was Graham Hancock's *Fingerprints of the Gods* (1995), which explicitly honored Donnelly and described a global culture of pyramid builders as White no fewer than a dozen times. In his early books, *Ancient Aliens* celebrity David Childress described White people as being the ruling race of the prehistoric world. He said that Whites founded Egypt and held Black and Brown people as slaves. In time, however, heightened sensitivity about racial matters caused writers like Childress either to downplay racial elements or, like Hancock, to replace a White master civilization with a Native American one.

## AFROCENTRISM AND ANCIENT EGYPT

A mirror image of the hunt for White Egyptians emerged among writers who identified as Afrocentrist. Not all these writers were themselves Black, though most were, and they took from Egypt's location in Africa the idea that the pyramid builders were themselves Black-skinned people from sub-Saharan Africa. The Afrocentrist movement began in the early twentieth century as a reaction to racist history that prioritized White experiences, but it drew on the sorts of extreme claims that had hitherto marked Victorian pyramid fantasies. In 1926, the Afrocentrist writer Drusilla Dunjee Houston published *Wonderful Ethiopians of the Ancient Cushite Empire*, which attempted to credit the ancient people of Ethiopia with founding Western civilization, including that of Egypt. For her, the pharaohs were sub-Saharan Africans and the pyramids were monuments to Black achievement. Greece and Rome only copied what ancient Africa originated, including, she thought, high technology like airplanes. She was hardly the only Afrocentric writer to make extreme claims about Egyptian high technology, but hers was one of the earliest and most influential in its genre. Her successors attempted to find ways to make such claims academically respectable, but they remain ideology, not science. At the most extreme end, the 1970s saw the rise of Kemetism, largely by African Americans, who sought empowerment by adopting a version of ancient Egyptian religion and iconography. One of the most extreme of the Kemetist groups was the Nuwaubian Nation, a Black supremacist group who combined Abrahamic religion, ancient Egyptian paganism, and ancient astronaut theories into a pharaonic-themed syncretic faith that considered the Giza pyramids sacred. The leader of the group, convicted child molester Dwight York, claimed that Black Americans were actually Native Americans because the Egyptians had colonized America and interbred with the Olmec, an ancient Mexican people. In the 1990s, the Reverend Louis Farrakhan, the leader of the Nation of Islam, attempted to rally African Americans to his cause by claiming Black Americans to be the descendants of the Egyptian pyramid builders and the originators of Freemasonry, and thus they were the founding force behind the United States, their birthright, a country born of Masons where an Egyptian obelisk stands at the center of the nation's capital.

A more sober argument along Afrocentric lines came from the pen of Martin Bernal, a Cornell professor who specialized in modern China until he developed an interest in his Jewish heritage and began seeking out connections between ancient Israelites and other Near Eastern peoples. In 1987, he published the first volume of *Black Athena: The Afroasiatic Roots of Classical Civilization* in which he argued that the Greeks derived their culture from Phoenicia and Egypt. Therefore, Egypt, as the mother culture, was the source of Western civilization. Bernal began from a correct observation—that ancient Greece wasn't isolated but was part of a broader eastern Mediterranean world in which Greece, Anatolia, Canaan, and Egypt interacted and influenced one another. But from this he drew an extreme conclusion unsupported by archaeological or scientific evidence, namely, that the ancient Egyptians had colonized Greece and had established an Egyptian culture there that would eventually evolve into classical Greece. The book was instantly controversial, and criticism of its extreme claims and lack of solid evidence were not helped by the author's admission in the second volume of the book that he wrote it with a political purpose in mind, to "lessen European cultural arrogance."

The drive to reject nineteenth- and twentieth-century Eurocentric scholarship animated many of the dissenting views of ancient Egypt at the end of the twentieth century and the beginning of the twenty-first, but as with so many correctives, they often tried to make too strong a case for the opposite, reproducing many of the same errors in reverse. In 2011, inspired in part by *Black Athena* and Afrocentrist literature, pyramid speculator Robert Bauval and his new writing partner Thomas Brophy published *Black Genesis*, a book they called a "testament of respect" for "all whose skin happens to be black." In the book, the pair argued that ancient Egypt was the gift of a lost and advanced sub-Saharan African civilization from the Mesolithic period, something like a Black Atlantis. They call them *Hamites* after Noah's son Ham. They worked from an actual archaeological finding that a Nubian people known as the Nabta Playa had tracked and measured the stars with a small stone calendar and had settled in Egypt's Nile Valley in the Mesolithic period. They then repurposed the old Egyptian story of the Followers of Horus, as Gaston Maspero and François Lenormant had conceived it, to make an Afrocentrist argument that the demigod Followers of Horus from predynastic Egypt were Black and had "civilized" Egypt and thus the Western world. To these Black gods, Bauval and Brophy attributed the Hermetic star knowledge of precession that had previously been assigned to the White gods of Atlantis. They claimed that pharaohs purposely left the Giza pyramids empty in honor of the Nabta Playa, whose heritage they supposedly drew upon to align the pyramids to the stars. In every case, modern authors were recycling late antique and medieval myths for modern times—and modern politics.

The shame is that there is a grain of truth to the claims, at least insofar as modern genetic research has shown that the critics were right—Egyptians were neither White nor Black. Those categories belong to modern culture and were not recognized in ancient times. Modern scholarship suggests ancient Egypt was a diverse society of many peoples, and genetic research has found that ancient Egyptians shared genetic relationships (in descending order) with the Middle East, the Mediterranean region, and sub-Saharan Africa. But too often that corrective to older racist views has been taken so far as to undercut the real facts with extreme nonsense, particularly a pernicious belief that culture is genetic and that one could revive cultural groups or rebalance the various ethnic and racial divisions of modern society if only a genetic link to Egypt could prove biological greatness. In the end, modern Egyptian and pyramid legends of almost every stripe were simply updated glosses on an old theme: appropriating the achievements of ancient cultures to claim glory and honor for oneself.

# CONCLUSION

ACROSS THOUSANDS OF YEARS, THE PYRAMIDS CONTINUE TO call out for explorers to probe their mysteries and search within them for the key that will unlock, if not a revelation, at least secrets about those who go questing for ancient truths. "If they could speak," a medieval Arab poet wrote of the Giza pyramids, "they would tell us what was at the beginning and will be at the end of time." This is perhaps an exaggeration. Instead, they would tell us what the people who gazed upon them imagined about themselves and the world around them. What we see from century to century is that the stories people tell about the pyramids are less about the pyramids than they are the hopes, dreams, and fears of the societies that spawned those tales.

The first set of transformations revolved around religion and the fear of early Christians and Muslims that the Abrahamic faiths seemed recent and transient compared to the timeless power of pagan wonders and their almost impossible antiquity. Late antique people tried to transform the pyramids into Christian monuments, and their efforts reflected their hope to find God revealed in the greatest of human achievements and their fear that Christian culture might not match the excellence of pagan antiquity. By making the pyramids monuments to God, they became proof that the Christian God transcended the pale claims of pagans. In the Middle Ages, Christian scholars tried to minimize the pyramids, ignoring them or treating them as Joseph's granaries, a reflection of medieval Europe's turn away from antiquity and toward the ethereal. By emphasizing heaven over earth, it became less important to deal with pagan remains. Islamic scholars, on the other hand, tried to recreate the pyramids as evidence of a vanished antediluvian world of scientific wonders whose glories anticipated those of Islam and presaged their restoration under the banner of the Muslim faith and Arab and Persian culture.

The second set of transformations saw the pyramids reimagined as talismans of mystery and occult wonder, an outgrowth of the rise in secular searches for knowledge that challenged received religious ideas. In the Renaissance and the Enlightenment, European scientists tried to find in the pyramids evidence of occult truths and hidden science, a reflection of the fits and starts by which the mystical medieval world was giving way to the secular culture of science in modern times. However, the growth of both scientific and occult approaches to the pyramids led to a division between those who accepted material facts and those who were uneasy with secularism and scientific materialism. The people of the nineteenth century were torn between scientific evidence for the pyramid's real purpose and a bewildering array of speculative ideas that had at their root anxiety about the decline of religious belief before the forces of science and secularism. Their efforts to find ancient truths, divine codes, and spiritual awakening within the Great Pyramid's walls served as an outlet for their fears about evolutionary theory and the declining power of the church. The empire imagined for antediluvians and Atlantis was a mythic precedent to the unprecedented imperial expansion of Victorian Europe.

After the world wars destroyed the Victorian world order, the new pyramid stories took on the color of their times, representations of the cultural anxieties of the postwar world. Long-standing modern efforts to find in the pyramids proof of the superiority of the White or Black race could not more clearly reflect contemporary racial anxieties, particularly during the middle twentieth century, when the US civil rights movement and global decolonization placed race relations in the forefront of ideas. Modern efforts to find evidence of benevolent space alien involvement

mirrored both the scientific aspirations of the Atomic Age and the uto-
pian hope—and paranoid fear—of the postwar period that a powerful
force might bring the world together as one. Similarly, the occult revival
that followed saw in the mysticism of the pyramids an anticipation of
the New Age spirituality that stood in opposition to what many now
saw as an oppressively conservative Christianity, defined by its most
extreme elements. Revived ideas about the pyramids' connections to a
globally interconnected world led by Atlantis and a lost civilization from
the Ice Age that had been destroyed by floods, fires, comets, or other
disasters were transparent reflections of modern anxieties over both
globalization and climate change. The pyramids alone, in this view, loom
as testament to how something of our own culture might withstand thve
disaster awaiting us.

This is the mark of a myth. The actual scientific truth about the pyramids—that they were the tombs of the pharaohs—remained unchanged
since the time of Herodotus, but also lacked the resonance and beauty of
a poetic myth. However, the stories told about the Giza pyramids, mostly
derived from Islamic tales told in the century on either side of the turn of
the first millennium CE, have proved infinitely adaptable to a wide array
of contemporary concerns century after century. Ultimately, the most
important factor behind the legends of the pyramids wasn't history but
contemporary culture. Hundreds of different legends circulated about
the pyramids, but the myths that attracted the most attention at any one
time just happened to be those that matched the anxieties and fears, or
the hopes and dreams, of the people investigating the pyramids. The
meaning of the pyramids isn't to be found in stone but in stories.

Precisely because the real history of the pyramids has become inseparable from myth, so many simply refuse to accept the findings of archaeology and even the testimony of the Egyptians themselves. In the 2010s,
a Franco-Egyptian team of archaeologists discovered a papyrus known
as the Diary of Merer. Merer was one of Khufu's officials, and he oversaw
the construction of the Great Pyramid. In the papyrus, he describes
how the Egyptians moved the limestone blocks for the pyramid from
their quarry by floating them down the Nile on boats and then up to the
pyramid along purpose-built canals, after which they were pushed up
wooden tracks to the construction site. Even this testimony from the

**Figure C.1.** The Great Pyramid has inspired thousands of years of speculation to find a story that would match its grandeur. *Library of Congress Prints and Photographs Division, LC-M33- 8925.*

actual builder of the pyramid was not enough to convince those who hold an abiding belief that the pyramid is an antediluvian relic of a lost civilization. Facts, ultimately, cannot overcome faith. And the myth of the pyramids, in all its many and varied forms, is a faith—a faith in an imaginary world where divine writ and powerful ancient truths promise safety and protection for those who believe in the pyramids, in the prophets, and in a higher power.

Ultimately, when we gaze upon the pyramids, we see what we want to see, whether it be history, faith, or fantasy (see fig. C.1). Perhaps nothing better captured the Rorschach test that the pyramids became than this fragment of a poem dedicated to the many lenses through which people strive to understand their meaning:

Was it a pious man who raised them as testimony to his piety,
Building the Pyramids for one of his idols?
Or is it the work of a man who believed in the return of the soul
To the body after leaving it?
Did he build them for his treasures and his corpse
As a tomb to protect them from the flood?
Or are these observatories for the planets
Selected by learned observers because of the excellence of the place?
Or are they the description of planetary calculations,
Such as those once done by the Persians and the Greeks?
Or do we have etched on their faces
A science that seeks to understand the mind?
In the heart that sees them, the need to know what their writing means
Arises as a desire biting at the fingertips.

While this might seem like the work of a modern "ancient mysteries" fan writing about the bewildering variety of pyramid "mysteries" on offer at any given Barnes & Noble or on the Amazon.com bestseller list, this particular poem was written by Fakhr al-Din Abd al-Wahab al-Masri in either 1257 or 1258 CE. Nothing has changed in the past eight centuries or for most of the eight centuries before that. Chances are that eight centuries from now someone will still be telling the same ancient stories about the pyramids. And someone will believe them true.

# INDEX

217

## Jason Colavito

researches the connections between science, pseudoscience,
and speculative fiction, with an emphasis on pop culture.
He is the author of numerous books, and he blogs regularly
about history, the supernatural, and popular culture.